Joanne Loy Jones
Christmas 1992
from Pastor Black & Gloydes

Songs of My Soul

Songs of My Soul

Devotional Thoughts from the Writings of

W. Phillip Keller

Compiled and Edited
by Al Bryant

WORD PUBLISHING
Dallas · London · Sydney · Singapore

Songs of My Soul

Copyright © 1989 by W. Phillip Keller

The King James Version of the Bible (*KJV*).

The Living Bible (*TLB*), copyright 1971 by Tyndale House Publishers, Wheaton, IL. Used by permission.

The Holy Bible, New International Version (*NIV*). Copyright © 1973, 1978, 1984 International Bible Society. Used by permission of Zondervan Bible Publishers.

The New King James Version (*NKJV*). Copyright © 1979, 1980, 1982, Thomas Nelson, Inc., Publisher.

The New Testament in Modern English (*PHILLIPS*) by J. B. Phillips, published by The Macmillan Company, © 1958, 1960, 1972 by J. B. Phillips.

The Revised Standard Version of the Bible (*RSV*), copyrighted 1946, 1952, © 1971, 1973 by the Division of Christian Education of the National Council of the Churches of Christ in the U.S.A., and are used by permission.

Library of Congress Cataloging-in-Publication Data

Keller, W. Phillip (Weldon Phillip), 1920–
    Songs of my soul : devotional thoughts from the writings of W. Phillip Keller;
compiled and edited by Al Bryant.
      p. cm.
    Includes index.
    ISBN 0-8499-0717-9
    1. Devotional calendars.   I. Bryant, Al, 1926– . II. Title.
BV4811.K38   1989
242'.2—dc20   89-9094
                                                      CIP

Printed in the United States of America

  01239 AGF 98765432

This compilation is for
four little Bryants:

Breanne, Britni, Jacob and *Jamie*

ACKNOWLEDGMENTS

The compiler wishes to thank the following publishers for permission to excerpt devotional thoughts from their books by W. Phillip Keller (Abbreviations for book titles are supplied for other than Word publications):

Bethany House Publishers:

A Layman Looks at the Lamb of God (LAMB), copyright © 1982 by Bethany House Publishers, Minneapolis, MN 55438
A Shepherd Looks at the Love of God (LOVE), copyright © 1984 by Bethany House Publishers, Minneapolis, MN 55438

Fleming H. Revell:

Walking with God (WG), copyright © 1980 by W. Phillip Keller
Gideon: Mighty Man of Valor, copyright © 1979 by W. Phillip Keller

Servant Publications:

As a Tree Grows (ATG), copyright © 1966 by W. Phillip Keller. Published by Servant Publications, Box 8617, Ann Arbor, MI 48107. Used by permission

Word Books:

David I: The Times of Saul's Tyranny, copyright © 1985 by W. Phillip Keller
David II: The Shepherd King, copyright © 1986 by W. Phillip Keller
Elijah: Prophet of Power, copyright © 1980 by W. Phillip Keller
A Gardener Looks at the Fruit of the Spirit, copyright © 1979 by W. Phillip Keller
Joshua: Man of Fearless Faith, copyright © 1983 by W. Phillip Keller
Ocean Glory (OG), copyright © 1980 by W. Phillip Keller
Salt for Society, copyright © 1981 by W. Phillip Keller
Sea Edge, copyright © 1985 by W. Phillip Keller
Sky Edge, copyright © 1987 by W. Phillip Keller
Still Waters, copyright © 1986 by W. Phillip Keller
Wonder O' the Wind, copyright © 1982 by W. Phillip Keller

Above all, I want to thank Phillip Keller for his friendship and example of godly living since first we met—and his encouragement and cooperation in the compilation of this book. Thank you, Phillip, for being you.

CONTENTS

FOREWORD

W. Phillip Keller has earned the accolade, "a dean among Christian writers," and is, indeed, one of a vanishing breed. Every word he writes goes through the crucible of his own experience and emerges finely honed and superbly polished. He does not waste pigment as he paints pictures with words. His descriptions of his experiences in God's great out-of-doors verge on poetry—and his ongoing declaration of awe and wonder at what Jehovah God has done in creation reminds the reader of David's poetic exclamations in the Psalms. The title, *Songs of My Soul*, truly describes the meditations selected for this book.

I have known Phillip Keller for some thirty years and I marvel at his dedication and disciplined approach to the writing task, obviously a labor of love on his part. Early and late he meditates on the Word of God and does not put pen to paper until he has digested a given passage or verse and wrung from it its unique meaning. Walking a deserted ocean beach or climbing a lofty mountain, he ponders, indeed ruminates and reflects, on the various facets of biblical truth until he is ready to put his conclusions into words. He does not parrot the commentators; instead he plows new ground and brings the lens of a lifetime of experience to bear on a given truth or passage.

Songs of My Soul brings together devotional thoughts from Phillip Keller's many books in a well-organized, easy-to-read daily format to encourage readers (whether serious Keller fans or those simply looking for a provocative and informative daily devotional discipline). A title and subject index in the back of the book also make it a valuable resource for serious Bible students.

Al Bryant

Songs of
My Soul

1 ——— Of Water and Roots

And the Spirit of God moved upon the face of the waters.
Genesis 1:2 KJV; *read Genesis 1:1–8*

There have to be those interludes in life when there sweeps over my mind, my thoughts, my emotions, my sensitivities, my disposition, my will, the refreshing effulgence of the living presence of God's gracious Spirit. He simply must come as surely and as strongly as any winter storm from the ocean deeps. He must sweep over my spirit from out of the wondrous depths of my Father's boundless love. As I begin this new year, I long for that refreshing.

Christ, when He was here amongst us in human guise, put it to us plainly. He encouraged us to seek, to knock, to ask. He assured us His warm and gentle Spirit would be bestowed on those who longed for His refreshing (Luke 11). Most of us are too timid, too shy, too hesitant to try.

But if we are to blossom where we are planted, then it is essential that we be watered where we are rooted. So many lives are like "adobe clay," hard as stone, tough as concrete, unyielding as a rock until touched by His grace.

Out of such unpromising materials our Father can produce a splendid show of colorful blooms. With the touch of His Spirit and the refreshing rain of His presence, our rugged, rocky souls can blossom like my bit of beach after the advent of the warm winter rains.

2 ——— The Wonder of the Waves

And God said, "Let the water under the sky be gathered to one place . . ." and the gathered waters he called "seas."
Genesis 1:9–10 NIV; *read Genesis 1:9–13*

If one goes to walk at the ocean edge when a heavy storm is under way, he must walk in quiet awe and humble wonderment. It is a sobering thought to realize that some of the huge walls of water breaking on the beach were waves born several thousand miles away, across the Pacific. They are not just a phenomenon produced by a local passing storm. Some of the surf bursting on my sun-kissed beach may well have started its movement in the grim, gray storms that surge around the Aleutian Islands, off Alaska. Or, at other seasons, they may have been spawned by a tropical typhoon 4,000 miles away in the South Pacific. This ocean is a mighty mass of water, within whose depths colossal currents flow, and across whose enormous breadth waves move in tremendous strength.

The ocean, perhaps more than any other part of the planet, reminds us that we are an integral part of the total universe. Earth is no more a mere island of matter in space, acting independently of and detached from all other bodies, than any man or woman is an island in society. Mysterious, little-understood magnetic attractions—of the moon, the sun, the planets of the solar system, and even remote stars—exert their pull upon our seas. No, we are not alone and on our own. The rise and fall of every tide upon the beach before my door is a striking reminder that we are all part of an enormously complex, interdependent universe, created and sustained by the powerful hand of my Heavenly Father.   (OG)

3 ———— The Story in the Stars

God made two great lights—the greater light to govern the day and the lesser light to govern the night. He also made the stars.

Genesis 1:16 NIV; read Genesis 1:14–19

If we are sincere in spirit, honest in heart, and open to truth, we must in intellectual integrity admit that all the remarkable interaction of stars, sun, moon, oceans, tides, surf, sand, and man is not mere chance. The laws of probability are prohibitively against such a supposition.

It is for this reason that when I go to walk alone upon the beach, as I have often done on winter days, it is with a genuine sense of sublime awe upon my spirit. There steals over me again and again the acute, intense, undeniable awareness: "Oh, God, my Father, You are here! This is but a fragment of Your exquisite artistry, Your magnificent mind, expressed to me in terms I can understand!"

My finite comprehension of the enormous expanses of outer space and of the interstellar systems may be strained and straightened beyond my ability to understand. But when the gravitational pull of the moon lifts 10 billion tons of water 10 feet on a rising tide and sends it bursting across my beach, I can grasp a little of the greatness of God. I may not be able to fully fathom what it means when astronomers tell me the light from some distant star, traveling at 186,000 miles a second, has taken 4,000 years to reach my eye. But I can lay hold of the loveliness of our Lord when I see that same clear, silver starlight shining on the edge of the surf that breaks endlessly before my door. No human hands have moved those waters; no human ingenuity has arranged this glory. It is from God, my Father.   (OG)

4 ———— A Mighty Mystery

And God created great whales, and every living creature that moveth,
which the waters brought forth abundantly, after their kind, and
every winged fowl after his kind: and God saw that it was good.
And God blessed them, saying, Be fruitful, and multiply, and
fill the waters in the seas, and let fowl multiply in the earth.

Genesis 1:21, 22 KJV; *read* Genesis 1:20–31

It has been suggested that the basic protein supply, plankton, offers mankind the greatest alternative food resource remaining upon the planet. Marine biologists debate this idea, because it has yet to be demonstrated that we can devise a system as efficient as that of fish and sea mammals for harvesting plankton from the ocean. Just as the most primitive crustaceans are more efficient than man's finest chemists in removing minerals from the sea, likewise lower forms of marine life are better able to utilize plankton as a source of protein than any sophisticated system so far designed by our scientific ingenuity.

This is an important concept for us to grasp. For though the ocean spreads out before us as a gigantic banquet table, still virtually untouched, teeming with billions upon billions of tons of plankton, no truly efficient means for partaking of this bounty has been found. Perhaps eventually the proliferating human population will compel men to devise some way of harvesting this so-called "sea grass" directly from the ocean currents.

Whatever the future may hold, for the present, we look out upon the ocean in quiet wonder. It is more—much more—than a mighty mass of water lying inert within its giant planetary basins. It is in truth a living, pulsing, moving, dynamic embodiment of myriad life forms. Within the oceanic environment, they live and move and have their being. Permeating every particle of this entire ecosystem are design, order, beauty, interdependence, and majestic mystery still beyond the mind of man to fully understand. (OG)

5 ———— The Wooing of the Spirit

And the Lord God formed man of the dust from the ground,
and breathed into his nostrils the breath of life;
and man became a living being.

Genesis 2:7 RSV; *read* 1 Corinthians 15:41–51

Throughout the Word of God the gracious Holy Spirit is likened to air, to atmosphere, to the wind. "The wind breathes where it will, and thou canst hear the sound of it, but knowest nothing of the way it came or the way it goes; so it is, when a man is born by the breath of the Spirit" (John 3:8, Knox Translation).

To every true child of God come continually the soft solicitations of the Holy Spirit. He comes with gentleness yet with an insistent desire to be allowed admittance into the innermost recesses of the life and heart and intellect. (ATG)

6 ———— Satan Invades Serenity

> *Now Satan was more crafty than any of the wild animals the Lord God had made. He said to the woman, "Did God really say, 'You must not eat from any tree in the garden'?"*
>
> Genesis 3:1 NIV; read Genesis 3

As God's people we sometimes delude ourselves into believing that we can live lives of serenity here on earth without fear of attack from the evil one. It simply is not so. Satan appeared in paradise to disrupt the sublime arrangements made for Adam and Eve. He appeared in the desert to assail our Lord and Master Jesus Christ in His great enterprise for our salvation. So he is bound to bother us. *Even in the most harmonious settings, the enemy of our souls is at hand to disturb.*

It is for this reason that the Spirit of God alerts us again and again to be on our guard against the evil one. Even our Lord, with enormous understanding, taught us to pray daily: "Our Father who art in heaven . . . deliver us from evil" (or the evil one).

7 ———— Who Do You Turn to?

> *Enoch walked with God; then he was no more, because God took him away.*
>
> Genesis 5:24 NIV; read Genesis 5:21–24

God has called to men across the centuries to come and walk with Him, because He wanted to share life with them. He had special insights and secrets to share.

Two people will not walk together, unless they have something in common to share. Parents and children, friends, lovers, business associates will walk with one another, often in close embrace, because there is something very personal, very private, very precious they wish to share.

So to be very practical and very honest it must be asked, is Christ your confidante? Do you, in a dilemma, turn to the telephone to call a friend or family member for counsel and encouragement? Or do you turn to God? Who is your closest intimate? Is it the Spirit of the Living Lord who resides with you?

If in truth, and not just in theory, we are walking together with God, we sense, know, and are acutely aware that He is our "alongside One." He is our companion, our counselor, our comrade on the path of life. It is to Him we turn always to share all the details and intimacies of our days. (WG)

8 ———— Exploring with God

[The Lord said to Abram:] "I will make you into a great nation
and I will bless you; I will make your name great,
and you will be a blessing."

Genesis 12:2 NIV; read Genesis 12:1–9

All my life I have been a keen walker, an enthusiastic hiker and ardent mountain climber. Always associated with these activities are the joy, exhilaration, and inspiration that come from exploring new terrain. There is stupendous pleasure in pushing back our horizons, getting a fresh glimpse of new ground. The thrill of new views and wide vistas over and across untrod territory is an exhilaration that stirs the blood, quickens the pulse, arouses ambition. The prompt response of every fiber in one's being is, "Come on—let's go!"

You will recall that over and over in God's record of His dealings with men, He showed them new vistas of what they could accomplish in His company. In ancient times He called Abraham outside his tent to look at the stars. He took Moses to gaze across the Jordan at the land of promise. He communed with Elijah at the brook Cherith.

Do you know anything at all about being in such close company, alone, with God, that He shares new vistas with *you*? Have you been invigorated, inspired, enthused (*entheo*—in God) by having Him open up before your wondering eyes worlds of possibility new and untrod yet by you? Have you sensed His Spirit saying to you, "I will bless you to the ends of the earth. I will enlarge your influence, extend your impact to ten thousand lives as we walk together"? (WG)

9 ——— Walking with God

> *He [Abraham] replied, "The Lord, before whom I have walked,*
> *will send his angel to you and make your journey a success,*
> *so that you can get a wife for my son from my own clan*
> *and from my father's family."*
>
> Genesis 24:40 NIV; read Genesis 24:32–51

We are astonished at the incredible life of Abraham. Called from his native homeland, he set out across the desert wastes to walk with God in explicit faith. He stood beneath the desert stars and responded positively to the still, small voice of God's Spirit, assuring him he would be the founder of a chosen, special people. He would be the father of a race through which "the Savior" would come. And Abraham walked with God in that quiet, strong assurance.

We see men like Moses, Joshua, and Caleb who, despite the deviation of their contemporaries, chose to walk with God. Across the desolate desert wastes between Egypt and the land of promise, for forty years they kept company with God. A thousand frustrations with their fierce temptations to turn back from the path set before them could not deter them from walking with God. (WG)

10 ——— Ponderings

> *[God said to Jacob:] "I am with you and will watch over you wherever*
> *you go, and I will bring you back to this land. I will not leave*
> *you until I have done what I have promised you."*
>
> Genesis 28:15 NIV

No two dawns are ever identical. Nor are the advents of any two days the same. Each bears a beauty uniquely its own. Each comes with freshness for a new beginning. Each carries the capacity for great adventure, stirring events.

Likewise it is in my humble, quiet walk with God. The imprint made upon the sands of time by this dawn are unlike those ever made before.

There stretches before me a strand of eternity upon which may be etched designs of divine inspiration. It is as clean, clear, and uncluttered as any stretch of beach unmarked by the tread of man. No one has passed this way before.

No one has lived in this moment in this special spot before this time. No one has left any mark upon this hour. The dawn announces a new day. It ushers in an untrammeled way. It waits to hear what God will say.

So I am handed a fresh scroll of unfolding time.

What will be inscribed upon it? What designs shall I draw upon the parchment of its hour? What mark or message will be left here of eternal worth and lasting merit?

These are questions that I, as a child of God, must ask and attempt to answer. This pilgrimage is a part of my daily walk with God. May I be in such close touch with Him that I will instinctively know His will, and walk as He would have me walk.

11 —— The Sound of the Surf

> Then Jacob awoke from his sleep and said, "Surely the Lord is in this place; and I did not know it."
>
> Genesis 28:16 RSV; read Genesis 28:10–17

A large part of the unalloyed fascination of the seashore is the symphonic variation of the melodies played upon it. There are days when the sea, under a brittle blue summer sky, barely whispers in soft notes of tiny wavelets caressing the sand . . . like the gentle tones of a violin string section. Other days there is the steady beat of breakers pounding the rocks like drums in the distance. Then there are times when with thundering notes there are the trumpet sounds of great waves rolling in from the deeps—the crash of their breaking on the beach like the clash of cymbals in the hands of the celestial music maker.

In all of this I find enormous stimulation, splendor and joy. The sound of the surf speaks to me at the greatest depths of my being. It is ever there, ever present, ever pervasive. Even though my thoughts and emotions may be preoccupied with other interests and activities, in the background there persists the eternal song of the sea.

Just so, our heavenly Father speaks to us in myriad ways as we live out our little lives in fellowship with Him. Sometimes His voice comes as loudly as the sound of thunder on a sultry summer night. At other times, His voice is as soft and subtle as a gentle summer breeze. I must listen quietly and closely or I may miss the blessing He has for me.

12 —— The Eternal Hills

> The blessings of your father are mighty beyond the blessings of the eternal mountains, the bounties of the everlasting hills. . . .
>
> Genesis 49:26 RSV; read Genesis 49

"The events He allows to intrude upon our little lives are not intended for our undoing," I murmured to myself in quiet soliloquy. "Rather they are intended to conform us to the greatness of His own wondrous character."

The sorrow, the suffering, the shaping of our lives would in time see the contours of our characters likened to His own lofty ideals and purposes for us as His people. Through the deep-cut valleys of our days His own sublime life could flow in refreshment to others who suffered as we did, who tramped the trail of tears that we had trod. . . .

This powerful process is as ancient as the earth itself and as eternal as the tides. It is as enduring as the rock over which the water runs. All of these are relative aspects of a planet which had a specific beginning in time and will come to a significant end in the future. But for the brief duration of our earth days it appears to us to be everlasting.

This is why poets, philosophers, and mystics have always turned to the eternal hills for uplift and inspiration. It is why they have sought the solace of the sea in their soliloquies. It is why they have written and sung of flowing streams and deep-running rivers.

13 —— Sensitive to the Spirit

> *For the Lord your God is a devouring fire, a jealous God.*
> *Deuteronomy 4:24 RSV; read Deuteronomy 4:15–24*

Because cedars are relatively thin-barked trees, readily susceptible to fire, they are a valid example of the Christian life. In my growth in God there needs to be a keen sensitivity to the reproof and correction of the Spirit. Otherwise, judgment, when it comes, will prove to be a burning experience. It will leave an indelible scar, like those on a charred tree, on my careless character.

"For our God is [indeed] a consuming fire" (Hebrews 12:29 RSV).

(ATG)

14 —— The Voice of God

> *When thou shalt hearken to the voice of the Lord thy God, to keep all*
> *his commandments which I command thee this day, to do that*
> *which is right in the eyes of the Lord thy God.*
> *Deuteronomy 13:18 KJV*

Running water, whether in waves, ripples, cascades or simple oscillation, brings with it a balm to weary bodies—a repose to high-strung souls and a quiet serenity to the human spirit.

Primitive men knew this instinctively. They sought solace and strength and inspiration from the voice of the waters. They spoke in awe and reverence of the singing streams and thundering seas. They came often to the water's edge not just for refreshment but also for the rejuvenation that the water music provided.

For me as a man, a great part of the pure pleasure derived from the sea edge is the loveliness of its sounds. For those not attuned to its music, unaccustomed to its rhythms, there may appear at first a restlessness to its beat upon the beach. But with further acquaintance and increasing intimacy the beach lover comes to know every nuance of the ocean sound, to enjoy the variations of its voice, to respond to the stimulus of its song.

In much the same way we need to be attuned to the voice of God. The Lord called upon the children of Israel to obey Him—and they disobeyed at their peril. I, too, need to be obedient to His voice. I need to listen to Him as carefully as I do to the ocean I love.

15 —— The Eternal God

The eternal God is your refuge, and underneath are the everlasting arms. . . .

Deuteronomy 33:27 NIV; read Deuteronomy 33:24–29

We speak glibly and rather facetiously of the eternal seas, but they are in truth not eternal nor enduring. Like the great mountain ranges of the world, so the oceans overwhelm man with their might and mass. But they are not enduring. They are inexorably subject to change and motion.

This truth comes home gently but surely to those of us who love the sea, who respond to its winsome call, who have fallen under its unique fascination. We sense that, at best, we are but pilgrims, passersby, wanderers who come briefly for the short span of our few years to live at the ocean edge.

All of us are transients. The tides, the waves, the wayward winds, the passing storms, the wheeling seabirds, the shifting restless sands, the schools of fish, the short-lived grasses and trees of marsh and dune are here but briefly. Is there no eternal meaning or message here for our questing spirits? Are we all but bare fragments of material, moved and shifted only in response to the physical, chemical, and biological forces around us? Is there no sense, meaning, or purpose for my short sojourn upon this planet that is hurtling through space? Are my years and thoughts and impressions to be carried away like bits of flotsam on the tides of time? Is there no direction to the deep and profound stirring of my spirit as I stroll by the sea?

Yes, there is. Deep does call to deep. There sweeps over my soul again and again the phrase "Oh, be still, quiet, alone, silent and know that I am God." (OG)

16 —— In Company with God

> *[The Lord said to Joshua:] I will give you every place*
> *where you set your foot, as I promised Moses.*
> Joshua 1:3 NIV; *read Joshua 1:1–9*

As God's people we are not armchair travelers. We do not walk by proxy. We set out to plant our feet on fresh ground. We set the soles of our boots on terrain never tramped over before. We are on the move. Nothing will deter or divert us from our destination.

The blood-tingling, pulse-quickening assurance given by God to Joshua, as he stood on the banks of the Jordan, thirty-four hundred years ago, is exactly the same to us today. Gazing out across the land of Canaan, flowing with milk and honey, God declared emphatically: "[Joshua] . . . go over this Jordan, thou, and all this people, unto the land which I do give to them, even to the children of Israel. Every place that the sole of your foot shall tread upon, that have I given unto you . . ." (Joshua 1:2, 3 KJV)

And Joshua did exactly what he had been told. He moved himself and a multitude of two million others with him across the Jordan and into the land promised to his people. Every step he took was an act of explicit confidence in God. He went places. He took territory. He walked in company with God. (WG)

17 —— Exhorted to Encourage

> *Be strong and of a good courage . . . be*
> *thou strong and very courageous. . . .*
> Joshua 1:6–7 KJV; *read Joshua 1:1–9*

As Christians one of our hallmarks should be that of courage and fortitude. All through God's Word He gives us enormous encouragement (read Joshua 1). He exhorts us to take heart, to be strong, to be courageous.

Our late twentieth-century society is notorious for its despair, its cynicism. The media is in the control of skeptics. Gloom and doom are dispensed in large doses from books, magazines, newspapers, radio and TV programs.

As God's people we are to encourage those around us. We are to show them there can be purpose, direction, and fulfillment in life. Let us draw alongside the weak and faltering to lift their hearts, fire their hopes, and transfer their attention from failing to our Father's faithfulness.

18 —— Godly Stamina

Have not I commanded thee? Be strong and of a good courage;
be not afraid, neither be thou dismayed: for the Lord thy
God is with thee whithersoever thou goest.

Joshua 1:9 KJV; read Joshua 1:10–18

In walking with God we are called upon to exercise ourselves. We are invited to invest something of our strength and confidence in Him. To walk with God is to trust Him. To join Him in life's journey is to invest our faith in His leadership and direction of our affairs.

Far too many present-day Christians consider walking with God some sort of soft, sentimental sensation that panders purely to their feelings. We do not walk with God that way. We are pilgrims and wayfarers on the rugged road of a rocky, unregenerate world—and the only way to walk it with God is in unshakable faith in His capacity to accompany us and encourage us all the way. This takes faith in His character. It will exercise us to the utmost. It is what develops godly stamina.

The Word of God to us today is exactly the same as it was to Joshua long ago. (WG)

19 —— A Step at a Time

Have I not commanded you? Be strong and of good courage;
do not be frightened, neither be dismayed; for the
Lord your God is with you wherever you go.

Joshua 1:9 RSV

God promised Joshua that every step he took, every spot where he set his foot down in quiet faith and simple obedience, would be given to him. (Read Joshua chapter 1 carefully.)

God does not ask you to climb the heights or cross the tough terrain in one giant leap. He knows you cannot. He asks you to take the journey with Him one step at a time.

By a definite, deliberate act of your will, decide to do the thing He asks you to do today—this hour—this moment. The instant you step out in quiet faith, to freely comply with His will, He empowers you to achieve His aims and ambitions for you.

Joshua stepped into the Jordan. God held back the river.

Joshua stepped out around Jericho. God flattened the walls.

Your part is to walk with God in unflinching faith, just one step at a time. His part is to prove faithful in performing everything He invites you to attempt. He always does. He cannot be unfaithful to Himself, to His Word, or to you.

Walk with Him unafraid, filled with confidence—quietly assured that it is He who can make your trip a triumph. (WG)

20 —— The Promise of His Presence

The angel of the Lord came and sat down under the oak in Ophrah that belonged to Joash the Abiezrite, where his son Gideon was threshing wheat in a winepress to keep it from the Midianites. When the angel of the Lord appeared to Gideon, he said, "The Lord is with you, mighty warrior."

Judges 6:11, 12 NIV; read Judges 6:11–18

The exploits of Gideon have been recorded for us in God's Word with authenticity and authority. They are more than the mere report of a most remarkable life under the direct guidance of God. Stimulating and inspiring as such biographical sketches may be, they demand more than our enjoyment of them.

Implicit in this narrative of a man "given to God" is the inescapable compulsion that calls us to action. There is no reason why in the last decade of the twentieth century, God's Spirit should not call some of us to become equally great men and women of valor.

The simple, penetrating truth is that God in Christ, by His gracious Spirit, does come to us just as surely as He came to Gideon under the tough, old oak in Ophrah. He does commune with us. He does challenge us to great exploits. He does call us to bold action in implicit obedience. He does promise us His presence, His power, His perseverance to accomplish the "impossible" in our tempestuous times.

The simple question is: "Will I respond in a positive way, empowered by Him, to do promptly the thing He instructs me to do?" If so, then titanic events will take place both in my own life, and in the world around me. (MMV)

21 —— Fire from the Rock

*The angel of God said to him, "Take the meat and the unleavened
bread, place them on this rock, and pour out the broth." And Gideon
did so. With the tip of his staff . . . the angel of the Lord touched
the meat and the unleavened bread. Fire flared from the rock,
consuming the meat and the bread. And the angel of the Lord
disappeared. When Gideon realized that it was the angel of
the Lord, he exclaimed, "Ah, Sovereign Lord! I have
seen the angel of the Lord face to face!"*

Judges 6:20–22 NIV; read Judges 6:19–24

God does not wrestle away our resources from us. He does not
uncurl our fingers from their grasping, tight clutch upon our possessions.
He waits, instead, for our hand to be opened by a generous, honest heart.

The angelic visitor, responding to Gideon's prompt and ready obedience,
reached out to touch the sacrifice. At once celestial fire flamed from
the rock consuming the bread and flesh in flames. Then the Lord vanished
from view.

But it was enough!

Gideon had been honored with the sign he sought.

It was the Lord God of his people who had met with him.

What he had offered had been accepted.

What he had given had been taken.

What he had done had been approved.

If a man will lose his life for the Lord, he will find it. Gideon had
given what he had. He had gotten God in return. He had turned over
what he owned to God, and God had reached out to touch and take it to
Himself. He would never be quite the same Gideon again. He had crossed
the "great divide." There was now no going back to his former lifestyle.
He was a man chosen, called, and appointed to signal service.   (MMV)

22 —— The Power of Humility

*The Israelites said to Gideon, "Rule over us—you, your son and your
grandson—because you have saved us out of the hand of Midian."
But Gideon told them, "I will not rule over you, nor will my
son rule over you. The Lord will rule over you."*

Judges 8:22, 23 NIV; read Judges 8:22–28

A man's usefulness to God is directly proportional to his willingness to be counted of little consequence in his own ability or estimation. It is the person who holds no great or grandiose notion of his own worth whom God chooses to achieve great exploits. The very basic reason for this is simply that his own self-importance does not interfere with the ongoing plans of God. The Lord has liberty and joyous freedom to use this individual how and where He chooses with enormous effectiveness.

At this stage in Gideon's meteoric career, he was maleable material in the Master's mighty hand. He was not blinded or distracted by any self-sufficient conceit. He was not interested in protecting either his own pompousness or prestige. He was simply a sharp and powerful sword in God's great hand.

Because of his implicit, unquestioning, and prompt obedience to the Lord's command, Gideon was now a man fortified with enormous faith. There remained not a shred of doubt in his mind that absolute and ultimate victory over Midian was assured. It simply could not be otherwise. God had given him the omen. He was bound to overcome. (MMV)

23 —— A Remarkable Bond

For the foundations of the earth are the Lord's;
upon them he has set the world.

1 Samuel 2:8 NIV; read 1 Samuel 2:1–10

There is in the ocean a remarkable bond that encircles all the globe. Its waters, though arbitrarily divided by man into separate seas, are really one. This flowing water, which is ever in flux, covers roughly three-quarters of the planet. It is in no sense static or stagnant. It is eternally active, ever in motion, relentlessly flowing with formidable force in great ocean currents. Yet it binds and unites all of the earth in a single unit.

The oceans encircle, touch, and caress every continent, every land mass, every island, every rock that protrudes from the sea floor. The ocean has this great glory of unifying the globe, shaping its coasts, tempering its climate, and in general contributing to the total environment in which life survives and thrives.

I can never stand alone high on a sea cliff, with the ocean roaring on the rocks below me, and not sense an overwhelming wave of genuine gratitude sweep through my spirit. There engulfs me the simultaneous sensations of my own insignificance and the glorious grandeur of the entire globe of which I am a minute part. There is imparted to me during these quiet interludes the indelible, irrefutable impression that "This is my Father's world."

Not only is there in it the moving, stirring, sublime majesty of mighty seas, but also the minute, heartwarming details of the exquisite artistry and care that have been bestowed on all living creatures who reside here. I am one of them, and He has been good to me. (OG)

24 —— Beyond Redemption?

Then David said to Nathan, "I have sinned against the Lord."

1 Samuel 12:13 NIV; read 1 Samuel 12

It might well seem to us at this point that David was indeed beyond redemption. Certainly for the casual reader with little if any spiritual understanding this episode in the king's life removes him from any further possibility of human respect. The inescapable verdict would seem to be one of absolute abhorrence—especially for one who claimed to honor the Most High. Certainly David's duplicity has brought endless reproach upon the man, and upon all of God's people, across the ensuing centuries. Only the grace of God and the unfailing faithfulness of His Spirit, still at work in David's life, could ever lift him again from the deep and terrible pit of evil in which he was mired. . . .

Only, only, only the redemptive mercy, the incredible pity, the eternal generosity of a compassionate, caring, loving, merciful God could possibly forgive his offenses.

This David saw!

This he now knew!

This he understood as his only hope!

He was utterly silent, subdued, smitten before Nathan. And it was at this point that God worked a miracle of redemption in his life. He can do the same for us at the low points in our lives.

25 —— Saul's Lack of Surrender

And Samuel said to Saul, "You have done foolishly; you have not kept the commandment of the Lord your God . . . for now the Lord would have established your kingdom forever. But now your kingdom shall not continue; the Lord has sought out a man after his own heart; and the Lord has appointed him to be prince over his people because you have not kept what the Lord commanded you."

1 Samuel 13:13–14 RSV; read 1 Samuel 13:8–15

What Saul had demonstrated at Gilgal was a stubborn, impetuous, strong self-will that insisted on asserting itself. He was obviously not suited to serve under the sovereignty of God. Again and again this trait would lead to his downfall. He was a man incapable of coming under divine control.

The principle is an all-important one for each of us. Will we wait patiently and comply with Christ's wishes? Or must we push ahead with our own ideas and insist on using our own initiative? Are we the ones who will "call the shots," or are we ready to respond in hearty good will to what heaven's royalty arranges for us?

To have our own way is to end up in disarray.

To quietly do our Father's will is to know strength and security!

26 —— Power to Follow, Grace to Lead

David grew stronger and stronger, while the house of Saul grew weaker and weaker.

2 Samuel 3:1b NIV; read 2 Samuel 3:1–27

Now that Saul had perished, Abner used all the military advantage and political power at his command to thwart David's legitimate rise to the position of national king. Even though Abner conducted a protracted and bloody campaign against David it was bound to fail, for in truth it was against the purposes of God for His people. This David had to believe in quiet faith. He had to trust God to do His own unique work behind the scenes to resolve the impossible impasse between the two rivals. At times it must have looked hopeless as Abner became stronger and stronger in Israel.

The Word of God makes it very clear to us that all who come to power in any area of human society do so only by the permissive will and purposes of God. It follows then that men and women rise or fall according to His wish.

Few of us truly believe this. But David did. He was confident that in His own good time Jehovah God would establish His kingdom in the nation and empower him to rule God's people both politically as a statesman and spiritually as a shepherd. This was God's covenant with him. He would carry it out.

As Christians living in the late twentieth century, we would do well to trust God in the same way. He it is who brings leaders to power in His own sovereign might. And we need to entreat Him earnestly not only for our own leaders, but for all those throughout all nations who hold sway over their fellows. This applies not only in the realm of politics, but also in business, in the church, in the media, in education and in science. Our God is able to work wonders behind the scenes, screened from our human view, if we will but trust Him.

27 —— The Power of the Imagination

David thought, "I will show kindness to Hanun . . . just as his father showed kindness to me. . . . " [But] Hanun seized David's men . . . and sent them away.
2 Samuel 10:2–4 NIV; read 2 Samuel 10

This is a compelling commentary on the power and potential for evil that resides in the human intellect. Of all living creatures on the earth, only man has the peculiar and powerful capacity to actually *imagine* things which are not, as though they really do exist. Used in its proper and appropriate way, the imagination can be a gift from God which can be most creative. The finest art, the loftiest literature, the most moving music, the greatest architecture, the latest inventions began in someone's inspired imagination.

Yet the same power, if not properly controlled by Christ, can be given over to the most insidious and destructive purposes. Instead of being used for uplifting and creative ends, it can drag one down into despicable behavior. It can distort thinking and give a false view of life. It can end in the indulgence of fantasies and self-deception that ultimately destroy the person.

Of course, Hanun was by no means a man whose mind was governed by God. The rash action and impulsive behavior of his imagination was to plunge his entire nation into terrible suffering, providing a classic example of how disastrous false imagination can be.

The Word of God speaks to this issue very emphatically. It gives us clear and categorical instructions as to how we should handle our imaginations. Unless brought under the control of Christ, they can readily become absolute monsters in our minds.

For the weapons of our warfare are not carnal, but mighty through God to the pulling down of strongholds; [mental] casting down imaginations and every high thing that exalteth itself against the knowledge of God, and bringing into captivity every thought to the obedience of Christ . . . (2 Corinthians 10:4–5 KJV).

28 —— The Scarlet Letter

*In the morning David wrote a letter to Joab and sent it with Uriah. In
it he wrote, "Put Uriah in the front line where the fighting is fiercest.
Then withdraw from him so he will be struck down and die."*

2 Samuel 11:14, 15 NIV; read 2 Samuel 11

Adding insult to injury, David dared to seal the orders, handed them
to Uriah in person, and commanded the dear fellow to carry his own
death warrant back to Joab in the battle zone. It was a dastardly deed! It
makes us despise David's action with profound loathing! This was a level
of disloyalty far greater than the most vicious behavior of brute beasts. It
was merciless and brutal, yet done with smooth, insidious subtlety. Is this
the action of "a man after God's own heart"?

One cannot help but ponder what the outcome might have been
had Uriah dared to open the letter, if but for an instant he had set aside
his loyalty to the king and broken the seal to read the royal orders. The
whole course of Israel's empire might have changed in an hour. In the
white heat of his flaming anger, Uriah might easily have returned to rush
at the king and use his valiant sword to sever the royal head. It would not
be the first time a monarch was murdered. David's very life and the entire
future of his nation dangled on the slim thread of Uriah's unwavering
loyalty.

The two men stand before us in blazing contrast. The foreign Hittite
so faithful to the very end. The cunning king so caught in dishonorable
intrigue of his own making.

The Spirit of the living God, in portraying the lives of God's people,
makes no attempt to mask their dark blemishes of character. With bold
strokes He paints them before our astonished gaze exactly as they are. He
never covers over the corruption of the human heart. He shows us what
we are!

29 —— A Perspective on Problems

*[David said:] "It may be that the Lord will see my distress and
repay me with good for the cursing I am receiving today."*

2 Samuel 16:12 NIV; read 2 Samuel 16:15–23

We do not blame our troubles and trials on others around us. We do
not blame them on Satan, as so many are taught to do. We do not blame

them on the cruel circumstances of our little lives. Rather we see our sufferings from our Father's noble perspective. We realize that they are the stern stuff He allows to come into our experience to conform us into His own beautiful character.

So in due time David and those with him crossed the burning Jordan plain. They came to the gentle, still waters of the river that flowed softly between its bushy banks. There in the lovely shade of the spreading trees they refreshed themselves and found solace for their spirits.

Beyond the river the king would find encouragement and support from old friends who stood with him amid his suffering and sorrow. Meanwhile back in the Royal City, in the providential arrangements of God, His Spirit was at work behind the scenes bringing the counsel of cruel men to an early end.

Just so, God can be at work in our little lives without our awareness. If we can accept adversity in this spirit, we will emerge stronger and better Christians from the tunnel of our travail.

30 —— A Song of Deliverance

David sang to the Lord the words of this song when the Lord delivered him from the hand of all his enemies and from the hand of Saul.

2 Samuel 22:1 NIV; *read Psalm 18*

At the time of David's restoration to the throne in Israel, he became acutely aware that the greatest need of his nation was not more military power or judicial administration but rather a turning back to God. He had sufficient spiritual perception to recognize that size and scale of state were of no significance to God unless the spirits of the people were in harmony with the wishes of the Most High.

He gives expression to this truth in the magnificent psalm recorded in 2 Samuel 22. There he proclaims boldly without apology to his people that it was the Lord who was his strength and his defense in the dark hours of his storm-tossed reign. His was not a peaceful reign. Far from it. Those years had been a time of upheaval and unrest both for himself and his people. He was erecting a mighty empire, but it was being built amid bloodshed, violence, intrigue and armed combat.

Still for David in the midst of the mayhem God was—"my rock"; "my fortress"; "my shield"; "my salvation"; "my high tower"; "my refuge—my Savior."

As we gradually approach the closing years of his tempestuous career it becomes ever more obvious that David's preeminent desire was to extol the greatness of God. His most compelling ambition was to exalt the honor of The Eternal One among his people. This became his consuming passion. . . . He was a man who above all else wished to do God's will. He was in truth a man after God's own heart. This his people all knew full well—and this they respected.

31 —— A Hymn of Praise

I call upon the Lord, who is worthy to be praised,
and I am saved from my enemies.

2 Samuel 22:4 RSV; read 2 Samuel 22:1-20

Every facet of David's life is clearly reflected in the two psalms set in juxtaposition in 2 Samuel 22 and 23. The first of these is in fact the same as Psalm 18 in the Psalter. It is commonly called "The Great Psalm." Quite obviously it was composed early in David's youth, prior to the time he was driven into exile by Saul's ruthless tyranny.

This magnificent poem is one of adoration and adulation for the Lord. It is an unabashed hymn of praise to the Most High for His part in preserving David during all his dangers. He ascribes to God all the credit and all the honor for his achievements. In it David foretells with the sure accuracy of a prophet all the mighty exploits he will yet accomplish as the leader of his people.

Yet it is without question a psalm written long before David had erred in his ways. It was composed before he had turned to violence, deception and intrigue in his career. In this poem David protests his own innocence. He disclaims any wrongdoing. He declares his own obedience to God's commands, the righteousness of his conduct before the Lord.

It moves us deeply to read such a manifest. For in the light of later events his testimony would change. . . . Later in life, David would confess openly and freely that he had in fact sinned grievously against God. He would plead for pardon. He would cast himself upon the mercy of the Most High. He would beg that God's gracious Spirit not be taken from him, even though He was so deeply grieved by David's terrible crimes committed against Bath-sheba and Uriah, his loyal officer.

And again, yes again, we are moved to the depths, for David was not alone in his sin. He speaks for all of us, for each of us has a past.

1 ———— Dark Days of the Soul

[David sang:] "You are my lamp, O Lord; the
Lord turns my darkness into light."
2 Samuel 22:29 NIV; read 2 Samuel 22:21–43

The birds were back. Their presence was a sure sign that winter was over. The dark days were gone; the long, dreary nights were behind. Each week it would become warmer. Every new day would be a little brighter. Each dawn held vivid promise of better things to come.

Contemplating all this it came home to me with formidable force that really it was all a precise replay of the recent, spiritual experiences we had passed through. There had been chilling days of sharp anxiety for those who faced death. We had known dark hours of sorrow for those who had bade loved ones farewell. There had been the grim vigil of those who endured the unknown future alone. All these were akin to winter in the soul and night in the spirit.

Sometimes it seemed the long nights far, far outstretched the brief days. Despair and darkness far, far outweighed the brief interludes of hope and cheer. The forlorn fears were far worse than the bright promises of renewal.

Yet behind the scenes of sorrowing, pain, and acute suffering our Father was still very much at work in the weariness of our winter. His faithfulness to His people would prevail over and beyond all the agony of their human despair. His concern and His care would change the impossible anguish into new and fresh opportunities to begin again.

2 ———— A Poet and a Prophet

Therefore I will praise you, O Lord, among the nations; I will sing
praises to your name. He gives his king great victories;
he shows unfailing kindness to his anointed,
to David and his descendants forever.
2 Samuel 22:50, 51 NIV; read 2 Samuel 22:44–51

David realized he was a gifted person. He knew he had been endowed with special talents from God. He refused to bury them in oblivion. He would not neglect them. They were to be used for the honor of God and to bless others. These capacities were not just to advance his own ambitions.

His abilities were bestowed to promote God's purposes upon the planet. The events of his life would prove:

- He was a gifted musician skilled in playing the harp.
- He was a talented composer of psalms, hymns and poems.
- He was an outstanding statesman of great diplomacy.
- He was a fearless, brilliant military man, a gallant general.
- He was an astute financier who amassed fortunes.
- He was a deeply spiritual person, a true "shepherd" to Israel.
- He was a prophet who spoke for God.

All these gifts he used in the service of Jehovah-God. As children of One who is greater than David, we should do the same!

3 ——— A Psalm from a Prophet

The Spirit of the Lord spoke through me; his word was on my tongue.
2 Samuel 23:2 NIV; *read 2 Samuel 23:1-7*

This statement was David's categorical claim to fame as one who foretold the future as surely as the prophets who preceded him. In this very psalm he proclaims the unbreakable covenant which God would make with him as a king in Israel. This covenant was that David's dynasty would endure; that through his lineage a Savior would come; that this Savior would in due time be the One to rule the entire earth. In all of this the coming of Christ was anticipated.

Proof that such events did indeed take place is provided in the genealogies given to us in the early chapters of both Matthew and Luke (see especially Matthew 1:6-17 and Luke 1:69). But beyond even this the numerous predictions which David made in Psalms 16, 22, 23, and 24 regarding the life and death of Christ are convincing evidence of David's major role as a prophet in the history of Israel.

It is astonishing yet wonderful to hear Peter on the day of Pentecost proclaim boldly to the huge crowds in Jerusalem that the very events they witnessed at Christ's crucifixion, death, burial and resurrection were those foretold by David. Unashamedly Peter repeated verbatim the statements made by David over a thousand years before in Psalm 16.

The truth of his prophecy came with such compelling conviction that over 3,000 converts were added to the band of disciples that day. It was the genesis of the New Testament Church. And its very beginning was the inviolate truth written by David under the unction of God's Spirit, so long before.

4 ———— The Servant-King

[David said:] "I will not sacrifice to the Lord my
God burnt offerings that cost me nothing."
2 Samuel 24:24 NIV; *read 2 Samuel 24:18–25*

It must be said that David's glory did not lie either in his gifts as a man nor his genius as a leader. His splendor lay in his willingness to be a servant to his people and to his God. He was in essence a living example of the magnificent grace of God active in the life of a man available to the purposes of the Most High.

What God could do for and through David, He is also able to do for any of us who will give Him the chance. Most of us are too stubborn to submit to His wishes. Then we wonder why our little lives are so useless, so impotent, so unavailing in the economy of Christ.

A great part of the impact of David's character on his contemporaries was its spiritual dimension. Even if some of those near to him, like Joab, were not men of faith in the Almighty, still David's own devotion to Jehovah God commanded their respect. He was not a man to hide his hope in the Lord. Consequently, the men under his command were keenly aware that David himself was a leader under God's command. This in part explains their unflinching loyalty and love to him. This is a unique quality found in very few leaders.

In his years of exile under Saul's tyranny, David had suffered with his people as few rulers ever do. He knew what it was to be oppressed, abused, and harassed by those in power. Accordingly he fully understood the feelings and fears of his fellow citizens. He was one with them in this common bond. Very much like this the Greater David, our Beloved Lord Jesus, the Christ, has lived among us, suffered with us, and is therefore touched with the feelings of our lot in life.

In truth David was not a monarch aloof from his men of war. He was one of them. He was their adored hero.

5 ———— David Deals with Death

When the time drew near for David to die,
he gave a charge to Solomon his son.
1 Kings 2:1 NIV; *read 1 Kings 2:1–12*

David's days drew to a close. His call "to go home" was at hand. He would not bypass death in the rare and wondrous ways accorded Enoch,

Moses, or Elijah. He was destined to die as most of us are. He would have to walk through the valley of the shadow of death about which he had written so poignantly in Psalm 23. This he could do with great dignity and quiet assurance because he would pass through the portals of eternity in company with the great Shepherd of his soul.

For the child of God, death is not a dread. It is but the doorway through which we step from this earthly dimension of time, space, and brief mortality into the glorious dimension of eternity and life everlasting. It is to be set free from sin, sorrow, sickness, and the despair of earth into the spectacular freedom of liberty in the life and light and love of the Most High who makes heaven our home, a realm of magnificent repose. What hope, what expectation, what assurance the Lord gives those who rest in His preparations for them!

6 ———— A Discerning Heart

> [Solomon prayed:] "Now, O Lord my God, you have made your servant king in place of my father David. But I am only a little child and do not know how to carry out my duties. . . . So give your servant a discerning heart to govern your people and distinguish between right and wrong. For who is able to govern this great people of yours?"
>
> 1 Kings 3:7–9 NIV; read 1 Kings 3:1–15

With the same undivided devotion that David had shown to the Lord God, Solomon set about his duty to erect the temple. His father had built a mighty empire to the honor of the Most High. He would build a magnificent edifice to the glory of God.

He simply could not do this with his own skill or using his own strength. He needed the same sort of divine direction that David his father had received from the Almighty.

In his compassion and loving concern for the fledgling king, God appeared to him in a dream by night. The story is well known, the account clearly documented for us by the Spirit of God. In the night vision Solomon is offered whatever supernatural help he might need.

In his humility of heart the young monarch beseeches God to bestow on him divine wisdom and supernatural understanding to rule Israel aright. God is so pleased He grants him this request as well as the promise of enormous honor and riches surpassing those ever known before.

Then there was added a proviso most people forget: "If you walk in my ways and obey my statutes and commands as David your father did, I will give a long life" (1 Kings 3:14 NIV).

This was God's estimation of David's life. It had set a standard of supreme consecration by which Solomon would be measured. From God's perspective David had lived a superb life.

7 ——— The Second Blessing

When Solomon had finished building the temple of the Lord and the
royal palace, and had achieved all he had desired to do, the Lord
appeared to him a second time, as he had appeared to him at Gibeon.

1 Kings 9:1–2 NIV; read 1 Kings 9:1–9

A second time the Lord God appeared to Solomon, just as He had before (see 1 Kings 3). He assured him that He, the Most High, had hallowed this sanctuary and that His presence would be pleased to reside there among His people. Then, wonder of wonders, He declared emphatically to Solomon exactly how highly He esteemed David—how he was a man of incredible integrity and uprightness in heart:

"And if thou wilt walk before me, as David thy father walked, in integrity of heart, and in uprightness, to do according to all that I have commanded thee, and wilt keep My statutes and My judgments: Then I will establish the throne of thy kingdom upon Israel forever, as I promised to David thy father, saying, There shall not fail thee a man upon the throne of Israel" (1 Kings 9:4–5 KJV).

All of Solomon's glory, all of his power, all of his dynasty depended upon conduct and character of David's caliber. What a superb accolade and tribute from God Himself!

8 ——— Faith in Action

And Elijah said unto her, Fear not . . . For thus saith the
Lord God of Israel, The barrel of meal shall not waste,
neither shall the cruse of oil fail. . . .

1 Kings 17:13–14 KJV; read 1 Kings 17:8–16

God does not indulge in embarrassing those who put their confidence in Him. He honors those who honor Him. He vindicates the faith of all who trust in His capacity to meet His commitments to them. He is pleased to find those who recognize His sterling character.

It is to such people that Christ comes and fills their lives to overflowing, not only with spiritual benefits, but also with moral and material resources beyond their fondest dreams.

The powerful prophet looked calmly and quietly at the distraught widow. His words were soothing, healing ointment to her tempestuous fears. "Don't be afraid. Don't worry. Don't panic. The Lord can and will supply all the flour and oil we shall ever require."

This was faith in action.

This was Elijah's powerful, positive response to the word spoken by God.

It demonstrated that he had an unshakable confidence in the character of Jehovah, God. He would come through. He would supply flour and oil, bread and butter, for all of them throughout the famine.

This was to exercise faith not only for himself, but also on behalf of others. His God was alive! His God was active! His God would deliver them out of their dilemma!

This was faith without fear.

It was straightforward obedience to the declared will and wishes of the Lord. It was the secret of Elijah's success, the key to the prophet's power.

9 ———— Winter Rains

> *And Elijah said to Ahab, "Go, eat and drink,*
> *for there is the sound of a heavy rain."*
>
> *1 Kings 18:41 NIV; read 1 Kings 18:36–46*

All through the winter months, there had been virtually no rain, no storms, no winter moisture. The whole earth lay parched, thirsty, dry and barren. I went early to a small rise overlooking the coast and there, stretched in the shade of a scrubby, wind-bent oak, reflected on how drought had ravaged the land in the days of Elijah.

Like him, after his great conquest on Carmel, I lay prostrate on the crest of the hill, casting my eyes out to sea. . . . In quiet confidence I bowed my face to the ground and pled earnestly, "O Father, refresh us again with a rain from the sea." It was a simple, single sentence prayer, spoken from the depths of a common man's spirit.

By evening great, gray banks of clouds began to move in off the ocean. They were being pushed toward shore by strong winds from the sea. As darkness descended, I went outside to stand in the gathering storm and I could feel the first drops of moisture falling on my face. Within a few hours thunder rumbled along the coast. Lightning flashed over the waves. Then the rain fell in torrents.

What a sweet sound! What a refreshing for the earth! What a renewal for all things living! The earth was restored!

10 —— A Noble Giver

Araunah said to David, "Take it! Let my lord the king do whatever
pleases him. Look, I will give the oxen for the burnt offerings,
the threshing sledges for the wood, and the wheat for
the grain offering. I will give all this."

1 Chronicles 21:23 NIV; read 1 Chronicles 21:18–30

In the plain language of a plain man, yet transmitting the impact and power of divine approbation, Araunah (or Ornan) smiled and said: "My Lord, the king, do whatever you see best. I give you my threshing floor. I give you my oxen for the burnt offering. I give you all my wooden tools and sledge to use for fuel to offer the sacrifice in this spot. I give it all to you and to my God!"

He held back nothing. There was no excuse that it would ruin his livelihood. There was no protest about how to support his family.

This was complete and immediate abandonment to the will and wishes of God. It was wholehearted relinquishment of all he possessed for the purposes of the Most High. It was pure, undefiled self-sacrifice for the good of others.

David was so deeply moved by Ornan's gesture he paid him six hundred shekels of gold. The equivalent value in today's currency is about $137,000. The king refused to offer a sacrifice that had cost him nothing. But by far the greater offer of a sacrifice had been made by this ordinary man, Ornan, doing an ordinary job, but set above all else to do God's will in an extraordinary way.

Wonder of wonders, that special spot was the very site on Mount Moriah where Abraham had offered his son Isaac to God 850 years before! Marvel of marvels, it was the very spot where Solomon would later erect the most beautiful temple ever to grace the earth! How God exalts those who honor Him!

11 —— The Divine Design

And Ezra said: "Thou, even thou, art the Lord alone; thou hast made
heaven, the heaven of heavens, with all their host, the earth and all
things that are therein, the seas, and all that is therein. . . ."

Nehemiah 9:6 KJV; read Nehemiah 9

We recognize that, amid the raging of gigantic ocean storms and movements of the sea, there is eternal change. We see coasts cut away and sculpted by relentless erosion. Land masses shift and buckle, to form enormous oceanic canyons or submarine mountains. Gigantic ocean currents, flowing thousands of miles, change their courses, alter climates, and bring life or death to continental littorals. Arctic and Antarctic ice caps freeze and thaw, expand and contract. Oceans rise in some periods of history, fall in others. Gigantic inland seas subside, to leave behind vast coastal plains. At other times the ocean returns, to inundate the land and bury immense land masses beneath its briny waves.

This has been going on for eons. The record is written clearly in the fossil remains of rocks now forming high mountain ranges. I have come across perfect specimens of seashells in limestone ridges at 10,000 feet elevation on the crest of the Canadian Rockies. Likewise I have flown across great wastes of the Sahara Desert, where, etched clearly in the desert sand, are the ocean deposits of a once-gigantic inland sea. Wave upon wave, dune upon dune of sea-formed sand stretches across the landscape as an incredible display of the ocean's relentless impact upon the planet.

None of this has happened in wild disorder. All of these changes occur under physical and biological laws of meticulous order and precision. On every side there is unmistakable evidence of divine design and supernatural programming. The elemental forces shaping the planet, moving the oceans, controlling the climate, determining the survival or extinction of species, are not random influences. They have been planned with precision. They have been programmed with meticulous attention to detail. They are proceeding in proper order, not by blind chance.   (OG)

12 —— Music in the Moisture

He bestows rain on the earth; he sends water upon the countryside.

Job 5:10 NIV; read Job 5:8–16

There is music on the moisture descending from above: a gift from God, my Father. I remember one such experience. . . . A diffused light filtered through the trees from an overcast sky. It was still raining, but very gently, quietly. The raindrops were barely audible on the deck outside. They scarcely dimpled the surface of the lake. Yet everywhere there was wetness, coolness and gladness.

Bird songs rang through the air with notes of crystal-clear beauty. Meadowlarks flung their melodies into the morning light with gay abandon. The songs splintered themselves on the great bluffs and echoed off across the lake. Swallows swept over the lake in graceful arcs, calling cheerfully to their newly fledged broods to follow them in their swift flight. The orioles chattered happily as they moved from tree to tree in search of insects drowsy with dampness.

With the coming of the rain, shrubs and trees and grass and reeds glowed emerald green. All their tissues were taut and turgid with moisture. Even in the somber gray light, they shone wet and smooth and satiny, charged with fresh life from within. New vitality and dynamic vigor moved in every living thing.

I slipped quietly out the door. Standing alone, inhaling deeply of the exquisite fragrance of soil wet with rain, deep and profound gratitude welled up within me for such a joyous interlude.

The rain had come! All of us together were singing thanks to God.

13 —— Of Weather and Wind

> *Blessed is the man whom God corrects; so do not despise the discipline of the Almighty.*
>
> Job 5:17 NIV; *read Job 5:17–27*

Often as I wander quietly along the foot of the seacliffs I am reminded vividly that my own life is just like they are. My own character is just as subject to change. There really is nothing about my person which cannot be altered by the passing of the seasons.

In other moments of quiet reflection, areas of our lives seem to be very similar to sand on the shore. Our minds and emotions are easily moved, played upon, and shaped readily by the current of events and circumstances God arranges around us.

The influence of people, the impact of the beauty of the natural world, the care and affection of family and friends, the attention of our associates, and the flow of time and study and knowledge shape our thoughts and mold our emotions rather easily.

But standing in sharp and solid contrast, like the bluffs above the beach, there tower over our lives the strong, formidable bulwarks of our tough wills. The hard rock of our apparently invulnerable volition is like a bastion of basalt against the storms of life.

Of course I can only speak with authenticity about this inner bastion of the will from my own personal perspective. Yet, from what I have observed in the lives of others, it appears to hold equally true for them as well. For ultimately, man's volition, tough and hard as it may appear, is subject to change under the impact of God's presence and the circumstances of change which Christ can arrange in our careers.

It is the man whose spirit has been shaped by the weathering wind of God's Spirit; whose hard heart has been broken by the breaking power of

29

our Father's love; whose tough will has been altered by the touch of the Master's hand, who becomes a beautiful character.

14 —— Broader than the Sea

> *Can you find the deep things of God? Can you find the limit of the Almighty? . . . Its measure is longer than the earth, and broader than the sea.*
>
> Job 11:7, 9 RSV; read Job 11:9–12

As with the ancient poet, we must cry from the depths of our being: "When I consider thy heavens, the work of thy fingers, the moon and the stars, which thou hast ordained; What is man, that thou art mindful of him? and the son of man, that thou visitest him?" (Psalm 8:3, 4 KJV).

My little life and your little life are not for nothing. Our short stay upon the shores of time is not a mockery. We are not here today, gone tomorrow because of blind fate or the whimsy of fickle fortune. Just as each grain of wave-washed sand; each stone, smoothed and rounded by the sea; each stick of silvered driftwood; each fragment of fragile flotsam; each shell shining in the sun contributes something of beauty and value to the passing scene, so likewise can my life and yours.

We are not here merely to serve our own little self-centered ends. I am not a cocky cockleshell, lying smugly on the sands of time, content to conclude that because I contain a thimbleful of seawater I hold the whole ocean in my embrace. Somehow I must see that, though I cradle a tiny part of the whole cosmos in my being, the entire cosmos in turn enfolds me within its embrace. Something of the gracious Spirit of God, my Father, does indeed deign to dwell within my spirit. But by the same token, I live and move and have my very being in Him whose presence and Spirit surround me on every side. (OG)

15 —— In the Hand of the Creator

> *In his hand is the life of every creature and the breath of all mankind.*
>
> Job 12:10 NIV; read Job 12:7–13

The immediate surroundings had that wild, neglected, uncared-for appearance that creeps over any piece of countryside that once was cultivated, then later abandoned. Ramshackle driftwood shacks, built from bits of driftwood and hand-split cedar shakes, cluttered the beaches. Assorted boats, some half-rotten hulks sinking in the sand with broken bottoms, littered the shore. Old fallen fences, overgrown with wild brambles and tangled roses, ran down to the tide flats.

Yet beyond all these unsightly intrusions on the scene, a mysterious mood of contentment and tranquility pervaded the place. I began to prowl around the property and found a very old, weathered "For Sale" sign half-buried in the underbrush. Obviously it had been left there years before by some real-estate agent who had given up trying to sell such a derelict spot. For me, it was like stumbling on a vein of high-grade ore. I had found exactly what I wanted. Beneath all the debris and clutter that defaced the landscape lay a bit of ocean-side land of exquisite beauty.

A few days later I was the delighted owner of 214 acres of abused and beaten land that lay encircled by the sea with over two miles of magnificent ocean frontage. That we were still solvent by only 54 cents after paying the full purchase price did not seem to deter our buoyant, youthful enthusiasm. We had found our homestead, and we would succeed.

In much the same way, our heavenly Father can take the flotsam and jetsam of our little lives and fashion from them a character and countenance that will please Him. (OG)

16 —— Hope for a Tree

At least there is hope for a tree. . . .
Job 14:7 NIV; read Job 14:7–12

Within the tiny seed, packed tightly inside the cone of the mature cedar tree, lies the minute life-germ implanted there through the complex and mysterious reproductive process of heredity.

When the cone has ripened and fully matured it opens under the impulse of sunshine, moisture, and moving air. The small seed is released to the wind and floats down to earth where it will find its seedbed upon the forest floor. Lying there so very small and insignificant, it holds within itself *life*; it possesses a potential cedar tree within its very germ. Yet to the untrained eye of the casual passerby it may appear inert and unpromising.

All that is required, however, is for the appropriate natural environment to exert its influence on the life within the seed and it will begin to be a tree. As the germ responds to the stimuli of moisture, warmth, air, and light which surround it, germination takes place and growth commences.

This is how a tree begins. This is how the life of a tree develops. But, what is life?

We really do not know! Immense sums of money and millions of man-hours of research have been spent attempting to discover what *life* really is. We know what it does and how it responds to various stimuli, and on this basis we have produced a fairly simple scientific definition for it: *Life is the capacity of an organism to correspond with its environment.* As a Christian, how am I responding to the "new life" within me? (ATG)

17 —— Of Stars and Mud

> *Is not God in the height of heaven? and behold the height of the stars, how high they are!*
>
> Job 22:12 KJV; read Job 22:21–30

God's people are realists. We recognize we are in a decadent society. We see corruption and decay everywhere. Yet amid the mayhem our spirits soar in hope. For our confidence is not in the community of man but in the goodness and graciousness of our God.

We are acutely aware of increasing anarchy. Yet we are intensely excited about the redemptive work of Christ rescuing men and women from the chaos.

We can challenge others to follow the Master. We can inspire them to serve God and serve men. We can look up and see the stars when others only look down and see the mud.

18 —— The Life-Giving Spirit

> *The spirit of God has made me, and the breath of the Almighty gives me life.*
>
> Job 33:4 RSV; read Job 33:1–7

Most of us know very little about walking in the Spirit. We are seldom energized by the reality of His presence at work upon us. We are so bundled up in the impedimenta of our human trappings that He is seldom given a chance to touch us at all. We are so insulated from His impact upon us by our preoccupation with our personal priorities, we know nothing of the stimulus that comes when we stand stripped and exposed before Him.

It takes a certain element of self-discipline to get out of a cozy home and take a tramp in the wind. It calls for courage to throw off the coat and open the shirt to let the cool breeze play upon the chest. It demands some discipline to inhale deeply of the sharp wind off the sea, to sense its vitality race through the veins, quickening the pulse. But it is worth it all to be fully alive.

So it is with the Spirit of God. He comes constantly to renew and refresh. He comes to encourage and invigorate. He comes to impart to us the resources of the Resurrected One.

It is in Him that we can find energy, power, vitality, the very dynamic for positive living . . . today.

19 —— The Breath of the Almighty

The spirit of God hath made me, and the breath of the Almighty hath given me life.

Job 33:4 KJV

Often, often, when I go out to hike in the hills, as I attempt to do every day, those moving sentences uttered by the prophet Nahum so long ago come to me with tremendous force. "The Lord hath his way in the whirlwind and in the storm, and the clouds are the dust of his feet" (1:3).

Yes, He is everywhere present. He is everywhere active and at work in the world. Very much alive, He is aware of all that transpires upon the planet and in the lives of its people. Most of us subscribe to this vague idea with mental assent. Precious few people consider the concept important enough to invest their confidence in the omnipresence of Christ. They refuse to have faith in our Father who is actually at work in every event that touches our lives. They do not sincerely believe God's Spirit is everywhere active.

This becomes very obvious in times of great stress or emotional turmoil. It is one of the tragic truths that strikes with great impact when we see men and women surrounded with excruciating sorrow or enveloped in overwhelming grief. It is as if suddenly they feel abandoned by God. In the surging storms of sadness or darkness that sweep over the soul, hope vanishes, faith flees and good will evaporates away. . . .

In such moments pious platitudes will not do!
We cannot mumble sweet nothings!
There can be no vague ideas!

The excruciating crisis demands formidable faith in the Living Christ. It calls for unshakable confidence in the love of our Father. It must have the consolation and assurance of God's gracious Spirit.

20 —— My Father's Weather Workshop

God thundereth marvellously with his voice; great things doeth he,
which we cannot comprehend. For he saith to the snow,
Be thou on the earth; likewise to the small rain,
and to the great rain of his strength.

Job 37:5, 6 KJV; read Job 37:1–13

All over the oceans, worldwide, there is the restless, never-ending, gigantic spawning of weather systems. Huge cloud formations arise, towering thousands of feet into the wide skies. Their proportions dwarf the earth's mightiest mountain ranges. In a single tropical storm, ten billion tons of water will be evaporated from the ocean surface, to rise forty thousand feet into the atmosphere. Driven and propelled under its own physical forces, it will sweep a thousand miles across the ocean, to unload its burden of moisture on some parched land mass.

Year in, year out, inexorably across the centuries, the ocean—in all of its unmatched glory and splendor—saturates the earth's atmosphere with moisture. It is the formation of these breathtakingly beautiful cloud patterns enveloping the earth that also helps to make life as pleasant as it is. The cloud layer in the earth's atmosphere helps to shield it from excessive solar radiation. It prevents undue desiccation on the surface of warm land. It gives rise to the glorious beauty of our skies. It plays a prominent part in the incredible loveliness of sunrises and sunsets that turn sea and earth to molten gold. It is the veil of exquisite whiteness that is drawn delicately across the face of the earth, causing us to gasp in ecstatic awe when we fly above it.

If we are people sensitive in spirit to the splendor of our world, such phenomena make us pause to give thanks to our Father. Scarcely a day passes that alone, lost in awe, I do not raise my eyes to the skies and give gratitude to God for winds and rain and clouds and waves and sunrises and sunsets. They are the weather workshop of the world—my world—my Father's world.

(OG)

21 —— The Enormity of Eternity

[The Lord said to Job:] "Where were you when I laid the foundation
of the earth? Tell me if you have understanding . . . who laid its
cornerstone, when the morning stars sang together,
and all the sons of God shouted for joy?"

Job 38:4, 7 RSV; read Job 38:1–15

I have often sat alone beneath the stars and moon, wrapped in the wonder of their enchantment. Their soft and silver splendor spread across the earth is free for the taking. It is lavished with love across the landscape. It is spread with exquisite artistry upon rocks and grass, upon trees and water. Everywhere one turns, the light of the night glows gently. It makes the earth a magic sphere, suspended in space, shining with reflected light that may have taken ten thousand years to reach it from remote stars in the depths of distant space.

With my finite mind and limited human perception, I cannot comprehend the enormity of eternity. Nor can I reach out to embrace the uncounted, unknown millions of stars, suns, and galaxies of the universe. But I can bow my soul before the beauty of dawn, breaking now across the eastern ranges, and whisper softly, "Oh God, my Father, You are here. . . ."

Man's puny pride, his arrogant intellect, his brazen bravado, have had no part in planning or programming this pageantry. It is strictly a divine production. Only God Himself could arrange such grandeur. It pulverizes petty pride.

For this I am glad.

It reassures me: *"Thou, God, changest not!"*

22 —— Deliberate Design

[The Lord answered Job:] Who set up the sea behind doors when it burst forth from the womb . . . when I fixed limits for it . . . when I said, "This far you may come and no farther; here is where your proud waves halt"?

Job 38:8–11 NIV; read Job 38:4–11

One of my favorite times to take a tramp along the tide line is at the ebb. If the sea is down and the waves are receding in gentle, graceful arcs, there is left behind a fretwork of fantastic patterns. These designs in the sand equal anything ever etched on the finest British bone china by a master craftsman. . . .

The surprising thing to me is the brevity of their beauty. Some are drawn and die within a few short seconds. The next wave washing up the strand will erase them in a moment. . . .

It is not the sand alone that responds this way to the moving water. In the foam and froth left behind every passing wave and wavelet, there are gorgeous, glowing types of embroidery that garnish the beach. . . .

Then there is the graceful movement of sand particles under the gentle pressure of the wind. They form shifting, drifting designs of graceful shape behind and around every stone, rock, shell, stalk of grass, or bit of flotsam flung on the beach. None of this is accidental or erratic. . . .

None of this is purely chance. None of this is merely blind coincidence. Each is an exquisite, intimate reminder that I live and move and have my being in a gorgeous environment ordered by a loving, caring, gracious Father. This is His world. He designed it. He set it in motion. He sustains it. (OG)

23 —— A Reason to Rest

And he shall be like a tree planted by the rivers of water, that bringeth forth his fruit in his season; his leaf also shall not wither; and whatsoever he doeth shall prosper.

Psalm 1:3 KJV; read Jeremiah 17:7, 8

Dormancy in a tree occupies a specific season. This season of rest is the one which just precedes the springtime of active and accelerated growth. It is really the time of peaceful preparation for the drastic demands of growth. It is the time of rebuilding worn-out cells and reconditioning tired tissues. All this is in preparation for the upsurge of the vigorous spring.

In a certain sense the period of rest is one of the most important throughout the entire year. It is the season when a tree becomes fully refitted for the exhausting demands that will be made upon it during the long rigorous growing season when new wood is added to its structure and fresh fruit is borne upon its boughs.

So we may say in all accuracy that in order to grow and flourish in season a tree must also rest and relax out of season.

Precisely the same principle applies in the total spiritual, mental, and emotional life of the Christian. There is an erroneous concept common to many children of God that to be effective they must be always active. There is the idea abroad that one must be always "on the go for God."

Yet even our Lord and Master, Jesus Christ, when He moved among us as the God-Man, found it imperative to withdraw from the activity of His busy life and take time to rest. Again and again we find Him slipping away to some quiet spot on a mountainside or across the lake where He could be alone and still for refreshment of body, mind, and spirit. These were interludes of quiet communion with His Father. (ATG)

24 —— Morning Moments

In the morning, O Lord, you hear my voice; in the morning I lay my requests before you and wait in expectation.

Psalm 5:3 NIV; read Psalm 5

Quiet morning moments are precious points in one man's brief life. Yet they are the essence of the eternal; for out of the endless, timeless immensity of eternity, God speaks softly, clearly, and specifically to the waiting soul: "Be still and know that I am God." The words are poignant and appropriate. His own gracious Spirit is present, to commune with the heart quietly humbled by the breathless beauty about him. In such interludes, my soul is stilled, my spirit is at rest. All is well.

Amid the ebb and flow of the shifting tides of human history, these eternal values remain. No one can rob me of the stars. No man can deprive me of the moon's majestic mood. No crisis of civilization can completely eclipse the stillness of the desert night. These remain and endure. They are beyond the grasp of rapacious men, yet they are freely available to the most humble heart, which briefly but sincerely is open and responsive.

25 —— What Is Man?

O Lord, our Lord, how majestic is your name in all the earth! You have set your glory above the heavens.

Psalm 8:1 NIV; read Psalm 8

In giant storms, the pressure of an ocean beating on solid stone can mount to more than 60,000 pounds to the square foot. That is the awesome equivalent of well over 30 tons of impact to one square foot of rock surface. The rock cannot long endure such battering and abuse. Some portion of it will break loose, to be flung against the shore and serve as a giant battering ram that is caught up in the waves, to grind and rumble against other boulders in the surf.

This explains in part why some of the most elaborate seawalls, ocean harbors, and coastal installations simply do not survive great storms. There have been instances where blocks of cement, stone, and reinforcing steel weighing more than a thousand tons have been torn loose, broken up, and shattered by relentless ocean storms.

The less obvious reason is, of course, the simple physical fact that in deep water any submerged object becomes increasingly buoyant. A giant boulder on the seabed, or a huge block of concrete below high water, is not nearly as heavy or immovable as we might imagine. The hydraulic action of the mighty inrushing waters that thunder and roar over the rocks lifts, shifts, and splits stone, concrete, and steel with impunity and disdain.

Again and again I have stood silently in awe beside a battered, broken seawall or shattered harbor wall. The immense power that pulverized the best of man's endeavors likewise pulverizes my human pride. The skill, science, and engineering expertise that were combined to try and tame the sea came to naught. Only a twisted, torn reminder of man's insignificance remains.

At such moments, there steals softly over my spirit those solemn strains from the Psalms:

O Lord our Lord . . . When I consider thy heavens, the work of thy fingers, the moon and the stars, which thou hast ordained; What is man, that thou art mindful of him? and the son of man, that thou visitest him?   Psalm 8:1, 3, 4 KJV   (OG)

26 —— The Glory of Our God

When I look at thy heavens, the work of thy fingers, the moon and the stars which thou has established; what is man that thou art mindful of him, and the son of man that thou dost care for him?

Psalm 8:4 RSV

It is not that He chooses to deprive us of staggering, mind-bending demonstrations of His splendor. Rather, the difficulty is that we are so slow of spiritual perception, so dull of divine insight that we are impervious to the remarkable display of His magnificent prowess all around us. Eyes we have that do not see and ears that do not hear.

An avalanche lily, pure as the finest gold, pushes its lovely bloom through the snow on some remote mountain meadow. We simply nod our heads in momentary surprise, then stroll on—never considering that no man's hand had any part in such a spectacle, such a complex creation. A skein of geese, hurtling across the loftiest ranges at a steady 60 miles per hour, hour after hour, dead on course, without the aid of computers or other electronic gadgetry, will find their winter haven 4,000 miles to the south. A gorgeous Olalla bush all aglow in glorious attire, no matter the season—graceful lacework in winter, perfumed blooms in spring, purple with fruit in summer, ablaze with gold in fall—to us dull mortals is all just "part of the scene."

O to have the scales of human skepticism stripped from our eyes, now dimmed by the madness of our man-made media! O to have the sensitivity of our spirits reborn after being so long imprisoned by the crude and crass culture of our cities! O to have the strings of our souls stirred once more by the splendor and the glory of our God and Father which in fact fill all the earth!

27 —— Communion with God

I will bless the Lord who counsels me; he gives me wisdom in the night. He tells me what to do. I am always thinking of the Lord; and because he is so near, I never need to stumble or to fall.

Psalm 16:4, 5 TLB; read Psalm 101

This sea edge is a unique spot of seclusion and privacy. It is a place where a person can sit lost in meditation, or take long walks thinking eternal thoughts, or repose in the sanctum of quiet communion with his Creator.

One does not have to be a saint, recluse, or mystic to partake of this environment. For it casts its special spell upon the most common of us common people. From barelegged boys sitting on the wave-battered black rocks, staring out to sea, dreaming dreams, to elderly gentlemen strolling softly in the sunset of their days, there emanates the contentment found in the quiet company of the ocean.

This tranquillity settles down into the soul and spirit as softly as a sea bird settles down upon the shore. There the gulls and terns and curlews and pelicans rest on the sand, preening their immaculate plumage in peace. The beauty of their bodies, reflected in the mirror surface of the wet and shining shore, is etched in soft shades of gray, brown, and ivory white.

The warmth of the sun, the softness of the sea air, the drift of haze and sea mist wrap this bit of beach in folds of quietude. It is a spot to come with a good book, with a thick terry towel, and an hour or two to stretch the body and stretch the soul and "extend one's spirit" to meet one's Maker in quiet communion.

28 —— Spiritual Exercise

I have set the Lord always before me. Because he is at my right hand, I will not be shaken.

Psalm 16:8 NIV; read Psalm 16

Walking together with God involves exercise. One of the great, wholesome benefits that comes from walking with a friend is the exercise it provides. And even though the trail may be steep at times, and the path rough and rocky, the interlude is a healthy, happy aid to our general well-being.

In this age of the automobile most of us do not walk nearly as much as we should for the benefit of our bodies. It is a splendid exercise and insures vigor and vitality.

I'm afraid the same is true in the spiritual realm. If we "walked with God" daily, our spiritual muscles would be stronger as well.   (WG)

29 —— The Secret of the Shells

As for God, his way is perfect; the word of the Lord is flawless.
He is a shield for all who take refuge in him.

Psalm 18:30 NIV; *read Psalm 18:20–30*

"Shell hunting" teaches me a profound spiritual lesson. There are often days when not a single unbroken specimen can be found anywhere on the sand. Only the thickest, heaviest, and toughest seem able to endure the grinding of the ocean mills.

Scattered here and there in sheltering crevices amongst the rocks one can sometimes come across a lovely shell. Half buried in the gravel, sheltered a bit by the surrounding stones, some of the more frail and delicate specimens do survive the breaking of the surf that roars around them if they've managed to land in a protected spot.

Perhaps it is because of their comparative scarcity on our coast that the shells cast up on our shore seem of special worth. It is because they are rather rare that they seem to possess a special value out of all proportion to their appearance. For many of them lack the ornate shapes or exotic colors of shells gathered in warmer waters.

Still, for me, finding these shells remains a happy fascination that has never diminished across the years. Somehow they are one of the beautiful bonuses that come to us from the bounty of the sea. They are gifts bestowed freely for the taking.

Just so, I sometimes discover spiritual treasure where I least expect it. Perhaps it is uncovered in the midst of a difficult experience, or in the wake of a devastating crisis. Lord, help me to be open to the lessons You would teach me along the way!

1 —————— Learn to Look for His Hand

The heavens declare the glory of God; and the firmament sheweth his handiwork. Day unto day uttereth speech, and night unto night sheweth knowledge. There is no speech nor language, where their voice is not heard. Their line is gone out through all the earth, and their words to the end of the world. In them hath he set a tabernacle for the sun.

Psalm 19:1–4 KJV; read Psalm 19

God communes with me through the people in whom He resides, through providential events and through His natural, created universe. These three means of communication are so obvious that they require little elaboration.

Almost all of us have met men or women who were obviously deeply and significantly walking with God. Without pretense or ostentation they made an enormous impact upon us. Through their character and conduct we got a new glimpse of God. We knew they had been with Jesus. They walked in company with God's gracious Spirit.

Just knowing them induced within our spirits an intense, inner desire to know and walk with God in the same way. Some of them God used to touch our lives and commune with us in tangible terms.

Then there are the circumstantial events of our everyday, common, human experiences whereby our Father constantly alerts us to His presence. His compassionate arrangement of our affairs with our best interests in mind stills our spirits and moves us to turn to Him in enormous gratitude. . . .

Learn to look for His hand in all the events of your life. Learn to thank Him for every incident. Adulate Him with your appreciation.

Finally there is the grandeur, the glory, the gentleness of our God shown to us in the created universe all around us. In stars and streams, in mountains and meadows, in grass and trees, in oceans and plains, He conveys strength, inspiration, and uplift to our seeking spirits.   (WG)

2 —————— Strength for Adversity

May the Lord answer you when you are in distress;
may the name of the God of Jacob protect you.

Psalm 20:1 NIV; read 2 Samuel 16:1–14

The one sure and unshakable assurance which remained at this stage in David's excruciating experience of flight from Jerusalem is best stated in his own words. "It may be the Lord will look on my affliction, and that the Lord will requite me good for his cursing this day" (2 Samuel 16:12 KJV).

The great and wondrous consequence of David's calm confidence in the living Lord was that in the midst of adversity he found enormous strength, inspiration and intimacy with God. It was at this time in his troubled life that he was given the imperishable lines of Psalms 20, 23, and 42. Of these, Psalms 23 and 42 have become my special favorites. Out of all the poetry this gallant man ever composed amid adversity under the inspiration of God's gracious Spirit, they stand supreme. They have encouraged and heartened uncounted millions upon millions of souls across thousands upon thousands of years.

What was the psalmist's great secret?

What was the basic bedrock of his belief?

What was the sure source of his strength amid such grief?

It is this: "Nothing that happens to God's child, no matter how excruciating it may be, does so by chance. Every detail is arranged by the knowing hands and understanding wisdom of God our Father. It is planned in love for our own good and His great honor. So all is well, as we walk with Him!"

It is this quiet assurance, this calm confidence in the living God which can insure that any child of God can triumph amid tragedy.

3 —————— Praise from His People

But thou art holy, O thou who inhabitest the praises of Israel.
Psalm 22:3 KJV; read Psalm 22:1–5

As we walk with God, we learn to recognize His hand upon us through His Word, through His Son, through His Spirit, through other people, through His arrangement of our affairs, through the beauty of His earth, through the impact of prayer answered! Then there springs up from within our spirits an overflowing fountain of praise, appreciation, and gratitude.

This is absolutely inevitable. It does in fact become the central, compelling motivation for a person's desire to please God; to walk with Him in harmony, to enjoy His presence, to love Him because He has first loved us, literally to live for Him.

Praise of this sort embraces the whole of my life. It is not the mere articulation of pretty phrases or pious-sounding platitudes. Genuine praise is an entire life lived in humble gratitude and wholesome appreciation for who God is and what He has done. It is a clean-cut, shining, simple walk with the most wondrous Friend in all the world.

This is what is meant by God inhabiting the praise of His people. He actually deigns, in magnanimous generosity, to come and reside with us. He lives with us, talks with us, shares life with us, loves us, enjoys walking with us. (WG)

4 ———— Beside the Still Waters

The Lord is my shepherd; I shall not want. He maketh me to lie down
in green pastures: he leadeth me beside the still waters.

Psalm 23:1, 2 KJV; read Psalm 23

For the soul sensitive to the uplift of quiet waters there come moments, breathless moments, when in truth the whole earth speaks in hushed tones: "O God, *You are here! Your presence fills this place! Your peace enfolds these skies.*"

And because He is there, my spirit, too, attuned to His, can find refreshment, renewal, and restoration in such a spot. This is not to indulge in some spurious imagination of the mind. Rather, it is to discover the wholesome healing of the entire person in the presence of the Most High.

This element of utter serenity, of complete stillness, of lovely tranquility in company with Christ, is a dimension of life that increasingly eludes us Americans. It is not that millions of us do not crave it. But it is unfortunately ever more difficult to find. The simple reason is that more and more multitudes are imprisoning themselves in large metropolitan centers where the roar and rumble of industry, traffic, and commerce never cease.

Added to this is the insistence of modern man that wherever he goes, even into the countryside and remaining wilderness areas, he must take his twentieth-century gadgetry with him. The thunder of all-terrain vehicles, the drone of aircraft, the scream of snowmobiles or power boats, the staccato rattle of dirt bikes all shatter the stillness and desecrate the solitude of those who seek it.

Nevertheless all is not lost. Here and there stretches of unspoiled terrain remain. For those who will take the time and make the effort, quiet spots can still be found where serene waters bask in the sun and reflect the gentle glory of the sky edge.

Lord, lead me beside the still waters!

5 ———— Serene—Not Stagnant

Because the Lord is my Shepherd, I have everything I need! He lets me rest in the meadow grass and leads me beside the quiet streams.

Psalm 23:1, 2 TLB

Still waters need not be a place of stagnation. Quite the opposite, they serve as a powerful magnet that attracts a startling array of wildlife. Their moisture provides a rich environment for all sorts of vegetation that lends lovely diversion to the dry arid region.

Here ducks dabble in the shallows. More often, they simply rest on the surface, looking almost like carved decoys reposing on a glass table-top, their smooth shapes reflected to perfection in the surface. A heron will often stand as still as a miniature statue carved in stone, waiting at the water's edge for a careless bit of prey to come his way. . . .

A whitetail doe steps out of the dim shadows of the black birches on the bank. Because I sit so still she has not spotted me. No stray eddy of air bears my scent to her twitching nostrils. Step by step, in silent but deliberate action, she moves into the strong sunlight. A fawn follows her. His spotted coat glistens gold and white in the bright light. Both doe and fawn dip their black muzzles in the cool waters. Only briefly do they pause to refresh their lips and throats. Then softly they turn away and step back into the dim, dark shadows of the trees.

It is an instant of delight—a scene of supreme serenity. It is a moment of joy, an uplift of the spirit. All of it is unplanned; none of it is arranged by man. It is a pure but gentle gift from God. In our common lives such simple incidents come as treasures beyond calculation. They are cameos of beauty, healing, love and restoration that remain etched on the memory, never to be erased.

6 ———— Healing from on High

He restores my failing health. He helps me do what honors him the most.

Psalm 23:3 TLB

Part of the reason that the sea possesses such potent healing proper-ties is its content of a saline solution. It carries in suspension not only salt, but also a multitude of other trace minerals. Some of these rare sub-stances are seldom found on land, yet they abound in the ocean.

The fact that the sea waters which wash over the coastline in a continuous scouring action are salty tends to sterilize and cleanse the shore. The salt actually counteracts decay of material that accumulates on the beach. It deters decomposition. It purifies and prevents undue putrefaction and pollution.

The result is that the beach is not only beautiful to behold, but it is also a lovely place to be. There is a fragrance, a pungent freshness, that permeates the air and quickens the senses. Part of this comes from the ozone off the sea. There is a rich and abundant supply of oxygen in the breezes that blow in off the breakers. They are charged with moisture and trace elements that sweep in over the shore in potent stimulation.

The sea water itself is a marvelous healing agency. Cuts, wounds, abrasions, sores, and skin blemishes are sterilized, cleansed, and enabled to heal with great rapidity. Even injured joints and torn ligaments, if bathed in the sea, then exposed to the warm therapy of the sun, will mend in wondrous ways. . . .

Everywhere, in a hundred ways, the ocean waters heal.

Often, as I stroll along the shore, or sit quietly contemplating the grandeur of the deeps, the Spirit of God reminds me that similarly He is my great Healer. It is He who restores my soul. It is He who renews my spirit. It is He who imparts to my life the health and wholesomeness of His own character.

7 ———— The Earth Is the Lord's

> *The earth is the Lord's, and the fulness thereof;*
> *the world and they that dwell therein.*
>
> Psalm 24:1 KJV; read Psalm 24

Suddenly a dense cloud of heavy fog moved up out of the distant valley below us. In a matter of moments it engulfed us in thick, dense folds of gray vapor. The sun was gone. And a darkness, almost like dusk, enshrouded the hills. . . .

I had often lamented the dreadful devastation of this particular range. Yet on this glorious day it had lain before us cloaked in pristine splendor. So I promised myself I would come there again to see it the following summer. And I did. . . .

What I saw cheered my spirits and lifted my morale. For a great healing had come to the hills. As I climbed the summit a pair of coyotes called across the open grasslands. A mule deer doe and her fawn bounded down the slope. A profusion of wildflowers flung themselves beneath the trees and over the ridges. A new forest would replace the carnage of cut-over country. Once again wildlife and wildflowers would flourish over a wasteland of old mine heaps and torn-up terrain.

This has always been our Father's way with the earth, so scarred, abused, and ravaged by man.

And likewise it is always our Father's way with the soul of man so wounded, torn, and scarred by sin, sorrow, and the sickness of our society.

Only in Him can there be found the help, the healing, the health that restores us from utter ruin.

8 ——— The Gracious Touch of God's Hand

The earth is the Lord's and the fulness thereof, the world and those who dwell therein; for he has founded it upon the seas, and established it upon the rivers.

Psalm 24:1–2 RSV

A profound sense of peace swept over me. It was every bit as real and palpable and strong as the incoming tide running across the golden sand. Here was intense inspiration of spirit, as tangible as the warm thermals rising against the sun-drenched ramparts of rock soaring above the beach. Everywhere there was beauty, splendor—the eternal impact of my Father's wondrous design conveyed to me in grandeur and loveliness.

At such moments—interludes of intense delight and keen spiritual perception—our inner souls long with exquisite yearning to know that somehow they shall endure. And little did I dream on that sun-splashed spring day, some years ago, that in God's own good time, my home would be perched on a height of land just a few hundred yards from this special spot, my bit of beach.

Such is the gracious touch of God's hand upon our little lives. It is His generous pleasure to give us dreams. It is His unique habit to help us see those fond hopes come to exciting reality and heart-pounding fulfillment. This is all part of the exquisite wonder of knowing Him as a dear companion.

9 ——— The Purity of His Presence

Who may ascend the hill of the Lord? Who may stand in his holy place? He who has clean hands and a pure heart, who does not lift up his soul to an idol or swear by what is false. He will receive blessing from the Lord and vindication from God his Savior.

Psalm 24:3–5 NIV

Release from my selfishness can come only from the constant impact of His life on mine. It is the result of the subjugation of my soul by His

Spirit. It is the counteraction of my inner corruption by the purity of His presence, the cleansing of my character by His cross.

It is the outgrowth of the deliberate surrender of my will to His wishes with glad abandon. It is that which happens when I allow the fullness of His wondrous life to sweep over me as the sea sweeps over the shore.

The daily impact of His life on mine brings vigor and vitality. It insures health and holiness to all of life. It assures well-being. . . .

It is just as dramatic as the action of the sea in sterilizing the shore to arrest putrefaction. It is the self-giving, self-sharing, self-sacrificing life of Christ that cuts diametrically across my selfish self-interests. It transcends the giant "I" in my soul, to pour itself out in service to God and man.

10 ——— Prescription for Peace

Where is the man who fears the Lord? God will teach him how to choose the best. He shall live within God's circle of blessing, and his children shall inherit the earth.

Psalm 25:12, 13 TLB; read Psalm 25:1–10

Peace that passes our human comprehension is not a quality of life which excludes us from the stresses and strains of human society. It is not a sheltered withdrawal from the wrongs that rack our world. Nor is it a cloistered existence in which we are cut off from the calamities and conflicts of our generation.

The place of peace to which God our Father calls us is that intimate inner acquaintance with Himself whereby we come to know so assuredly: "O Father, You are here! All is well!" This is the personal, private encounter with Christ which brings serenity amid the storms of life. It is the pervading influence of His own Spirit, so profound He speaks peace even in the midst of earth's most formidable pressures.

The peace He provides is not such as the world supplies. His peace is of eternal duration. It is as timeless as the tides that shape the sea edge and form my bit of beach. In His peace my soul finds strength, my days find deep delight.

11 ——— The Grace of God

The secret of the Lord is with them that fear him; and he will show them his covenant.

Psalm 25:14 KJV; read Psalm 25:11–22

Whether my hours on the beach are taken up with reading a book, enjoying a brisk stroll, lost in quiet prayer or simply stretched in the sun thinking long thoughts, the ocean music surrounds and enfolds me with its melodies. It is superior to any stereo sound. It comes to me clearly with the utmost fidelity, untarnished by human technology.

. . . a large part of the wonder of this music from the deep is that it is there free for the listener. There is no charge for admission to this concert. There is no limit to how long one cares to stay and enjoy it. It has neither beginning nor end. Freely it is given, freely it may be received. One can come heavy in heart, downcast in soul, weary in spirit, yet go away renewed. Often after a quiet interlude by the sea my steps turn toward home revitalized and invigorated by the music of the morning. As it sweeps over me in wave upon wave of inspiration, hope, and uplift, my spirit and soul are energized by the eternal music of the spheres. My whole person is at peace with the benediction of God my Father's blessing.

David must have felt this same kind of peace when he returned from walking with God. The grace of our God is a limitless sea available to His children.

12 —— A Lesson from the Stones

For in the day of trouble he will keep me safe in his dwelling; he will hide me in the shelter of his tabernacle and set me high upon a rock.

Psalm 27:5 NIV; read Psalm 27

In His own special way God has often spoken to me distinctly through the stones on my bit of beach. In their beauty and attractiveness I have been made to see that some of the choicest treasures in life come to us through a long history of hardship.

Small shining stones are not shaped in a day. They are not formed in a single storm. They do not emerge to lie shining in the sun from the turbulence of one night's tide.

They are the end product of a long and painful process that has gone on for countless years and scores of stormy seasons. Small smooth stones once stood as sturdy rock ridges or rugged bedrock. Broken and battered by countless thundering seas, they have been shaped to ultimate perfection in the rolling mills of tide and surf. Their smooth surface emerges from the rugged rasping of sand, the grinding of gravel in the rock tumbler of the tides.

Our lives, too, are like that. It takes the hard and sometimes shattering events of life to break our hard hearts. It takes calamities and losses to crack and fracture our bold, brave facade. It takes the surge of sorrows, the grinding of grief to shatter our proud spirits, our tough, hard wills.

13 —— Cleansing from the Sea

The voice of the Lord is upon the waters; the God of glory thunders, the Lord, upon many waters. The voice of the Lord is powerful, the voice of the Lord is full of majesty.

Psalm 29:3–4 RSV; read Psalm 29:1–4

The outward grandeur of the breakers is not their only greatness. For within the waves themselves there goes on a magnificent cleansing movement of the beach.

This inner action of the sea upon the shore is seldom understood by those who come there only casually. It is as if the curling foam, with countless flying fingers, combs and scours the sand for any debris or silt that pollutes the shore. Caught up in the scrubbing, scouring, washing action of the rolling breakers, every trace of the contamination is borne away into the sea itself.

As the waves wash across the sand and crash around the rocks, they retreat in ceaseless motion, carrying off the silt and mud that may have marred the shore. In wondrous ways the ocean currents carry this burden of sediment in suspension. Lifting it from the land, the waves finally lay it down in the remote depths of the ocean's own immensity. Thus the sea deposits the accumulated filth of the years in faraway ocean canyons.

It is a perpetual process. The poured-out power of the breaking waves washes the beaches . . . with meticulous care. It is the life, the energy, the dynamic of the sea that spills out upon the shore to cleanse it from all its contamination.

14 —— Strength through Separation

The voice of the Lord breaketh the cedars; yea, the Lord breaketh the cedars of Lebanon.

Psalm 29:5 KJV; read Psalm 29:5–11

I can recoil from the apparent disaster of God's discipline, growing bitter, scarred, and cynical. Or I can reach out to grasp Him, spreading myself penitently in His presence to grow stronger than ever: this because I realize it is He who has done it in love.

Some of the finest and most noble cedars stand all alone, set apart among their crowded fellows. The man or woman who grows mighty in

God discovers, too, that he must be set apart from the clamorous commotion of the common crowd. (ATG)

15 —— New Beginnings

For his anger lasts only a moment, but his favor lasts a lifetime;
weeping may remain for a night, but rejoicing comes in the
morning. When I felt secure, I said, "I will never be shaken."
O Lord, when you favored me, you made my mountain
stand firm; but when you hid your face, I was dismayed.

Psalm 30:5, 6 NIV; read Psalm 30

There just have to be times in a person's life when the past is past, when bygones are bygones, when the gaunt, gray, forlorn memories of a former glory are buried under the supernatural loveliness of a new life from above.

For all of us there have to be new beginnings. There have to be fresh moments when we stand on a new height of land and look with widening eyes upon fresh vistas of our Father's great intentions for us. He and He alone can come down upon our soiled souls, our grieving spirits, our wounded hearts to enfold them in His wondrous ways.

16 —— My Times Are in God's Hand

But I was trusting you, O Lord. I said, "You alone are my God;
my times are in your hands. Rescue me from those who hunt
me down relentlessly. Let your favor shine again upon
your servant; save me just because you are so kind!"

Psalm 31:14–16 TLB; read Psalm 31:14–24

No two days were ever exactly the same on my bit of beach. Part of its great appeal lay in the ever-changing appearance of its shoreline.

The subtle play of sunlight and shadow on the cliff faces altered their contours. Some mornings the rugged rocks seemed softened by the muted shades of the rising sun. They glowed warm, golden, wrapped in sunshine and serenity.

Other days the same rock buttresses stood gray and forbidding in the fog and mist that swirled in off the sea. The shoreline looked almost black, dark with dampness, soaked with sea spray.

Always, always, always the ocean is at work on the land. Summer and winter, spring and autumn the changing tides rise and ebb, shaping the character of the coast. Their force is utterly relentless—their power immeasurable—their titanic thrust untamed.

Great mysteries surround the majestic, awesome action of the tides. With incredible precision they move billions of tons of water from surface to surface upon the sea. They are the reflection of gigantic energy within the cosmos that knows no rest, that never slumbers, that never sleeps.

In the same overshadowing way, our Father watches over His children, quietly overseeing the events of their lives that they might accomplish His purposes for Him.

17 —— Established by the Word of the Lord

By the word of the Lord were the heavens made, their starry host by the breath of his mouth. He gathers the waters of the earth into jars; he puts the deep into storehouses.

Psalm 33:6, 7 NIV; read Psalm 33:4–11

There are some aspects of the ocean that twentieth-century technology has opened up to our understanding with tremendous interest. One of these great discoveries is that all the water of all the oceans is in fact one gigantic fluid. It is in constant motion and movement, circulating by means of colossal currents from pole to pole and clear around the earth.

The ancient idea that each ocean or great inland sea, such as the Mediterranean, was more or less a self-contained body of water, restricted roughly within its own continental basin and boundaries, is no longer valid. We now know for a fact that these great oceans actually flow into one another in gigantic subsurface rivers that make the Mississippi, Nile, or Amazon seem like mere trickles in comparison. . . .

God, very God, is the One who established the sea and "gathers the waters of the earth." And, wonder of wonders, He is my heavenly Father who will "comfort (y)our hearts and stablish (us) in every good word and work" (2 Thessalonians 2:17 KJV). (OG)

18 —— The Surge of the Sea

By the words of the Lord the heavens were made, and all their host by the breath of his mouth. He gathered the waters of the sea as in a bottle; he put the deeps in storehouses. . . . For he spoke, and it came to be; he commanded, and it stood forth.

Psalm 33:6, 7, 9 RSV; read Job 23

The innermost response of my spirit to God's magnificent presence is, "O Lord, my Father, my Creator, my Most High God! You are here! All is well!"

Human language is strained to describe the sense of ecstasy, the upwelling of blessing, the surging tide of serenity that floods over my soul in such moments. This is an interaction between God and a common man made doubly precious because I was once a stranger to this One. I knew nothing of the inspiration of His Spirit. I was ignorant of and oblivious to the impact Christ's character could make on mine.

Just as the ocean sculpts and shapes my bit of beach with the rise and ebb of every tide, so there sweeps now across my soul the surging impulses of God's own gracious Spirit. The powerful current of the very life of Christ sweeps through my mind, my emotions, my will to do His own wondrous work.

Still I sense profoundly that I am, like my bit of beach, but a single soul on the bare edge of God's great love. But I am there—open, exposed, vulnerable, susceptible to every incoming surge of His Spirit, able to be altered, waiting to be worked upon, shaped and recreated daily by the impulse of His presence.

The beach does not shape itself! It is a reflection of the movement of ten thousand ocean tides. It is the product of the ocean's might and power. It is the superb piece of artistic craftsmanship that emerges from the ocean's endless sculpting.

Nor am I a self-made man. For there has played upon my life the eternal impact of the love of God in Christ which has shaped my character with eternal perseverance.

19 —— The Music of the Stars

By the word of the Lord were the heavens made,
their starry host by the breath of his mouth.

Psalm 33:6 NIV; *read Psalm 33*

God chooses to speak to us earthlings in various ways. His thoughts and intentions toward me as His child are clearly articulated in many modes. We speak freely of "hearing His voice" and being attuned to His purposes. The Scriptures are replete with references to the songs of love that come to the bride from the Beloved. There is the sound of the Shepherd communing with His sheep.

In music moods as numerous as those produced by the ocean upon the shore, God's gracious Spirit plays upon the shore of my soul. Sometimes He speaks to me in the softest whispers. It may be a gentle suggestion from His Word, the kindly remark of a caring friend, the refrain from a song, the momentary impact of an exquisite sunset or the serenity of a star-studded night.

In that fleeting, sublime instant, my spirit, quietly responsive to Christ's presence, is sensitive to His voice. I sense acutely I have heard from Him. He is here. All is well. The music of His companionship cheers me. The melody of His good will assures me He is near. He has spoken to my spirit.

20 —— Our Great Creator God

He merely spoke, and the heavens were formed, and all the galaxies of the stars. He made the oceans, pouring them into his vast reservoirs. Let everyone in the world—men, women, and children—fear the Lord and stand in awe of him. For when he but spoke, the world began! It appeared at his command!

Psalm 33:6–9 TLB

Just as the sea absorbs into itself all the debris from the shore, bearing it away into the fathomless oblivion of its own depths, so Christ bears in His own person all the wrongs and ill will of our contaminated characters. He receives into His infinite forbearance all our wretched attitudes, our contorted decisions, our negative impulses. In their place He pours out His love, His care, His forgiveness upon us—new each day—wave upon wave.

The unique disclosure, given to us by His own Spirit, goes beyond even this, namely, that all our sins and all our iniquities are carried away into the depths of the sea of His forgiveness, not only to be buried from view but also forgotten forever. Only God our Father could be so gracious. Only He could be so magnanimous. Only He could be so utterly astonishing.

To use the theological terminology of the New Testament, "He hath made him to be sin for us, who knew no sin; that we might be made the righteousness of God in him" (2 Corinthians 5:21). What an exchange!

21 —— Surviving by Surrender

Blessed is the nation whose God is the Lord, the people to whom he has chosen for his own inheritance.

Psalm 33:12 KJV

March

The seeds and spores of ferns and flowers, grass and shrubs, trees and herbs blow across mountain ridges on the wind to take root in the rock and gravel. And so out of the most austere setting of ice, snow, gravel, and stone there has emerged beauty, elegance, and grandeur of divine design.

In the whole realm of outdoor art, there is a profound return to the reality of natural beauty. As a people we are rediscovering the inherent glory of God's creation. In a most wholesome trend, we are turning away from the confusion and meaningless expression of abstract art.

But beyond all this there lies at even greater depths the profound spiritual perceptions which we need to discover as a modern society if we are to survive. Those principles are absolutely basic to any human understanding of what our Father's ultimate objectives are in shaping our lives to His ends. . . .

In my own search for spiritual reality in the midst of so much sadness, my footsteps have been led back again and again to the wonders of the natural world. As with our Master, I find true understanding in such simple things as water, rocks, trees and skies.

This must inevitably be the case. As the supreme Creator it was He who brought the earth into being. It was He who first conceived of things as lovely as sunsets, birds on wing, clouds against the sky, or water shaping stone. And it was also He who brought man into being with all his convoluted character. As we surrender our chaotic lives to Him, He can bring serenity and peace where confusion once reigned.

22 —— Bounty from My Father's Bonus

The young lions do lack, and suffer hunger; but they that seek the Lord shall not want any good thing.

Psalm 34:10 KJV; read Psalm 34

One day I went to walk alone on the shore. In mid-winter it appeared desolate, empty, and forlorn. Its mood exactly matched the melancholy of my own emotions. I had been seriously ill for several weeks. Strength was slow to return. Responsibilities and work were falling far behind, overwhelming me with their pressures.

As I strolled alone along the sand, suddenly my attention was arrested by a magnificent snow-white heron soaring on the thermals above the beach. Herons seldom do this. Usually their flight is slow, ponderous, and heavy. Yet this beautiful bird sailed in utter serenity, scarcely moving a wing, gliding in rhythmic circles against the brilliant blue sky. Finally it soared down to settle sedately on the crown of a wind-tossed Monterey cypress clinging to the cliffs.

At once my spirit was inspired. My emotions were moved. My whole being was galvanized by the splendor and glory of this sight.

Out of the silence, out of the stillness, out of the serenity of that moment my Father spoke to me in accents only His: "My son, you are not forgotten. I am here to help, to heal, to lift you above the burdens of life!"

I needed no more. I had seen a vision of beauty. My life had been enriched by the bounty of my Father's bonus. I think I experienced the same awe and wonder that David did when he wrote, ". . . they that seek the Lord shall not want any good thing."

23 —— Bruised but Not Broken

A righteous man may have many troubles,
but the Lord delivers him from them all;
he protects all his bones,
not one of them will be broken.

Psalm 34:19–20 NIV

Most of us don't want to be broken in the storms of life. We much prefer to protect our personalities from the stresses and strains of our days. We would rather, much rather, be tough and rugged and self-assured than contrite before Christ, repentant in soul before His Spirit.

No, as the rocks resist the action of the sea that surrounds them, so we resist the movement of our God who enfolds us in His encircling care. We see the impact of His presence upon us as something shattering, painful, and at times very unpleasant.

Many of us would like to avoid the mills of God. We are tempted to ask Him to deliver us from the upsetting, tumbling tides of time that knock off our rough corners and shape us to His design. We plead for release from the discipline of difficulties, the rub of routine responsibilities, the polish that comes from long perseverance.

We are a restless generation. We of the West want and insist on instant results. We demand a quick fix. We look for shortcuts and immediate results. We are quite sure we can be a rough slab of stone today and a polished gemstone tomorrow.

But God's ways and our ways are not the same. His patience is persistent. His work is meticulous. His years know no end. His perception of time is that one day is as a thousand years and a thousand years as but a single day.

The shattering of rock, the smoothing of stone, the polishing of a jewel in the sea requires eons of time. Can I then expect the breaking of my hard heart, the smoothing of my spirit, the shaping of my character as it is conformed to His own to be any less time-consuming?

24 —— Shaping the Soul

Many are the afflictions of the righteous: but the Lord delivereth him out of them all. He keepeth all his bones; not one of them is broken.

Psalm 34:19, 20 KJV

The pounding of the surf, the crash of giant waves, the working of the wind, the rivulets of winter rain, the lashing of seasonal storms off the sea, the variation of temperatures from day to night—all erode, sculpt, and shape the character of the cliffs.

Some of these bold bluffs may have withstood ten thousand storms. But then one day a giant fault will appear in the cliff face. In time a thundering avalanche of rock, soil, and debris will crash to the foot of the rampart. Rocks, rubble, and scattered stone will lie shattered on the sand.

It takes time and hundreds of tides to wear this material away. The running of the sea currents, the rasping of the sand, the softening action of the sea water will do their unceasing work to beautify the beach again. For the cliffs, like the sand, are in eternal flux. They know only endless change. They are at best the passing reflection of an ever-changing seascape.

Yet, in a wondrous way, this is all a part of the eternal fascination of the sea edge. There is nothing static or sterile about it. Subject to the action of the ocean, it is being altered from strength to strength, from glory to glory, from character to character. It is not stale, but stimulating.

In much the same way the Lord works on the lives of His children, shaping and refining them so that they can become His instruments for sharing the story of His love with a broken and bleeding world.

Lord, shape me and use me after Your will.

25 —— Lessons from the Sea

The good man does not escape all troubles—he has them too. But the Lord helps him in each and every one.

Psalm 34:19 TLB

Sometimes the most beautiful beach is the one which has endured the most severe storms. The most attractive sea edge has been exposed to the fiercest force of flood tides. The most spectacular seascapes are sculptured by the most sweeping wave action.

My very natural human reaction is to try to avoid the storms of life, to hide from the abrasive action of daily events, to retreat from the incoming impact of God's providential presence in my affairs.

But let me not!

As I recognize my Father's kind hands at work upon my life, I shall be quietly content to expose myself to Him. It is in the sure knowledge that He knows full well the best way to make me attractive to His eyes that I shall rest beneath His strong hands. In His presence I shall find peace. No matter what storms, trials or stress are brought to bear upon my soul I shall see them as His tools for shaping my character into a winsome piece of His workmanship.

Because He is here, active, patiently at work on me, *all is well!*

26 —— A Bonus from the Sky

Your love, O Lord, reaches to the heavens, / your faithfulness to the skies. Your righteousness is like the mighty mountains, / your justice like the great deep.

Psalm 36:5 NIV

The best of blessings do not always come in crowds.

There are those still, quiet moments when, alone in gentle communion with Christ, I sense and see the momentary glory of His person. The intense nearness of His Spirit as soft, yet sublime as any tern on wing, moves my spirit. And again I know, "O Father, You are here! I have been enriched by Your beautiful bonuses."

As with the lone and sometimes solitary sea birds on the beach, there are times when we must search and seek for the bonus blessings of our God.

27 —— A Word from the Waves

Your love, O Lord, reaches to the heavens, your faithfulness to the skies.

Psalm 36:5 NIV; read Psalm 36

A remarkable principle that the ocean beach has impressed upon my spirit is one shaped by the action of the waves upon sand. I see it repeated a hundred thousand times when I walk softly between the tides. It is there for any passerby to see. Yet most of us have never been open or receptive to it.

Every wave or wavelet that surges across the sand seems to run up the beach in threatening fashion. The water foams and froths ominously.

March

It comes swishing up the sand, hissing menacingly. It seems intent on shifting and sweeping everything before it. . . .

Yet, mysteriously, wondrously, incredibly, I have seen those same threatening waves come to a quiet end. Their energy spent, they simply sink into the sand. The water not soaked up recedes gently, to be reclaimed by the next incoming wave. The threatening presence is lost and dissipated in the matrix of the great white beach. Only tiny bursting rainbow bubbles and a vanishing fleck of foam remain to remind one of the menace.

It seemed so real, so overwhelming, so all-engulfing. Yet it came to nothing.

Life, too, is like that. So many of the events or things we fear often come to nothing. Initially they may appear, like a rising wave on the sea, intent on sweeping right over us. We are sure they will engulf us in calamity and chaos. We are terrified at times that they will fling us off our feet, to toss us up, crumpled and broken, on the beach of life.

Yet again and again, like waves that run out of energy, to spend themselves softly on the sand, the threats of our days fade away. They look so menacing, they appear so formidable; we want to turn and run from them. Yet time tames most of them. They dissolve into nothing. Lord, help me to remember this word from the waves. (OG)

28 —— At High Tide

Thy steadfast love, O Lord, extends to the heavens, thy faithfulness to the clouds. . . . How precious is thy steadfast love, O God! The children of men take refuge in the shadow of thy wings.

Psalm 36:5, 7 RSV

There are days and there are times when only the high tide of God's overflowing goodness can put right all that is wrong within. Most remarkably, those looking on will know and sense the impact of His life on mine. For I am His bit of beach!

At high tide the surging ocean asserts itself with awesome power upon the open shore. Likewise in my life, the impact of God's pervasive Spirit, if allowed to do so, can move in majestic might upon my soul and spirit and body.

As the full weight of the sea currents change and shape the coast, so Christ, in control, recreates me as a man. He alters the contours of my character and conduct.

At full flood the tide turns the entire beach into a glistening expanse of water, brilliant as a sheet of beaten silver. And thus it is my

Father enfolds my common life in the generous love and purity of His own perfection.

Little wonder John cried out from the depths of his yearning spirit: *"He must increase, but I must decrease!"* (John 3:30 KJV).

29 —— Where Is Your Sanctuary?

> *Never envy the wicked! Soon they fade away like the grass and disappear. Trust in the Lord instead. Be kind and good to others; then you will live safely here in the land and prosper, feeding in safety.*
> Psalm 37:1–3 TLB; read Psalm 73:21–28

The sea edge is in very tangible truth one of God's great gifts to His earth children—not just exclusively for man, but also for all his brothers of paw, wing, flipper, or shell. It is a place to be shared, relished, cherished, and preserved. For here one can find wholeness, soundness, health, and beauty amid a troubled world.

The hours spent in peace here are hours of healing. They are interludes of serenity for the soul, times for making one whole in the world of fragmentation and bruising abuse. The moments slip away softly, their motion as smooth as the murmuring movements of the sea, caressing the conscience, mending the mind, stilling the spirit.

There are those who rather naively insist that our Father can be found only in the formal and sometimes rather august surroundings of a man-made sanctuary. But my contention is that He is more often met in the majestic amphitheater of His own wondrous creation. He cannot be confined to structures of steel, concrete and glass devised and erected by the efforts of man.

He comes softly to meet the soul open to receive Him upon a stretch of sand, along some leaf-strewn forest trail, across a summer meadow deep in the sun-splashed daisies, or on a storm-blasted mountain ridge.

30 —— Delighting in God

> *Take delight in the Lord, and he will give you the desires of your heart.*
> Psalm 37:4 RSV; read Psalm 37:1–4

How does one delight in God? Here are a few simple suggestions. Use those same five physical senses of your body that the world exploits to intrude into your life, to make yourself aware, instead, of God.

Use your eyes to read His Word—to study it. Use them to revel in the sublime beauties of His creation around you.

Use your hearing to listen to the sounds of wind, waves, streams, bird song, the laughter of children, great music. Take your body where these can be found. Revel in them.

Use your sense of smell to inhale the fragrance of flowers, fresh earth after rain, ozone off the sea, hay curing in the sun, orchards in blossom. Thank Him for every perfume.

Use your taste buds to relish clear, cool water, delicious food, the delicacy of fresh fruit and vegetables. All come from Him.

Use your sense of touch to feel the smoothness of a rose, the roughness of tree bark, the warmth of sand between your toes, the luxuriance of grass and pine needles beneath your feet, the hand of your wife, husband, child, or sweetheart.

Every good and perfect gift comes to us in generous measure from our God. On every side He surrounds us with an overwhelming outpouring of His loving provision for our bodily welfare. Submerge yourself in His generosity. Let an upwelling stream of gratitude and delight pour from you in ardent appreciation for His presence that surrounds you on every side. (WG)

31 —— A Light in the Dark

Commit your way to the Lord; trust in him, and he will act; He will bring forth your vindication as the light, and your right as noonday.

Psalm 37:5, 6 RSV; read Psalm 37:5–11

A Christian must understand that darkness may invade his personal life. We are given no guarantee by God that all our days on earth will be nothing but brightness. It is an inexorable law of life, as sure as the rotation of the earth, that for all of us there are going to be some tears and sighs, some sorrow and sadness, some dark periods of disappointment and despair.

Often these are times and events over which we have no control whatever. They come as swiftly and surely as darkness in the desert. How am I going to respond to their apparent oppression? How will I react to these seeming reverses that come to me as stimuli in disguise?

Am I going to rebel against them because they bring a sudden lull into my feverish activity, because they bog down my busy life, because they curtail my ambitious aspirations?

Or will I accept them calmly as coming from the hand of my Heavenly Father for my own well-being? After all, it is perfectly possible to walk in the dark unafraid, undisturbed, and undismayed—"for thou art with me" (Psalm 23:4 KJV). (ATG)

1 ——— Our Father's Faithfulness

*For evil men will be cut off, but those
who hope in the Lord will inherit the land.*

Psalm 37:9 NIV

Across the long years of my life, God's Spirit has taught me some unforgettable truths from watching birds in flight. During quiet walks along the sea edge Christ has brought home to my innermost spirit powerful parallels learned from the ocean updrafts. My Father has used the splendor of soaring birds to show me something of His own wondrous faithfulness.

For the birds along the beach, and for me as a man, life has all sorts of weather. Just because I am a child of God does not exempt me from the downdrafts of disaster, the cross currents of calamity, or the dark, rainy, dreary days of distress. These are as much a part of the warp and woof of life's tapestry as are the sun-filled days, brisk with warm sea breezes.

The climate may be fair or foul. The winds of change may be offshore or onshore. The days may be bright or bleak.

But the ocean is always there. Its presence and its power are ever at work, seen or unseen. And ultimately its influence is beneficial and beautiful.

The birds know this. But most of us human beings forget the faithfulness of our Father. Quietly, calmly, the birds adjust their behavior to the changing pattern of their surroundings. We humans, however, fight and buck the setbacks of our surroundings. We fret and worry over the fortunes and misfortunes of our little lives. We insist on trying to soar and sail away into the heights when we should just sit still and wait upon the wind of God's Spirit to lift and guide us.

Most of us modern Christians know precious little about waiting patiently for the Lord. We prefer to use our own high-powered technology to be on an "eternal high."

2 ——— Relishing the Moment

But the meek shall inherit the earth. . . .

Psalm 37:11 KJV

In our Western world we place too much emphasis upon attaining, achieving, ambitions. We are overly concerned and preoccupied with motivation. Somehow we feel we must make our mark.

In this inner intensity we deprive ourselves of the special delight to be found in the actual process of achieving.

So much of our enterprise, rather than being a labor of love, becomes a burden to endure. We do not "relish the moment." We do not find pleasure in our work.

But the meek man does. Though he toils, it is with a twinkle in his eye, a whistle on his lips, a tune in his spirit. For he is inheriting the earth. His service is a joy and not a penance.

3 ——— Treasures in Trusting

And he hath put a new song in my mouth, even praise unto our God; many shall see it, and fear, and shall trust in the Lord.

Psalm 40:3 KJV; read Psalm 40:1–10

Human spirituality does not consist only of creeds, churches, biblical knowledge or good deeds. It is made up as well from the humble art of learning to see and find the impress of my Father's hand in all the land. It is woven into the warp and woof of our little lives by sweet associations in the company of Christ, who cares about sparrows, lilies, and shells from the sea. Human spirituality comes to us afresh every day by His gracious Spirit who touches us with the impress of wind and surf and sea and sky and a thousand glorious sunsets over the shining shore of our days! All for free! All for the taking!

If we will but pause in mid-stride to pick up the treasures of our God from between the tides of time we can become richer in spirit than we ever dreamed.

4 ——— A Contrite Heart

For troubles without number surround me; my sins have overtaken me, and I cannot see. They are more than the hairs of my head, and my heart fails within me.

Psalm 40:12 NIV; read Psalm 40:11–17

David had the remarkable capacity to repent of his wrongs whenever he became acutely aware that he had sinned against God. He was not haughty or arrogant.

He was a man capable of enormous remorse. His outpouring of genuine sorrow for wrongs committed touches us to the depths. He is not given to excuses or putting the blame on others. He knew his personal responsibilities and when he failed in them he took the necessary steps to put things right with God and man.

Such people the Most High picks up again and again. He restores them to fellowship with Himself! He heals the wounds and reestablishes them in peace and prosperity. He forgives and forgets the failings and folly of the past. He honors such a contrite spirit.

5 ———— Fire on the Mountain

God is our refuge and strength, a tested help in times of trouble. And so we need not fear even if the world blows up, and the mountains crumble into the sea.

Psalm 46:1, 2 RSV; read Psalm 46

Out of fire on the mountain, new life will emerge. New growth will come. A fresh forest will be re-created.

Perhaps the most dramatic demonstration of this process in modern times is the renewal of life on the devastated slopes of Mount Saint Helens. Biologists and environmentalists have been startled and delighted to see the incredible resurgence of new life in areas utterly devastated and burned over by the volcanic eruption.

Our lofty western mountains have been born and shaped by fire. Their very character and contours are the end product of burning. Their grand silhouettes against the sky, their mantles of forest cover, grassy ranges and glorious alp-lands all have been shaped by fire. Even the shining "silver forests" of stark, fire-scorched trees with their blazing carpets of native wildflowers came to beauty by their burning.

O Father, I pray that Your fire will burn the dross from my life so that Your life can emerge in me!

6 ———— Meeting on the Mountain

There is a river whose streams make glad the city of God, the holy habitation of the Most High.

Psalm 46:4 RSV

As the sun warmed my body, caressed my face and sparkled in the stream, I was struck with the remarkable potency of the river that flowed beside me. Everything it touched it transformed. There was vigor and vitality in every tree, shrub, blade of grass or mountain flower that flourished on its banks.

It was as if in loud, clear tones it stated boldly, "Life-life-life!" Here was the source, the strength, the surge of life itself poured out, spilling over, quickening everything it touched. From this singing, spilling, shining stream came the vitality of all the vegetation of the valley. Even more than that, beyond the forest, grass, and flowers were the birds that dropped down here to drink; the wildlife that came here to slake their thirst; the solitary person who came to find new life to face the future.

"O Lord, my God, how Generous You are; how gracious to this weary one; how merciful to a man deep in distress!" The words were not spoken aloud. They were the profound inner expression of a spirit being renewed by the gracious inflowing presence of the Living Christ.

He had come to me in the solitude of a high mountain stream and renewed my spirit. Vigor, vitality of divine origin swept into my soul bringing life—life from above—from the edge of the sky, from Himself.

7 ———— Solitude by the Sea

> *Be still, and know that I am God: I will be exalted among the heathen, I will be exalted in the earth.*
>
> Psalm 46:10 KJV

Sometimes along the ocean edge there is remarkable solitude. There is a sense of stillness greater and more majestic than mere silence. It is the hush and quietness of a small fragment of the planet still in its pristine state. It is the solace of a bit of beach not yet polluted or ravaged by the grasping hand of man.

Strolling on this ocean strand I sense that I am alone, yet not alone, one solitary man moving quietly, gently in awe before The Most High. It is not that I have earned or deserve the privilege of such precious privacy. But rather it is the fundamental fact that I discipline myself to take the time to seek the stillness of this shore. It is there for others to share. Yet few deliberately seek solitude.

Many are afraid to be alone with their thoughts. They are intimidated by the idea of spending several hours in stillness, allowing God's spirit to speak to them.

I have been ridiculed, both privately and in public, by those detractors who insist that the measurement of a man's usefulness is how busy he is. It is the unwritten rule of our contemporary society, both within the church and outside it, that our effectiveness is directly proportional to how much we are on the go—for God, or man.

The truth is, our Father calls us at times to come apart and be still before Him. Christ calls us to commune with Him in meditation and quiet contemplation of His character. The Holy Spirit calls us to serenity and rest so that we may be sensitive to His wishes.

8 ——— Renewal in Solitude

> *Be still, and know that I am God; I will be exalted*
> *among the nations, I will be exalted in the earth.*
>
> *Psalm 46:10 NIV*

The joyous renewal that comes to the anguished soul in solitude assures me again and again of my Father's care that enfolds His earth children. If we are to know His compassion, if we are to sense His touch upon our torn spirits, if we are to feel the caress of His hand upon our wounded hearts, we must seek Him in solitude.

It is no accident that His Spirit speaks to us with such clear perception as the psalmist wrote: *"Be still and know that I am God . . . I will be exalted in the earth"* (Psalm 46:10).

We modern people live so much amid turmoil, tension and the trauma of a fractured world. So, when death strikes or illness of terminal nature tears away the fragile fabric of one's thin veneer of invulnerability, most men and women know not where to turn for shelter. It is as if they stand exposed, naked, stripped and shattered by the suffering and sorrow that has swept over them in a whirlwind of horror.

Again and again I have been through the storms of suffering with other human beings who really wondered if there would or could be a way out. Was there a place of peace? Was there some spot of stillness for the soul?

My answer over and over is, "Yes!" But one must search, and seek, and find it in the presence of Jesus Christ, who is from everlasting to everlasting, who changes not across the centuries, who is eternal, Creator of heaven and earth, yet also Creator of my complex character.

9 ——— In the Summer Silence

> *Be still and know that I am God.*
> *I am exalted among the nations,*
> *I am exalted in the earth!*
>
> *Psalm 46:10 RSV*

Most of us want an instant fix. We want immediate renewal. We demand an overnight remedy for all our hurts.

We will not give God in Christ either the time or opportunities to bring us back from the bleak disasters that overwhelm us. Instead we turn to every sort of human device or manmade technology in an attempt to find consolation and comfort amid the chaos of our calamities.

The one great lesson I have learned above and beyond all other amid the great distress of recent months is this: *Be still, be quiet, be calm, and know that I am God!* It takes time to do this. It means one must, by a deliberate act of the will, learn to repose confidently in Christ . . . to rest assuredly in the faithfulness of our Father.

He is our hope.

He is our healing.

He is our helper.

The wondrous work which He accomplishes in our souls is done in silence. It is nothing less than the persistent incoming of His own Presence to generate in us new life, new vitality, new confidence to carry on. He actually transmits to us His hope, His love, His energy, His ability to begin anew.

10 —— How Great Thou Art!

The Mighty One, God, the Lord, speaks and summons the earth from the rising of the sun to the place where it sets.

Psalm 50:1 NIV; *read Psalm 50:1–6*

Often as I move along the shore it appears so utterly beautiful, so completely perfect, so exquisitely lovely that it is akin to walking across a painted stage setting. On one side the blue Pacific stretches away to the horizon. Along its fringe of beach, the rolling surf lays a lacework of immaculate white across the golden sand. On the other side, the shoreline itself undulates above the brown, buckskin cliffs in a gorgeous carpet of green grass and blowing wildflowers.

The wildflowers come in many hues and shades. There are brilliant beach peas of flaming pink. I have gathered some of their seed and planted them in my own garden. What a show they made, spreading out into huge clumps of bursting blooms. The tough and hardy ice plants, turgid with the winter rain, burst into colors as varied as a rainbow. There are yellows, reds, purples and pinks, some of them so prolific they appear as rugs of flowers flung at random over the cliffs and rocks.

My heavenly Father made all this and so much more! What more can I do than say, "O Lord my God—How Great Thou Art!"

11 —— An Attitude of Gratitude

*I don't need your sacrifices of flesh and blood. What I want from you
is your true thanks; I want your promises fulfilled. I want you
to trust me in your times of trouble.*

Psalm 50:13–15 TLB

It was a veteran missionary working amid the awful poverty, squalor and degradation of India's poor who taught his children early, "Learn to look. Observe quietly. Think long thoughts. Find what is beautiful. *Give humble thanks.* Recall it to mind often. Refresh your soul in the gentle stream of our Father's bounty!"

To do this is to live with an attitude of gratitude. It is to discover fragments of loveliness in the most ordinary events of life. It is to search and seek and seize every evidence of bonuses bestowed by the gentle hands of our loving Father.

We of the affluent twentieth century have had our sensibilities seared, our appreciation jaded, by the easy overabundance of our days. Few, few amongst us know anything of the humble art of a lowly heart that can find inspiration in the soaring flight of a gull or the exquisite shape of a shell or the song of the surf.

We of the West have, by our crude and crass culture, become so conditioned to look for the sensational and spectacular in our experiences that we miss seeing the stars while looking at our spacecraft. We know so little of the sublime, because we are so attuned to the clash and crash of our civilization. We prefer crowds and mass displays to the enrichment of soul or uplift that can come to the person prepared to spend a few moments alone in company with Christ.

12 —— The Legacy of a Life

*Have mercy on me, O God, according to your unfailing love; according
to your great compassion blot out my transgressions. Wash away
all my iniquity and cleanse me from my sin.*

Psalm 51:1, 2 NIV; *read Psalm 51:1–12*

The legacy of David's life was a brilliant endowment that enriched all of Israel during his rule, but much more than that, it has been an inspiration to all of God's people of every nation across thousands of years.

We can safely say that not more than half a dozen other men have ever made such a spiritual impact on human history.

It is important that we should understand clearly the secrets of David's success. . . .

David was not perfect. He was not a plaster-cast saint with a halo around his head. He was a passionate man with lights and shadows in his character. But, most importantly, he was a man *totally available to God and His purposes*. God has difficulty finding such individuals. Most of us, by a deliberate decision of our wills, refuse to relinquish our selves to the Lord. We insist on controlling our own careers rather than capitulating to the control of Christ.

We are determined to make all our own choices in life, rather than submit in humility to the gracious sovereignty of God's gracious Spirit.

In essence this is personal pride. Such people God resists! It is, therefore, little wonder that the majority of men and women who claim to be God's people achieve little for Him.

13 —— Whiter than Snow

> *Cleanse me with hyssop, and I will be clean;*
> *wash me, and I will be whiter than snow.*
>
> Psalm 51:7 NIV; read Psalm 51:1–9

Snow begins to fall. Ten million times ten million drifting flakes, each perfect and distinct in pattern, float down out of the heavy overcast. They drift down through the trees, settle among the shrubs, adorn every twig, cone, blade of grass or stone upon the ground.

The storm is not noisy. It does not come in with roaring force or thundering tones. It is almost imperceptible, yet utterly irresistible. Flake by flake, moment by moment, hour upon hour, it impresses itself upon the entire landscape.

Nothing escapes its impact. The whole world is suddenly transformed by the pervasive whiteness. Everywhere the contours of the countryside are softened and smoothed with the enfolding mantle that crowns every stone, stump or broken fence rail. . . .

Nothing stirs.

The land lies immaculate in its dazzling splendor.

It is a moment of magnificent splendor.

A total transformation has come over the earth.

Exquisite loveliness has erased every scar upon the land. The last trace of waste, the worse signs of damage and devastation are covered over by the gracious mantle of gleaming purity.

Lord, heal my life with Your cleansing touch!

14 —— The Carving of Character

*Cleanse me with hyssop, and I shall be clean; wash me, and
I shall be whiter than snow. Fill me with joy and gladness;
let the bones which thou hast broken rejoice.*

Psalm 51:7, 8 RSV

There is a rare and unique quality to smooth stones shaped under
the impulse of flowing water. The stones speak of long years of wear.
Each is a silent tribute to great spans of time during which water was at
work on the rock. It tells of patient, quiet subjection to the abrasive forces
of the natural world.

Even more stunning and arresting than the small stone fragments a
mountain man can carry home are the exquisite stream beds carved out of
solid rock. Only in the highest streams that have their source at the sky
edge may the ultimate beauty of this kind be seen.

Their water, at the eternal verge of freezing, carries in suspension
stone worn so fine it hangs suspended in the stream like thin milk.
Millennia after millennia the ice-fed freshets flow relentlessly from their
mountain source of snow and ice to carve an ever-deepening channel
through the upthrust rock formations.

This is a picture of the way God works to carve the character of His
chosen children. The lessons of life can create magnificence or meager-
ness, depending upon the way we react to the shaping hand of God. Lord,
carve the character You want me to have—and may I be the person You
want me to be.

15 —— Renew a Right Spirit

*Create in me a clean heart, O God; and
renew a right spirit within me.*

Psalm 51:10 KJV

As I stood alone upon a snow-mantled mountain there came to me
clearly the awareness that my Father, in His mercy and generosity, could
again make all things bright and beautiful in my life. It was He who could
erase the resentments at the grievous loss of my friends. It was He who
could heal the deep hurt of seeing so much suffering. It was He who
could cleanse away the criticism of so much pain and pathos.

Yes, there had been scarlet stains upon my soul. It was not a question
of hiding them from Him. Rather it was a time to admit them openly, to

lay them honestly before Him, to see that only the profound outpouring of His own wondrous life could ever cover them completely with the purity of His presence.

I came down off that snowy ridge a man renewed with a right spirit within me. I had met my Master at the edge of the sky. And in His own winsome way a tremendous fall of fresh snow, His righteousness, was enfolding all my life and outlook.

All would be well! Hope came afresh.

Not only was there hope for today, but even more exciting, hope for the years ahead.

16 —— True Riches

The sacrifices of God are a broken spirit: a broken and contrite heart, O God, thou wilt not despise.

Psalm 51:17 KJV; read Psalm 51:10–17

It is the meek person who discovers with great delight that God loves to draw near to the contrite and broken in spirit.

It is the man humble in will, obedient to the overtures of God's Spirit, who becomes acutely aware of God's presence. And though he himself may be of the earth, his sojourn here is rich and replete with the gracious companionship of Christ.

Even though he may be poor in material possessions, his inheritance in the constant comradeship of God can enrich his earthly days beyond human ability to express.

17 —— A Humble Heart

The sacrifices of God are a broken spirit; a broken and contrite heart, O God, you will not despise.

Psalm 51:17 NIV

David, because of his humility and contrite spirit, was sensitive to God's Spirit. He was a man with "a broken heart." That phrase does not mean the center of his emotions had been grieved by sorrow of an intimate sort. In the Scriptures, a "broken heart" is a will that has been trained and disciplined to do God's will. The expression is used in the same sense as we speak of a horse "being broken to the saddle" or an ox "being broken to the plow" or an ass "being broken to bear burdens." It means to be harnessed or yoked.

Our service to the Almighty is not predicated upon some soft, sentimental, fickle, human emotion of a broken heart. Our usefulness is directly dependent on our being disciplined in will and spirit to do God's will no matter what that means.

Our Lord spoke clearly of counting the cost to follow Him—and work with Him. That cost is suffering as He does.

Most modern Christians only look for a comfortable way of life. They only serve if they happen "to feel like it." They know little of disciplined devotion to God, even less of literally laying down their lives, their strength, their time, their money, or their ambitions for the sake of others.

But David did! He demonstrated this again and again in the life he lived out before his people in his declining years. His was a life of amazing self-sacrifice.

18 —— "Birds of Joy"

I said, "Oh, that I had the wings of a dove! I would fly away and be at rest—I would flee far away and stay in the desert; I would hurry to my place of shelter, far from the tempest and storm."

Psalm 55:6–8 NIV; read Psalm 55:1–8

Here and there like a solitary rascal of a raven tumbling gleefully in the wind, a sudden spectacle of fun and good cheer would tumble through my sometimes gloomy thoughts. Borne on the wind of God's powerful Spirit some joyous word of encouragement or little experience of ecstatic delight would sweep into my life to dispel my melancholy.

There were hours, yes, sometimes even days or maybe even weeks, when the crows of craven fear and apprehension seemed to crowd in upon us. The ragged cries of cowardice and black regret seemed to gang up on us. But we found a place of peace, a spot of strength as we settled down quietly to be still and know the presence of the Living Christ who abides with us always. Eventually the harassments of the opposition would fade away and we would know the rest of those who trust in God.

Some of the most unpromising circumstances became suddenly brighter when . . . they were invaded by unexpected bits of light. It astonished me to see how one unexpected knock at the door, a letter from a long-forgotten associate, a bit of fun with a friend, a hilarious cameo of humor could come winging into the day to drive away the despair.

There were a dozen ways in which our Father arranged for "birds of joy" to return, bringing with them hope and healing for the deep hurts of my wounded heart. In His mercy, love, and compassion He had ways of bringing light and love back into the gloom.

19 —— God's Majesty and Might

> Be exalted, O God, above the heavens!
> Let thy glory be over all the earth!
>
> Psalm 57:5 RSV; read Psalm 57:1–5

To me, it seems God's majesty, His might, His splendor are as magnificent as any seascape. In quietness as I contemplate His character it equals and surpasses in grandeur anything known to man. The extent of His glory fills the earth.

As I am drawn to Him by the irresistible magnetism of His own greatness, there are pensive moments when in awe and wonder I sense that at best I can only really experience "the edge of His life." There is a dimension at least in my earth life, in which He will never be known to me in all His magnificence. With my human fallibility and spiritual limitations I shall never fully comprehend the length or depth or breadth of His infinite, amazing love.

But, what joy, I still can touch the edge of His glory. I still am drawn before His Majesty, I am moved by the touch of His life upon mine.

20 —— Emmanuel!

> O God, my heart is quiet and confident. No wonder I can sing your praises! Rouse yourself, my soul! Arise, O harp and lyre! Let us greet the dawn with song! I will thank you publicly throughout the land. I will sing your praises among the nations. Your kindness and love are as vast as the heavens. Your faithfulness is higher than the skies.
>
> Psalm 57:7–10 TLB; read Psalm 57:6–11

Not all the hours at the sea edge pass in glad praise.

There are times of tears. There are sessions of intense intercession when a solitary soul pleads with His God for a world gone awry. There are acute moments of pain when deep remorse and genuine repentance are wrung out from a broken heart and contrite spirit that has grieved Christ's Spirit.

Yet for me, such encounters are more profound, more purifying, more redemptive than any service in a sanctuary.

The whole earth and sea and sky are pervaded with the presence of The Most High. Everywhere I turn there is impressed upon my still spirit the power of His majesty. Awed, amazed, stirred to the utmost depths, I stand silent, alone, serene.

A man has met his God.
A soul has been refreshed.
All is well, for God is here. Emmanuel! "God with us!"

21 —— On Higher Ground with God

> *O God, listen to me! Hear my prayer! For wherever I am, though*
> *far away at the ends of the earth, I will cry to You for help.*
> *When my heart is faint and overwhelmed, lead me*
> *to the mighty, towering Rock of safety.*
>
> Psalm 61:1, 2 TLB; read Psalm 61

If certain of us are going to be shaped into special specimens of rare quality, it calls for some suffering alone. Rugged strength is not developed in the soft security of our associates. There has to be that deep grounding of our lives in the very bedrock of Christ's character if we are to endure the blasts of adversity.

Christian leaders speak too easily, too glibly, too romantically of "getting into higher ground with God." It is almost as if they are inviting their listeners to take a stroll into a summer rose garden.

To get onto a higher life with the Risen Christ demands great discipline from the disciple. It calls for separation from the world's soft and cozy associations. It means strong self-denial, standing alone in noble, lofty living. It entails suffering, sorrow, pain, and the drastic endurance of adversity.

Christ came to us as "a man of sorrows and acquainted with grief." He was one cut off from the comfortable, easy companionship of His contemporaries. He stood alone in His suffering that He might prove to us the unfailing fortitude of the living God. Despite the worst the world could hurl at Him, He emerged triumphant—beaten, broken, bruised on our behalf, yet able to bring us to Himself in great glory. Lord, make me more like You!

22 —— Sunrise over the Sea

> *You answer us with awesome deeds of righteousness, O God our*
> *Savior, the hope of all the needs of the earth and of the farthest seas,*
> *who formed the mountains by your power . . . who stilled the roaring*
> *of the seas, the roaring of their waves, and the turmoil of the nations.*
>
> Psalm 65:5–7 NIV; read Psalm 65

For ocean lovers, sunrise and sunset are perhaps the most poignant interludes of the entire day. These hushed hours bring to the beach a unique aura of splendor and stillness that speaks to the innermost spirit of man. They are moments in which all sense of time is temporarily set aside, to be replaced by awe, wonder and quiet reflection that extends into eternity.

This is especially true of sunrise over the sea. For in this hour of early dawn the shore lies stripped of all human life. The clash and clamor of all human intrusion is stilled. The feverish activity of modern man is absent.

Peace pervades the realm of sea, sky and shore. . . .

The long, slender fingers of early dawn reach out from the central palm of the rising sun to stretch themselves across sea and sand. The whole seascape is caught up and wrapped in a golden glow.

If there are random clouds above the horizon they will burn bright with changing colors of crimson, purple and yellow.

A peculiar hush lies heavy over the shore. The sand is swept clean by the overnight tides. And all the world lies fresh, burnished, new as if for the first time it came clean and fresh from the Creator's hand. And in fact it has!

This is a majestic picture of what it means to be cleansed by the crimson blood of our Savior. Fresh from the Savior's touch, we go out to fulfill His will in a needy and lost world. Lord, help me to walk so close with You that I can serve in Your strength!

23 —— A Serene Stillness

O God of our salvation . . . who dost still the roaring of the sea, the roaring of their waves, the tumult of the peoples.

Psalm 65:5, 7 RSV; see Matthew 8:26

Just down the country road that winds through our valley is one of the largest radio telescopes in the west. It was located in that lovely mountain basin because of its seclusion. No aircraft are allowed to fly over the area. No chain saws, snowmobiles, dirt bikes, or all-terrain vehicles are permitted.

Here unusual peace prevails. And most of the time a serene stillness enfolds the valley.

As more and more people crowd the planet, it is inevitable that they must adjust to the ever-increasing noise of their civilization. This is especially true of larger metropolitan areas and industrialized urban centers. In those places noise is a way of life. It is a major part of the pressure which makes existence for millions stressful and painful—even though they may not be aware of this tension in their man-made environment.

In such a setting, try as he or she may, it is most difficult for any individual to think long thoughts—to meditate quietly over eternal verities, or even consider carefully the ultimate destiny of day-to-day decisions.

This explains why all through human history, if men were to be set aside for special service to their people, it was demanded that they first find some solitude and stillness where they could commune with their Creator. The ancient patriarchs, the flaming prophets of former times, the seers with burning eyes and great visions, the chosen saints with their profound spiritual perception were variably those who had found the stillness of the high places, there to listen quietly to the soft solicitation of God's Gracious Spirit.

24 —— The Message of Springtime

Then shall the earth yield her increase; and God, even our own God, shall bless us. . . . Yea, the Lord shall give that which is good; and our land shall yield her increase.

Psalms 67:6; 85:12 KJV

In our western mountains and desert valleys some four thousand diverse species of wildflowers carpet the countryside. In frontier days, before the advent of the pioneer's plow and the range rider's hordes of "hooved locusts," the earth glowed with the glory of fields of flowers. The display now is much less dramatic, much more subdued, altered by the invasion of cheat-grass, gray sage, knapweed, and other noxious plants.

Still for those of us who search out the secluded valleys and climb the steepest slopes there are spots where the upland flower fields are a majestic spectacle. In some areas hundreds of acres are blanketed in blossoms of every possible hue. Whole ridges are alive with masses of blooms too beautiful to describe with mere words. . . .

No wonder we want to walk for miles, to climb a hill, to laugh in the sun, to sing in the breezes that blow so softly, to throw off our jackets and bare our faces to the touch of spring.

Everywhere there is new life. The zest of renewal reassures us: All will be well. The coming of April flowers, the refreshment of spring showers, the sheer loveliness of shining cumulus clouds towering high against the sky edge relaxes our pent-up bodies. We rejoice in the wonder of it all. Somehow, suddenly, we are at rest.

The poet, Robert Browning, said: "God's in His heaven/All's right with the world." That's the message of springtime!

25 —— God Is Here!

Then the land will yield its harvest, and God, our God, will bless us.

Psalm 67:6 NIV

Is it possible that amid all the mayhem around us God is actually bringing beauty out of the barrenness of our lives? Is He creating something of consummate loveliness out of our chaos? Is He in fact actually fashioning us to His Own character?

The unequivocal answer is, "*Yes, He is!*"

Somehow we simply must see this!

Again and again as I have sat alone by a singing mountain stream that flowed strongly over the hard bedrock, the acute awareness has come home to my soul. "That, God, is exactly how Your Own eternal, perpetual life flows over me!"

There is a river of divine energy that emerges ever from the very person of the Eternal One. It flows over the entire universe. But more particularly it moves relentlessly over me, around me, as a person. It exerts its influence and power in wondrous ways, some of which may not be even understood or known.

The eternal grace of God manifest in the outpouring of His kindness, compassion, patience, and care, whether I deserve it or not, flows fresh and unfailing to me every day. The abundance of His life, His love, His light surround me on every side in joyous effulgence, whether I respond to their stimulation or not. The stirrings of His sweet Spirit surge over my spirit in a dozen ways, carried to me continuously by the constant coming of His presence to bring comfort, consolation, and encouragement, whether I am even aware of Him or not.

Across the years and across the tears, He is here!
Ever, always, His quiet assurance is "*I come to you!*"
Our difficulty lies in discerning His presence with us.

26 —— Answer Me, O Lord

Answer me, O Lord, out of the goodness of your love;
in your great mercy turn to me.

Psalm 69:16 NIV; read Psalm 69:13–21

The abundant gifts of God our Father to us His earth children come to us constantly . . . as continuously as the change of every tide, the shifting of every sea current. But they become ours only if we are there to absorb them into our little lives.

The bounties, mercies, and benefits of the Lord are new every day. They are swept along the shores of our daily experience to replenish and renew our strength as God's people. The point is I must be there to partake of the life presented for my perpetuation.

The process is a dynamic, daily interaction of any living organism with its environment. Life proceeds and is preserved only so long as there is continuous correspondence between the individual body and the biota surrounding it. The day the creature ceases to draw and derive its life from its surroundings, it dies.

So it is whether it be a scallop, a fish, a sea bird or a seal. Each has life only by virtue of the fact it is feeding on the abundance supplied by the ocean around it.

Precisely the same principle applies to me—and others who claim to possess the life of God. He surrounds me on every side with the overwhelming abundance of His life. It is He who is the very environment in which I move and live and have my being. If I am to know His life, if I am to experience the energy of His presence, if I am to drink the dynamic of His Spirit then it is imperative that daily I must draw upon His divine provisions.

27 —— Sunrise and Sunset

But you, O God, are my king from of old; you bring salvation upon
the earth. . . . The day is yours, and yours also the night;
you established the sun and the moon.

Psalm 74:12, 16 NIV; read Psalm 74:12–17

Sunset is an hour for quiet reflection. It is the particle of time poised briefly for a brief review of what was done this day. The afterglow closes the chapter, putting a period to the writing of my journal.

Eventide is the time for taking stock of how the day was spent. It calls briefly for a serious evaluation of the manner of my conduct. It speaks softly of work well done, of progress made, of the touch of God's hand upon my life.

It must be hard indeed for skeptics, atheists, and agnostics to view sunrises and sunsets. The splendor of their glory, the beauty of their colors, the intensity of their inspiration that comes from our Father's loving heart, are to the unbeliever nothing more than mere chemical and physical responses to external stimuli. No wonder their world is so bleak, their despair so deep, their future so forlorn.

But for God's child sunrise and sunset are very special. They are intense interludes of quiet communion with the living Christ. They are moments of majesty in which our Father displays His love and might. They are scenes of spiritual exaltation in which His glorious spirit lifts us to wondrous heights of pure joy in His presence.

28 —— The Way through the Sea

Thy way was through the sea, thy path through the great waters;
yet thy footprints were unseen. Thou didst lead thy people
like a flock by the hand of Moses and Aaron.

Psalm 77:19, 20 RSV; read Psalm 77:11–20

Strange as it may sound, though I was born and grew up hundreds of miles from the ocean, and was for years a stranger to it, I have come to love it. The ocean has drawn me to itself and won my total allegiance.

I really am an ocean lover. In profound ways the sea has wooed my soul. It has made me a part of its own life.

Just as much as the waves breaking on the smooth sand are an integral part of this wondrous world—or the gulls gliding along the cliff face, or the seals thrusting through the currents—so am I, as a solitary man, leaving the footprints of my small steps on the ocean edge.

All is passing. All is in motion. All is change—new every day, fresh in every way. None of it will stay. Only the ocean endures, eternal, unending in its movements.

So it is that these deep reflections and long thoughts move smoothly but surely into the realm of my spirit. In His own gracious and gentle way God has spoken to me more emphatically through parallels in the sea than any sermon in a sanctuary.

29 —— Streams from the Rock

He split the rocks in the desert, and gave them water abundant as
from the seas; he brought streams out of a rocky crag and
made water flow down like rivers.

Psalm 78:15, 16 NIV

I love to spend time sitting quietly in meditation beside mountain streams. Here water has been at work for a very long time indeed. The change from season to season may seem imperceptible. Still the shaping, the smoothing, the sculpting goes on steadily.

Often these little high mountain streams are adorned with the most remarkable trees, shrubs, and flowers. At the high altitude the only trees that can survive are often small and stunted by the stern and rugged weather at the edge of the sky. Beaten down by winter winds, blasted by blizzards bearing tons of snow in their teeth, the little trees take root in some crack of the stone and draw their sustenance from the stream. They resemble bonsai trees, shaped with supreme care to match the elegance of the water-worn streambed.

Here and there a clump of wildflowers will find a sheltered foothold beside the running water. Plants of pioneer species, especially hardy and tough enough to endure the stormy climate of the remote ridges, bloom here in quiet glory. Again and again I have paused in astonishment at the loveliness of water willow herbs, northern fireweed, and clumps of mountain anemone that decorate the verges of these ancient rocks.

In simple truth such spots are the natural "Gardens of God." No man designed them. They were not arranged by human imaginations nor brought into being by our horticultural ingenuity. They are the end product of eons of time during which year upon year ever-increasing loveliness has been brought out of the most unpromising material.

30 —— Freed from the Penalty and Power of Sin

He cleft rocks in the wilderness, and gave them drink abundantly as from the deep. He made streams come out of the rock, and caused waters to flow down like rivers.

Psalm 78:15, 16 RSV; *read John 4:7–15*

In Scripture, *to drink is to believe.*

First, I believe that by Christ's shed blood the *penalty* of death which would otherwise be mine for past sins has been canceled at Calvary.

Second, I claim a daily energizing through the resurrection life of Christ made real in me by His Spirit. This keeps me from the *power* of sin and evil, which would otherwise stunt my Christian life.

The moisture which a tree took in last week will not suffice for today. Likewise I, too, must draw daily on the water of divine life—even on Christ's refreshing stream.

This process of receiving continuously the very life of Christ is to be made keenly aware of His presence and power within. I have the work of Calvary cleansing me from the *guilt* of sins, and I have the resurrection life of Christ (made real in me by the Spirit) ever keeping me from the *grip* of sin. Thus I live a triumphant life of true health and holiness in God. This is how I rise above the world.   (ATG)

1 —————— The Caring Creator

*Even the sparrow has found a home, and the swallow a nest
for herself, where she may have her young—a place near
your altar, O Lord almighty, my King and my God.*

Psalm 84:3 NIV; read Psalm 84:1–9

There are certain values in life that money and material wealth can
never purchase. Gold and silver, stocks and bonds, bank accounts and
investment securities are not sufficient to assure peace of mind or serenity
of spirit.

What price can be placed upon a life of simplicity, free from the fret
and strain of trying to keep pace in a man-killing society? What will a
person give in exchange for the quiet ecstasy of living gently in harmony
with the seasons? What consolation can surpass that of the secure inner
assurance that this indeed is my Father's world, in which He cares for me
with intense personal interest?

I am constantly reminded that this caring is not confined or directed
only toward us human beings. It embraces and enfolds the whole world
around us: the trees and shrubs, with their foliage shining in the sun; the
soft, sweet, fragrant grasses and flowers that flourish on our hills; the
birds that build their nests and rear their young all around us; the insects
that hum in the sun and flit across the lake; the wild deer and mountain
sheep and mink and beavers and bears whose realm we share. All these
remind us that we are friends and neighbors. As the ancient Indians
would say, we are all "brothers beneath the sun."

We delude ourselves if we believe our Father cares only for human
beings. His assurance to us is otherwise. It is He who clothes the flowers
of the field in great glory; He knows when a fledgling falls. He is the
Creator of all!

2 —————— Sun and Shield

*For the Lord God is a sun and shield: the Lord will give grace and
glory: no good thing will he withhold from them that walk uprightly.*

Psalm 84:11 KJV; read Psalm 84:10–12

The Word of God states it plainly: "The Lord God is a sun . . ."
(Psalm 84:11 KJV).

He is the source of all life, both physical and spiritual. He surrounds
us on every side with the radiance of Himself.

Spiritual light, divine light, God-given light, can reach our hearts in a number of ways.

First and foremost there is the earthly life, ministry, death, resurrection, and message of Jesus Christ. He was the literal expression of divine life and light in human form.

Second, there is the written Word of God in Scripture, which again is referred to as light.

Then there is the spoken message and live reality of godly preachers, teachers, and Christian friends conveying light to our hearts.

Finally there is the realm of nature, which reveals the unity, beauty, and wisdom of the character of God Himself.

Through all these media light is continually being shed about me. Now the important and crucial question is: Do I respond to the light that falls upon my heart and mind? Do I turn toward it? Do I reach out for it and hold myself in readiness to react to its stimulus? (ATG)

3 ———— The Place of Peace

I will hear what God the Lord will speak: for he will speak peace unto his people, and to his saints; but let them not turn again to folly.

Psalm 85:8 KJV; read Psalm 85:8–13

Our God is everywhere present in His universe—even in our bustling canyons of brick and iron that roar with the thunder of our vaunted technology. He is even in our ghettos of grime, and in our luxury condominiums crammed with their ceaseless sound and fury.

The problem is most people will not take either the time or trouble to find their "place of peace." They cannot be bothered to seek an oasis of serenity in the desert of their drab days. They have never discovered the healing stillness of some quiet spot where they can meet God and know Him in gentle meditation.

Crowded, pressured, driven, desperate, they rush on and on!

It takes time to draw aside from the society of man.

It takes time to enter deliberately into the presence of God.

It takes time to commune with Christ as friend.

For some people such time is simply not available. They feel it is wasted, thrown away, spent for naught. They would prefer to expend it on something much more stirring and exciting—like a football game, a soap opera, or perhaps even the fluctuations of the stock market.

There is a certain discipline of soul, a setting of the will, a determination of spirit required to meet with God's Spirit in a place of peace. It calls for much more than merely feeling like it. It demands a deliberate act of faith that in such a spot I shall meet my God. Such meetings are not encounters arranged by the church, denomination, or assembly of God's people to which I belong. Rather they are a private rendezvous planned purposely, carried out quietly, between my Father and me.

4 ———— A "Blameless" Walk

For the Lord God is a sun and shield; the Lord bestows
favor and honor; no good thing does he withhold
from those whose walk is blameless.

Psalm 84:11 NIV

Gradually as the sun moves in grandeur across the sky, the hours of the day are flooded with light, warmed with pleasure. Then slowly as evening descends the burning orb of fire settles softly into the sea, as though settling down gently for the night.

The brilliant banners of tattered clouds, tinged with intense red, rose, and pulsing scarlet hues, remind us that the day is done. What has been done has been done!

There can be no replay of this day, except in fleeting memory. There can be no rewriting of the script etched upon these hours. With the indelible ink of eternity there has been inscribed upon the page of this eternal sheet of time either something of value, or only what is vain.

If I look upon each day as a gift from God, how will I change? In what ways will my attitude alter and my perspective brighten? O Lord, help me to walk before You "blameless."

5 ———— The Promise of Peace

Let me hear what God the Lord will speak, for he will speak peace to
his people, to his saints, to those who turn to him in their hearts.

Psalm 85:8 RSV

In utter silence of spirit I lay prostrate. In total quietness of soul I remained silent. In complete surrender of body I did not move a muscle.

I, a mere man, was alone with my Maker.

It was from Him that I had come.

It was to Him that I would return.

He and He alone was from everlasting to everlasting.

Only in Him was there life eternal that could surmount all the exigencies of my little life. Like the breeze from the snowfields, His very life enfolded me on every side.

From the day of my creation He had breathed into my being the very breath of His own eternal Spirit. All my life He had sustained and supported me by that same still Spirit that surrounded me on every hand and pursued me along every trail I took. Now in the face of my friend's death He, the Gracious Spirit of the Eternal God, in wonder and awe opened my tear-dimmed eyes to behold again the glory and hope our Father gives His children as they cross over to the other side.

He and only He could prepare for us a place of peace.

The struggle and strain to survive would be over.

All would be well.

All is well!

He was here . . . Peace!

6 ——— Peace in God's Presence

> *Thou dost rule the raging of the sea;*
> *when its waves rise, thou stillest them.*
>
> Psalm 89:9 RSV; read Psalm 89:1–9

For me, the ultimate in solitude is often found on the wave-washed shore, several hundred yards from my front door. There I go with a towel to spread on the sand or rocks, a small well-worn Bible or a good book, and a spirit of eager anticipation ready to listen, eager to respond to the impulses of Christ's Spirit. Never does He disappoint me. For it is there we meet in quiet communion, one with another.

Being alone on the beach has some remarkable advantages not apparent to the stranger. There are no interruptions in these precious interludes—no telephones, no doorbells, no mail delivery, no one calling for attention, no neighbors' dogs, or police sirens, or roaring motorcycles, or raucous radio noises.

Peace pervades the shore. The song of the surf fills the air. A sublime, intense sense of God's presence is everywhere.

In this arresting atmosphere I feel wonderfully free—open before my Father, relaxed in communion with Christ, uplifted by His wondrous Spirit.

As He speaks to my spirit, there is often an audible response on my part. In such a setting I can give thanks aloud. If so impelled I can hum a hymn or sing a song of joyous praise and exultation in the greatness of my God.

The gulls don't mind my melodies. Sometimes a seal will raise his head above the surf to see whence the sounds come. Occasionally the ground squirrels scrambling along the cliff face will stop to whistle in the wind at my singing.

But we are all sharing this sea edge as friends together. Great and small our Father formed us all. This is a fragment of the firmament that we revel in and rejoice over with endless gratitude.

7 ———— A Beauty of Soul

O Lord God Almighty, who is like you? You are mighty, O Lord, and your faithfulness surrounds you. You rule over the surging sea; when its waves mount up, you still them. . . . Your arm is endued with power; your hand is strong, your right hand extended.

Psalm 89:8, 9, 13 NIV

After every storm, after every high tide, after the powerful action of the combers that have cleansed the beach, there remains behind remarkable beauty. Not just the outward splendor of a wave-washed shore sparkling in the sun, but an intimate beauty of delicate design etched upon the sand, carved upon the cliffs.

This character of a coastline is ever changing. It never remains static. It does not become sterile and stale. Each new day makes a difference in its design. Every high tide alters its outline. Endlessly the sea edge is shaped into a myriad of fascinating seascapes. . . .

In much the same way our Father fashions and shapes the lives of His children, working upon our minds, spirits and wills, to do His good pleasure, to reflect His love to those whose lives we touch.

8 ———— Walking in the Light

Blessed are the people . . . who walk, O Lord, in the light of thy countenance, who exalt in thy name all the day. . . .

Psalm 89:15–16 RSV; read Psalm 89:15–18

Most of us have never learned the humble though powerful practice of concentrating on Christ. Outside, walking alone, away from the usual surroundings which remind us of our feverish workaday world, we can give our hearts a chance to center their interest and affection on Him.

It is a simple, humble habit. Perhaps it is too ordinary for most people.

But to walk with God means just that—daily.

This in essence is the secret of rest. It is the time of waiting, of communing with God the Father, of coming to Christ, of being inwardly conscious of the Holy Spirit's gentle voice entreating me to lift up my soul to Him who, when He was among us, said, "Come unto me, all ye that labour and are heavy laden, and I will give you rest" (Matthew 11:28 KJV).

And having come, I will be refreshed and fitted for new growth in God during future days. (ATG)

9 ——— A Titanic Transaction

[God promised David:] My faithfulness and my steadfast love shall be with him, and in my name shall his horn be exalted. I will set his hand on the sea and his right hand on the rivers.

Psalm 89:24, 25 RSV; read Psalm 89:24–33

At the ocean edge a titanic interchange goes on endlessly. The ocean waters—clear, clean, fresh and pure—pour out upon the polluted sands. There they pick up the decaying debris, the bird feces, the fallen feathers, the flotsam and jetsam that would otherwise stain the shore. In their grasp the grime is gone, transported away into the ocean deeps. In place of the pollution there is left behind by the breakers, shining sand, and polished rocks.

So the breakers restore the beach, cleansing its shoreline and leaving the sea edge bathed in pristine purity.

Reflecting quietly upon this titanic transaction between sea and land, I have been deeply moved by the profound parallels that lie between my soul and God. As I meditate upon the majestic mysteries of His dealing with me I can clearly comprehend some similarities that have helped me understand the magnificence of His person, the magnitude of His intentions toward me.

For just as the ocean is ever at work breaking itself over my bit of beach, so my Father's unfathomable love is ever in action spilling out upon my sin-stained soul. Had He chosen, as well He might, to confine His compassion to Himself, I would never have known the cleansing, caring impact of His life on mine.

10 ——— Life on the Highest Plane

He that dwelleth in the secret place of the most High shall abide under the shadow of the Almighty.

Psalm 91:1 KJV; read Psalm 91:1–10

Every tide that rises along the ocean edge brings life in abundance. Microscopic plankton, one of the planet's greatest protein sources, abounds in these rich waters. Sea weeds and ocean plant life of a hundred kinds flourish along this coast. They are all an intimate part of the wondrous web of life that thrives in the biota along my bit of beach.

Each is a gift from the sea. Each is a daily bestowal from the ocean deeps. Each is provided in innumerable abundance for all who will accept it.

As the afterglow dimmed gently along the shore I turned my steps toward home. I inhaled deeply of the pungent ozone on the evening breeze. With one long, last lingering view I watched the well-fed gulls preen themselves upon the sand. All was well and we were at peace.

In that brief evening interlude life—new life, fresh life—had come to me as well from the bounty of the sea. A new surge of well-being coursed through my bloodstream. A rich stimulus of inspiration swept into my soul. A profound sense of the presence of the Most High engulfed my spirit in quietude and serenity.

11 —— A Sermon in a Seed

The righteous will flourish like a palm tree,
they will grow like a cedar of Lebanon.

Psalm 92:12 NIV; *read Psalm 92:12–15*

When the tiny, viable seed finds itself surrounded by stimuli such as moisture, air, warmth, light, and others which comprise its total environment, it responds. It germinates. It begins to grow. One day a slender rootlet emerges and starts to grow down into the soil. Soon after, a frail shoot pushes out and upward reaching toward the sun. A seedling is underway! If all goes well its root will penetrate the forest floor while at the same time its first frail leaves will spread themselves in the air. Slowly, surely, and with quiet persistence it grows first into a seedling, then a sapling, then a sturdy tree, and at last a forest monarch.

All this growth, all this maturity, is the outcome of correspondence between the tree and its environment.

In truth it may be said that not only does the tree penetrate directly into its environment but also that the components of the environment actually enter intimately into the tree, thus producing normal growth. This is correspondence between the two.

Now, just as the parent cedar produces certain cones carrying viable seeds implanted with the life germ of a new cedar, so God the Father, by His Holy Spirit, implants in the hearts of those who believe the very life of Christ, the LIFE of God Himself from above. (ATG)

12 —— Like a Cedar of Lebanon

The righteous shall flourish like the palm tree;
he shall grow like a cedar in Lebanon.

Psalm 92:12 KJV

The cedar boards and beams of Solomon's temple were produced from living trees that had grown in the high mountains. So, likewise, through the growth of godly character it is intended that I should become a fit habitation for God Himself. To be suited for this noble service, my life must possess qualities comparable to those of the cedars of Lebanon.

What are these special characteristics, and why was it imperative that cedar be used in the temple?

First of all, this timber is rich-grained, lustrous, and beautiful to behold. Is this true of my character? Is there a glow, an attractiveness, to my life?

Second, cedar has a delicate aroma, a delightful fragrance. This perfume permeated the whole building. Are those around me conscious of the fragrance of Christ in my character?

Third, the cedar is famous for its repulsion of insects of all sorts. Moths and beetles and termites avoid it. Its presence has a purifying influence. Does mine, in a sordid, corrupt world?

Fourth, the cedar of Lebanon is a very durable wood, being quite impervious to decay. If my character is Christlike it will have this enduring quality. It will not be weak or soft or rotten. (ATG)

13 —— The Fruit of Flourishing

The righteous will flourish like a palm tree, they will grow like a
cedar in Lebanon; planted in the house of the Lord,
they will flourish in the courts of our God.

Psalm 92:12–13 NIV

The sea surrounds and engulfs every living form of life that is to be found along its coastline. The ocean brings life, energy, stimulation, and vitality to every crustacean, every marine organism, every fish, every sea bird, every marine mammal. But each in turn, to survive and thrive in this watery world, must derive its life from the sea.

It is not enough to be surrounded by the great ocean waters. There is more to life in the sea than merely being swept to and fro in its changing tides. Each life form must be open, receptive, fully exposed to accept and absorb life and energy from the currents of the cosmos. Otherwise it becomes a shell or skeleton cast up on the shore.

So it is with the child of God.

Daily, hourly, momentarily Christ comes to us surrounding us with His Spirit. He brings to us in immeasurable abundance the resources needed for our eternal living. Yet there remains my responsibility to open myself to Him; to allow His Word ready entry to my mind, emotions and will; to permit His Spirit to invade my spirit, penetrating and vitalizing my intuition, conscience, and communion with Him.

Only in this way—in stillness and quietude, in obedience and faith, in loving allegiance—can I ever know what it is to have His life, and have it more abundantly . . . now and forever.

Let my soul beware that, like some empty shell or sunbleached skeleton, it not be cast away upon the sands of time—dead to Him, who comes to give me life.

Always, ever, I must be open, available totally to His incoming. Thus I thrive and flourish with His life.

14 ——— A Sublime Sanctuary

> *For the Lord is a great God, and a great King above all gods.*
> *In his hand are the deep places of the earth;*
> *the strength of the hills is his also.*
>
> *Psalm 95:3–4* KJV; *read Psalm 95:1–7*

I can recall with utter clarity the last time we climbed the faint, high, snow-covered ridge visible from my windows. It was mid-January. Winter had clamped its hard, icy grip upon the country. Deep snow had fallen. The whole upland world was a spotless white. We climbed steadily toward the summit. . . .

Step by step, as if in slow motion, we took turns breaking trail through the deep snow. It hung heavy in the dark brooding trees. It clung to our boots, dragged heavy on our pantlegs, slowed our upward progress. Wisps of white vapor drifted about our faces from the heaving of our lungs and exhalation of our breath.

At last we broke out above timberline. And just as we did, the winter sun, too, broke out from behind the low-hanging winter clouds. Suddenly the whole upland realm was wrapped in blinding light and ultra whiteness. One could only see by squinting the eyes to mere slits. The world was wrapped in beautiful brilliance. Then as we reached the sun-swept meadows, pristine whiteness swept away beneath our gaze to the very edge of the sky in every direction. It was as if we were suspended in space where time stood still and not a single sound stirred in the great eternal silence.

It was as if momentarily we stood reverently, almost breathlessly, in the sublime sanctuary of the Most High. Neither of us spoke. It would have been a desecration. An interlude in time, it was a moment in our lives when eternity could be sensed in the soul, known by the spirit. For with intense awareness we were aware: "O God, our Father, You are here! The majesty of Your might and the glory of Your presence fill the earth and sky!"

15 —— Seen from the Summit

> . . . *the Lord is a great God, and a great King above all gods.*
> *In his hand are the depths of the earth; the heights*
> *of the mountain are his also.*
>
> *Psalm 95:3–4* RSV

Hiking in high-country places puts a certain strenuous demand upon one's strength and stamina. It is not a gentle stroll in the park. It calls for fortitude, for discipline of mind and muscle, for vigor of spirit to push toward the summit. Life is like that.

Often the climb begins with a rather tedious trail at the foot of the mountain. This leads through thick timber, windfalls, and steep switchbacks where only here and there a distant glimpse of peaks encourages one to press on.

Bit by bit the trees begin to thin out. With increasing altitude the timber becomes more stunted, broken and beaten down by wind, snow, and fierce ice storms. Here, too, the air becomes thinner, less charged with oxygen. Vistas widen, distant views quicken the pulse, and the air is pungent with the perfume of pine, fir and spruce.

Then the trail breaks out above treeline. Sweeping alpine meadows of short grass, lowly heather, glowing wildflowers and broken rock beckon the climber to move higher. Here is the sky edge. This is where heaven seems to touch earth. It is a realm as yet unravaged or ruined by the hands of man.

Finally, for the hardiest of climbers there stands the summit. All sheathed in ice, snow, and giant rock buttresses, its peaks comb the clouds, or, if the weather is clear, stand stark and beautiful against a brilliant blue sky.

There is a stimulation, an uplift, an all-engulfing enthusiasm which energizes the soul in such a setting. The person who has spent time at the edge of the sky is never, ever, quite the same again. He or she has tasted the thrill of the lofty landscapes and learned to love them through intimate, personal contact.

16 —— Living Waters

In his hand are the depths of the earth; the heights of the
mountains are his also. The sea is his, for he made it;
for his hands formed the dry land.

Psalm 95:4–5 RSV

In a private, deliberate act of profound faith I lifted my face toward the slanting rays of the late afternoon sun and spoke softly: "O my Master, my Friend, my Father, I take of Your very life and drink it to the depths!"

In that moment I sensed the surge of His gracious Spirit flowing into mine to renew and revitalize my ravaged soul. The dynamic of divine life was restoring me.

A compelling awareness swept over me. It was the persistent power and vitality inherent in the flowing waters beside me. They poured over the rocks in gushing torrents that tumbled the small stones along the stream bed. The flowing action wore away rock, shaped stones, and carved ever deeper in the hills the channel to the sea.

So it is with the great good will of God. It is an irresistible force in the universe that flows steadily to shape the destinies of us all. His intentions toward us are grand and good and noble. It is His great, persistent power that shapes our history and directs our days.

17 —— Waves at Work

The sea is his, for he made it, and his hands formed the dry land.

Psalm 95:5 NIV

On the seashore, nothing remains static. There is an eternal flux. Perpetual change transforms the pictures from hour to hour, minute to minute. The next restless, rising wave lifts, moves, alters, and refashions the scene. It reshapes the pattern, resculpts the sand. Yet equally wonderful is the realization that none of this is done in wild, discordant abandon. There is a sublime harmony and unity in every design etched upon the beach. The waves are at work in compliance with the eternal laws of the universe—moving, singing, swirling beneath the baton of a cosmic conductor.

At other times the music and movement of the surf is almost terrifying in its intensity. Under the majestic impulse of mounting winds and ocean storms, it climbs to a rising crescendo. The great walls of water boom and break on the beach in giant thunderclaps. There is the roar of tumbling water, the power of the rushing waves surging up the sand, the hissing foam, and the fury of their impact on the land.

What assurance to know the One who holds all this in His mighty hands! (OG)

18 —— Gifts from the Sea

For all the gods of the people are idols; but the Lord made the heavens. Honor and majesty are before him, strength and beauty are in his sanctuary.

Psalm 96:5, 6 RSV

There are gorgeous undulations left upon the sea edge by the ebbing tide. The cutting, swirling, rhythmic movement of the ocean currents shapes the contours of the tide flats and sand dunes into smooth, soft curves that soothe the eye and still the soul. It seems almost an indiscretion to step upon their pristine perfection.

Here and there the dainty web of a crab's tracks or a sea bird's footprints add to the intensity of their lingering loveliness. Especially in late evening or at early dawn, when the long, low light accents their smooth forms, their beauty is so sharp, so stabbing, it almost pains.

Even the smoothing of stones, the polishing of rocks, the fashioning of driftwood by the oscillating action of the waves leaves one lost in wonder, awe and quiet gratitude for such gracious gifts from the sea. Everywhere one walks there is left the impress of the tides that work, often unseen, upon this bit of beach. . . .

All of this beauty on the beach, all of these rare and delicate designs, all of the exquisite sea-edge forms are the fashioning of the tides. Every ocean current that swirls along the coast cuts and chisels as surely as any sculptor's tools. Every wave or wavelet washing against the land rasps and shapes with relentless artistry. Every ton of sea water pressing upon the beach compresses the shore into a special seascape.

So it is, too, with the impact of the presence and power of God Himself upon my soul. It is the eternal persistence of His splendid Spirit that, working upon my mind, emotions, and will, gently conforms them to His own wishes.

19 —— In the Presence of Power

Let the heavens be glad, and let the earth rejoice;
let the sea roar, and all that fills it.

Psalm 96:11 RSV; read Psalm 96:7–13

Only those of us who have lived in close and intimate contact with the mighty ocean currents fully appreciate their remorseless power and tumultuous energy. Day and night, year after year, it is expended all around the earth; yet, strange to say, scarcely any of it has ever been harnessed or turned to useful purposes.

Often, as I have stood watching the breakers burst in white foam along miles of beach, the question has come to me: "Why has not some of this energy been harnessed?" It seems almost incongruous that scientific technology of the twentieth century has virtually left untouched the stupendous store of energy exerted by ocean tides and currents. The eternal, inexorable movement of literally trillions of tons of water every day of the year represents an expenditure of energy that dwarfs man's most sophisticated schemes.

It matters not whether we contemplate the might and magnificence of the magnetic and gravitational forces that oscillate the oceans on a worldwide scale, or whether we see but a single small segment of this energy expended in one spot in one fierce rip; on every hand, there is overwhelming power present.

This power, of which we are aware, humbles our haughtiness. It sobers our spirits. It exalts our souls in quiet reverence. For me, as a man, it bids me bow myself in wonder. "Oh, my Father—this is Your world. You made it. You sustain it!"   (OG)

20 —— God Sometimes Deals in the Darkness

Clouds and thick darkness are round about him,
righteousness and justice are the foundation of his throne.

Psalm 97:2 RSV; read Psalm 97

Darkness brings dew and refreshment to the foliage of the tree. In a mountainous country like Lebanon, where the forests lie close to the sea, nighttime brings its banks of cloud and mist and fog that enshroud the trees in refreshing coolness, saturating the cedars with mineral-laden moisture from the ocean deeps.

In short, darkness is the time during which a tree restores its strength, replenishes its energy, refreshes its fevered life, and finds respite from the heat and activity of the day.

Among Christians there is a decided aversion to darkness. Probably this is because in the Bible darkness is so often associated with evil. Because of this we draw back from the very thought of darkness as if it could contain nothing but ill.

God, in His infinite wisdom and mighty power, can use the darkness to enrich my life and strengthen my walk. Lord, help me to realize that fact in the face of my darker days. (ATG)

21 —— The Breakers of God's Love

The Lord hath made known his salvation: his righteousness hath he openly shewed in the sight of the heathen. He hath remembered his mercy and his truth toward the house of Israel: all the ends of the earth have seen the salvation of our God.

Psalm 98:2, 3 KJV; read Psalm 98

Like the breakers crashing every few seconds upon the shore, so His love comes sweeping over my soul from out of the eternal depths of His own infinite being. Over and over, His life is broken on my behalf.

Christians, it seems to me, speak too glibly, too lightly, too flippantly of the cleansing blood of Christ. They treat it almost as a talisman that can be called upon in a moment of extremity.

It is more, much more than that! It is instead the eternal, everlasting, endless life and love of God Himself being poured out in unrelenting power upon us poor mortals. His majestic body broken on our behalf, spilled out in ten thousand times ten thousand actions of self-giving, self-sacrifice is for our cleansing—for our salvation.

Not until we, in awe, wonder, and humility, see the grandeur of His generosity that allows His pure life to surge over our pollution will we ever repent. Only then can we begin to grasp even a little of the wondrous work the breakers of His spilled-out love can effect in our experience.

22 —— A Legacy of Love

Serve the Lord with gladness! Come into his presence with singing!

Psalm 100:2 RSV; read Psalm 100

One of my dear friends is an elderly widow who lives in an austere retirement center in the very heart of the city. Endless traffic and crowds of pedestrians press in around her residence in a constant cacophony of noise and confusion. The halls she walks are dim, dark, haunted by aged people who for the most part have given up hope. Her own tiny room is almost like a narrow cell with a limited outlook between the building's concrete walls.

Yet in such a stark setting this loving lady pours out the perfume of her gracious personality upon every life she touches. Every day she is fit enough to get out, she takes walks to pick any stray flowers, or leaves, or even decorative wayside weeds she can find. These she brings back to share with others who are shut-ins or others in the hospital. . . . Her tiny figure is filled with laughter, fun and the joyous optimism of one who loves her Father and revels in His company. The sunshine of the sky, the wonder of the stars, the fragrance of flowers, the healing touch of trees and grass are reflected in the gentle love pouring from the soul and spirit of this saint.

Wherever she goes, she leaves behind a legacy of hope, of cheer, of good will to those she meets. Through her little life there radiates to all around her the character of Christ, the gentle glory of God. She, too, is a living miracle, a divine demonstration of our Father's life touching and transforming her life at the edge of the sky.

23 —— Of Prayer and Praise

> *Bless the Lord . . . Who satisfieth thy mouth with good things;*
> *so that thy youth is renewed like the eagle's.*
>
> Psalm 103:1, 5 KJV; read Psalm 103:1–5

Have you ever watched an eagle get ready for flight? At first, almost imperceptibly, but growing ever stronger, he feels the warm air currents rising around him, lifting gently from the valley floor past his perch.

Presently the regal bird spreads his wings and launches himself confidently into space. At once the thermal currents are bearing up beneath his wings and he rides them splendidly. By deliberate effort the eagle keeps himself in the center of the updrafts, rising higher and higher, borne aloft, mounting ever upward until he is lost to sight.

What a sublime etching this is of the Christian in his relationship to God. On the outstretched wings of prayer and praise he launches himself out upon the promises of God, depending on the great updrafts of His faithfulness to bear him up.

It takes courage to do this. A daring act of faith is required for us to let go of the limb to which we have clung for so long and launch ourselves fearlessly into the great open space before us.

By the discipline of keeping his wings outstretched to catch every eddy of air, the bird rises with ease. So the Christian, if he would overcome, must school himself continually to spread his heart before God in an attitude of never-ceasing prayer and praise, looking to Christ, "the author and finisher of our faith" (Hebrews 12:2 KJV).

The updrafts of God's faithfulness are forever. It is up to us to rest upon that faithfulness. This we can do only by holding ourselves in the center of His purpose through a deliberate and continuous attitude of prayer and praise.

24 —— Bountiful Bunch Grass

> *He makes grass grow for the cattle, and plants for men to cultivate —bringing forth food from the earth.*
>
> Psalm 104:14 NIV

So deep, so far reaching, so extensive is the bunch grass root system that intensive scientific studies have shown a single plant to have up to seventeen miles of rugged roots! Little wonder this sturdy species can withstand so much grazing, so much trampling, so much abuse from reckless ranchers who often allow livestock to overgraze the range.

Year after year the bunch grass patiently puts out new growth. Season after season it sends up fresh shoots to shimmer in the sun. Generation after generation its golden glory cloaks the high country to gladden our spirits and nourish all those who rely on it for sustenance.

Cattle come down off the bountiful bunch grass ranges in fall, so fat, so well nourished that they appear to have been stall-fed on grain. The rich protein content of the grass makes it some of the finest forage in all the world. Even when it is bleached and glowing bronze it bears within its fibers a level of nutrition seldom matched by any other plant material.

When winter storms blanket the ranges in snow, deer and mountain sheep and range horses will seek out the open, southwest slopes to feed on the sturdy bunch grass clumps. The tough fibers, so rich in protein, like well-cured hay, will fuel their inner fires, fighting off the chilling cold.

Yes, in spring, summer, fall and even in winter, bunch grass is beautiful. It is the gentle healer of the hills, the sustainer of life, the golden carpet flung so freely over the land by our Father's generous care.

25 —— On the Wings of the Wind

O Lord my God, thou art very great! . . . who makest the clouds thy
chariot, who ridest on the wings of the wind, who makest the
winds thy messengers, fire and flame thy ministers.

Psalm 104:1, 3, 4 RSV; read Psalm 104:1-4

Life for God's child is sometimes like a storm at sea. Just because we belong to Him, we are not exempted from the dark storms and heavy winds of life. We must, and can expect, that in the short sojourn of our brief years here there will be some gales of adversity, some "blows" off the open seas of our days.

But the stirring truth remains that for those of us who know and love Him, our Father is always there with us. As the ancient prophet Nahum declared so boldly: "The Lord hath his way in the whirlwind and in the storm, and the clouds are the dust of his feet" (1:3 KJV).

He is ever active in our affairs. He is ever reliable in arranging the circumstances of our lives behind the scenes. He is ever near us moving on our behalf to bring about changes that are intended for our good. In the darkest hours we find Him closest.

26 —— Springs in the Valley

Thou makest springs gush forth in the valleys; they flow between
the hills, they give drink to every beast of the field. . . .

Psalm 104:10, 11 RSV; read Psalm 104:5-13

Clear, cold, pure water pouring out of the high country in constant, abundant supply is one of the exhilarating joys of the sky edge. Singing streams, tumbling waterfalls, roaring rivers all rumbling down their valleys are as eternal as the snowfields that comprise their source.

As long as winter and summer, springtime and autumn move majestically across the mountains, so will the snow-fed streams refresh the hills and nourish the valleys below. In the flowing water there is life and power and renewal for the earth, a beautiful picture of the spiritual sustenance available to the Christian.

In our rugged northern ranges the snow and rain have their origin in the uncharted, windswept reaches of the vast north Pacific. From out of the immensity of the ocean depths great winds pick up their burden of moisture and carry it aloft across the coast to set it down upon our western slopes. There in giant drifts of snow, some eighty feet deep, the precious moisture seeps into the soil and percolates gently into bubbling springs and melting freshets.

From just such a rich resource comes the eternal treasure of our God to His needy children here on earth.

27 —— Healing for Wounded Hearts

> *He makes grass grow for the cattle, and plants for men to*
> *cultivate —bringing forth food from the earth . . .*
> *and bread that sustains his heart.*
>
> *Psalm 104:14, 15 NIV; read Psalm 104:14–23*

Most of us behave as though God did not exist. We act as if He were not here. In fact, in our puny pride we demand He prove Himself by some strange sign or wonder.

But our Father does not function in that way. He does not indulge us with dazzling fanfare. He does not turn to stunning theatrics to impress us with His power.

Instead, He proceeds quietly to restore our souls just as He restores the ravaged hills. He brings His own wondrous healing to our wounded hearts in the same way He heals the flattened forests and binds up the broken ranges. He renews our spirits exactly as He quickens again the streams and springs of the high country—*by the gentle incoming of new life amid the desolation . . . yes, the miracle of His own life at work in the world.*

28 —— Trees above Timberline

> *The trees of the Lord are watered abundantly,*
> *the cedar of Lebanon which he planted.*
>
> *Psalm 104:16 RSV*

It is of more than passing interest that trees above timberline are not a part of the full forest of the lower slopes. They are rugged individuals set apart from the common crowd that make up the usual stand of timber. Isolated from their fellows, they are often rooted in some remote spot where they must stand alone against the storms. They do not enjoy the shelter of ten thousand other trees that might offer respite from the wind or shade from the sun.

Their life is spent in the solitude of the sky edge.

Their seasons are passed in the rare upland realm of the alp-lands.

Their life must be lived in the maelstrom of stress at the extreme edge of survival.

And in the economy of God, the same is true of those who are willing to live separated lives, apart from the common crowd of our human society. There is such a thing as being too sheltered by our "comfortable culture"—too coddled by our contemporaries, too indulged by our affluent age. Lord, give me the courage to "stand alone" where it counts!

29 —— It Began with God

> *Thou (God) hast made the moon to mark the seasons;*
> *the sun knows its time for setting.*
>
> *Psalm 104:19* RSV

We begin our life with God in a strong and buoyant season, sometimes called our "first love summer." But it is usually followed by the subdued events of a fall season during which a much more mellow mood engulfs our souls. Then come those severe storms of sorrow, the tough trials of pain and parting, the winter winds of adversity. Our faith is tested. Our confidence in Christ is constricted. But as we endure, spring comes again. We are renewed. The truth and credibility of Christ's resurrection power engulfs us. We are assured of His everlasting hope and life. Love springs anew within our spirits. Faith flames bright again. All is well, for *He is here!*

30 —— Bounty from the Sea

> *Yonder is the sea, great and wide, which teems with things*
> *innumerable, living things both small and great.*
>
> *Psalm 104:25* RSV; *read Psalm 104:24–26*

There is no question that as time goes on and modern oceanography opens new concepts or devises new techniques for understanding the ocean, it will prove to be a veritable storehouse of wealth. This is not only because of its capacity to hold mineral wealth, but also because of its ability to produce a profusion of life forms, some of which may well contribute to the survival of the proliferating human race upon the planet.

A typical demonstration of this has been the relatively recent discovery of enormous oil and gas deposits beneath the ocean floor. Just how these have been formed is still a matter of theory, speculation, and conjecture. Nonetheless, the fact remains that the petroleum and gas reserves of the world have been the grand and glorious work of the ocean across millennia. Today that productivity heats our homes, fuels our factories, works our farms, transports us swiftly across oceans, land, and skies.

All of this is an integral and inescapable part of the ocean's glory. She has bequeathed us, under God's good hand, a bounty beyond our wildest expectations. (OG)

31 —— Our Steadfast Father

> *The glory of the Lord shall endure for ever:*
> *the Lord shall rejoice in his works.*
>
> Psalm 104:31 KJV; *read Psalm 104:27–35*

All about me there may be the ebb and flow, the rise and fall of changing seasons, changing scenes, a changing world. "But You, oh, my Father, remain ever the same. You, oh, Lord are from everlasting to everlasting."

The ancient psalmist put this wondrous assurance into the following lines:

> O Lord, how manifold are thy works! in wisdom hast thou made them all: the earth is full of thy riches. So is this great and wide sea, wherein are things creeping innumerable, both small and great beasts.
>
> Psalm 104:24–25 KJV

As the tides change, as the winds veer from point to point on the compass, as the sand creeps across the coast, as the clouds cross the sky, there comes again and again this vibrant, joyous assurance to the spirit of God's child: "Oh, Father, You are here! You are eternal! You are sure and steadfast! Against this glorious, scintillating backdrop of sea and sky and shore, You stand strong and steadfast. In You my confidence is calm and sure. In You my heart glows bright with hope. You are forever and forever!" (OG)

1 ——— Stilling the Storm

Then they cried to the Lord in their trouble, and he delivered them from their distress; he made the storm be still, and the waves of the sea were hushed.

Psalm 107:28–29 RSV

Only God will or can bring beauty out of it all. Only He can bring help to our helplessness. Only He can restore joy for our sorrow. There is no other word of consolation or cheer that I can bring to those in dark places.

It may well be asked, how can you be so sure? My simple reply is based upon three indisputable aspects of life. The first is the inviolate truth of our Father's own Word to us as His people. Untold millions of individuals in their hour of sorrow have found faith and courage and calm strength coming to them from God in the midst of the storm.

Secondly, there has been my own private, moving discovery across the long years of my life that I am never alone in the times of trial. Christ has always been there in the turmoil of excruciating events which appear to be so threatening. . . . I have seen Him dimly, but alive!

Thirdly, there is the subsequent result of all the storms and clouds and wild winds that sweep about us. At the hour they seem so tempestuous. But at a later date their benefits are clearly seen.

For . . . out of the storms there comes to the high country the cleansing, the refreshment, the moisture, the sustenance that eventually renews the mountains. Here, in truth, new beauty is born that adorns the high ridges with a mantle of shining white. Out of the stormy weather spills moisture that refreshes the alpine meadows, the lofty forests, and sky edge rangelands.

Only because of clouds and mists and surging storms does moisture percolate through the soil to feed the mountain springs, enliven the upland streams, replenish the roaring rivers, and fill the lakes anew.

Out of what appears to be death, new life emerges.

2 ——— In the Company of Cliffs

He stilled the storm to a whisper; the waves of the sea were hushed.

Psalm 107:29 NIV; read Psalm 107:28–32

The rising and falling tides, the eternal impact of water on stone, the gnawing and grinding of boulders against basement formations, the rasping erosion of sand- and rock-laden waves chisel away at the cliffs night and day. Slowly, slowly, but ever so surely, they are undercut. Then in some fierce blow, with rain beating against the sodden banks, the whole structure will start to shift. The end is a thundering, slithering mass of earth that slips into the sea.

In one spot where I especially love to stroll, this attrition of the land lies ever before me in stark reality. Embedded in the sand are huge slabs of concrete walls, built to protect the cliffs. They lie twisted, broken, wave-worn, lodged at crazy angles to the surf. Here, too, there are once-proud gravestones, slabs of chiseled marble, and broken Grecian columns that once were the pride of their owners. Now they lie buried in shifting sand, garlanded with seaweed, and grown over with barnacles.

All this reminds me again and again that there is nothing permanent upon the planet. All is change. On every hand there is constant movement and refashioning. Yet, strange to say—as with mountains, so with ocean bluffs—I have found here moments of great repose and enormous uplift of spirit.

There is something very comforting, very reassuring for us human beings in the company of cliffs. For one thing, they have the capacity to close out all the clamor and cacophony of our contemporary world. A man or a woman who seeks solitude, who longs for a spot in which to think "long thoughts," who seeks temporary relief from the relentless tension of our times, can find it in the company of the sea cliffs.   (OG)

3 ——— Sea Walls and Sand Piles

> *Praise the Lord! For all who fear God and trust in him are blessed*
> *beyond expression. Yes, happy is the man who delights*
> *in doing his commands.*
>
> Psalm 112:1 TLB; read Psalm 112:1–4

The battering of a thousand storms, the pounding of ten thousand tides, the eternal erosion of the ocean currents can combine to reduce sea walls to rubble. Now the cement, reinforcing steel, bricks, wire, tangled pipes, and broken mortar stand in wild disarray as silent reminders of how absurd it is to try to keep the sea at bay. Even the most ingenious sea walls eventually crash down to collapse in broken wreckage.

All is for naught. All is but passing. All is change!

The very first home we were shown for sale on the Santa Barbara coast was threatened by the collapsing cliffs on which it was built. . . .

Today the lovely house stands in awful peril, only a few feet from the edge of the precipice. In time, it is bound to collapse and crash to the beach below.

What happens in such horrendous terms to oceanfront homes also occurs with regular frequency to the charming sand castles built by children on summer holidays. . . .

Pausing to watch the action of the waves, washing either over the wreckage of sea walls or the crumbling ruins of a small sand castle, a profound sense of pathos sweeps over me. I cannot seem to ignore them. It is impossible for me to pass them lightly.

They speak to me in terms so clear and emphatic, my attention is always arrested. For here, before my gaze, in sharp, stabbing severity, stand parables of spiritual truth.

You simply cannot stop the sea. It is relentless. It is irresistible! Just so, you cannot continue to ignore God and His claims on your life. Lord, help me to listen and hear Your Voice!

4 ——— Dawn Follows Darkness

Our God is in heaven; he does whatever pleases him.

Psalm 115:3 NIV; read Psalm 115:1–3

Again and again across the passing seasons of my years, sunrises and sunsets have induced me to think long thoughts about God, eternity, the brevity of my little life, the coming of Christ, the guidance of His Spirit along the shores of time.

Often I reflect upon the beauty of sea and sky and sand. Amid the musings of my spirit I realize that at best such glory is but a tiny glimpse, a fleeting foretaste of the wondrous splendor that awaits the children of God. What joy Christ sets before us! What intense and exciting hope He gives us! What tremendous longing He instills in our spirits for that realm where He will be the source of all light!

So dawn follows darkness. Sunset follows day. Our short sojourn here is marked off in the steady rhythm of the seasons, tides, moons and sunsets. Each is a beautiful reminder—"O my Father, You are nigh! Your glory fills the whole earth! All is well with my soul! In Your presence there is joy forevermore!"

5 ——— Of Healing and Holiness

Blessed are they whose ways are blameless, who walk according to the law of the Lord. Blessed are they who keep his statutes and seek him with their whole heart. They do nothing wrong; they walk in his ways.

Psalm 119:1–3 NIV; read Psalm 119:1–8

The unique disclosure given to us mortal men in God's Word is that at best we are corrupt. Our pride, our so-called self-righteousness, our perverseness are a pollution in the presence of the impeccable Person of Christ. There is a formidable force of decay and inner soul degeneracy within man.

Only the counteracting agency of the very life of God Himself can ever purge away our self-centeredness. Only the inner, sterilizing, sharp action of the self-sacrificing cross of Christ can eradicate my human corruption. Only the Spirit of God can enable me to see that my wrongs and wounds and selfish preoccupation can be corrected and healed by the touch of His life on mine. Only His love sweeping into my soul can sterilize it.

6 ———— The Secret of Renewal

Remember your word to your servant, for you have given me hope. My comfort in my suffering is this: Your promise renews my life.

Psalm 119:49–50 NIV; read Psalm 119:49–56

There have been times in my life when I found a banquet in the pages of God's own promises to me as His child. There was life and there was spirit embedded in my Father's word for me. Where before it seemed death was so dominant, now suddenly vital life sprang up anew. Where previously despair prevailed, now, radically, incredible love came to my soul. Where in the winter of my darkness there was such a long night, now in wonder and joy the brightness of new light and hope came alive.

Nor were these just passing whimsies or transient sensations that would delude and discourage those of us who passed through the dark shadows of the valley of death. They were much more permanent and enduring than that. Like the straggling skeins of great winged geese searching for a spot to nest, so the coming of Christ's gracious Spirit, of the Comforter, had arrived to take up permanent residence in the labyrinth of my life.

With fresh awareness and acute intensity there swept over my spirit those ancient, unshakable, marvelous words of old: "*Be strong and of a good courage; be not afraid, neither be thou dismayed; for the Lord thy God is with thee whithersoever thou goest*" (Joshua 1:9 KJV).

There, in essence, was the secret to renewal. The presence of the Most High would enable me and my friends to surmount every sorrow. He it was who would bring spring to the soul again. Because of His great faithfulness, joy would come once more to the spirit.

7 ——— The Blessings of Affliction

Do good to your servant according to your word, O Lord; teach me
knowledge and good judgment, for I believe in your commands.
Before I was afflicted I went astray, but now I obey your word.

Psalm 119:65–67 NIV; *read Psalm 119:65–72*

There will be faults and cracks in the character of the man who has withstood the endless stresses of many changing tides. But under the great, good hand of God, each mark, each line, each change in the contour of his character will but enhance its appeal. It is under the shaping, chiseling forces of life's varied experiences that Christ can sculpt us into magnificent masterpieces if we will but let Him. These are the well-worn tools of His trade for turning out beautiful souls. His Spirit can work wonders on the rough stone of our tough wills, bringing them into lovely conformity to His own will.

It is this sort of person, who, standing tall, despite the worst weather, reflects back something of the warmth and wholesomeness of Christ. As the sandstone cliffs with open face to the southern sun create their own marvelous mini-climate on the coast, so the man open to the impact of the "Sun of Righteousness," reflects something of God's love to a weary world around him.

8 ——— Help from the Hills

I lift my eyes to the hills—where does my help come from?
My help comes from the Lord. . . .

Psalm 121:1, 2 NIV; *read Psalm 121*

It is not surprising that the Most High met with people like Noah, Abraham, David, Moses, Elijah, and others in the high places. Even our Lord Jesus Christ often communed with His Father on the hill slopes and chose to reveal some of His greatest truths to His followers while on the mountains.

Like the sea, mountains often convey to us mortals the impression of immense durability. Yet they are subject to constant change. Weathering and erosion change their appearance. Still our Father uses them to speak emphatically to us earth children in flashes of spiritual insight.

Life in the high country can be most stimulating. The slopes challenge our strength, test our muscles, harden our bodies. The sweeping vistas and serene solitude energize our minds, quicken our souls, and toughen our resolve. The grandeur and glory of the lofty peaks with star-studded skies sharpen our spirits and stir us to contemplate deeply the supreme issues of life.

It is in the quiet interludes on some remote ridge against the edge of the sky that God's eternal Spirit can speak with stunning clarity. There away from the crush and commotion of our culture He, Christ, God very God, can commune with us at great depths. In the stillness and solitude of the hills and valleys it is possible to know our Father and understand His eternal intentions for us.

9 ——— Am I Not Worth More than a Bird?

He will not suffer thy foot to be moved; he that keepeth thee will not slumber. Behold, he that keepeth Israel shall neither slumber nor sleep.

Psalm 121:3–4 KJV

Watching the sea birds, there are times when their numbers are so great I am overwhelmed with the impact of their presence. I cannot help but pause and stand in awe, overwhelmed by the myriads of wings soaring against the sky or the smoothly burnished bodies resting quietly on the sand. There are birds on every side—birds above, birds around me, birds before my feet.

So it is with life. There are days when the marvelous blessings of my Father come winging in upon me in such abundance I can scarcely comprehend the outpouring of His generosity. There are the days when in awe and wonder I can only lift my heart in praise, my spirit in adoration, for all the bounties He bestows upon the beach of my life.

The benefits come from far and near. Some are letters, phone calls, messages from friends in the family of God that stir my spirit, quicken my pulse, inspire my outlook. Others are close at hand—the loveliness of the land, green hills after the rain, warm earth after the storm, sunshine through the clouds, the beauty of the flowers, the voice of a friend, the smile of a stranger, the companionship of a dear one.

Like the birds along the beach, each is designated and ordered of God to enrich my days and enliven my world. They are gifts from the sea. They come at no cost. They charge no fee. They are there, free for the one who will pause to receive their uplift and inspiration.

Other days on my beach are not as replete and full with birds or obvious blessings. Still, some are always there. It may take a little time to find a solitary curlew or a single tern. But they are to be found. And in the spread of a mottled pair of wings with gorgeous tan feathers or in a single flash of white wings over the waves there lies enormous inspiration.

10 —— The Winds of Change

He makes clouds rise from the ends of the earth; he sends lightning
with the rain and brings out the wind from his storehouses.

Psalm 135:7 NIV; read Psalm 135:1–7

I vividly remember camping on a remote and lonely beach in Mexico when a severe sandstorm developed on the shore. So fierce and violent were the wind gusts that only by moving my vehicle down into the lee of a deep draw and turning its tail to the wind did it manage to survive the storm. Even then, the velocity of the wind-driven sand was sufficient to strip all the paint from any exposed metal. Every corner and crack of the vehicle was packed solid with flour-fine grit. And it took an entire day of hard, tedious labor to remove the sand from the engine, where it had been blown in and deposited in solid masses by the blinding storm.

Tempestuous winds of this wild nature will steadily build dune upon dune. There are strips of shoreline on the Oregon coast where entire successions of forests have been buried, one beneath the other. Lowly, tough, hardy beach grasses may briefly bind the shifting sand until a few stunted, misshapen trees take root. For a short spell the vegetation may hold the beach against the onslaught of the wind, but eventually the moving sand will again engulf the struggling trees. Remorselessly, it will begin to bury them beneath its burden of sand and silt. Finally they are entombed, swept over, haunted by the howling gales and whining winds. In all this there lies a somber, startling lesson. It makes me pause and marvel.

Along the beach I see and sense a dynamic microcosm of all of life. From the dawn of time—geologic time, when the first gigantic tides of earth swept inland on raging floods that covered thousands of miles of coastal plains—the biota has ever been in flux. Here I discern and discover that nothing remains the same. There is everywhere about me change, cataclysmic change. The shifting sands, the drifting dunes, the sea-rasped rocks, the chiseled coastline, the wind-wracked trees all declare eloquently that here the only constant is *change*. How thankful we should be that our God does not change. (OG)

11 —— Knowing God

The Lord is near to all who call upon him,
to all who call upon him in truth.

Psalm 145:18 RSV; read Psalm 145:8–20

So it is in coming to know God, to walk with Him in spirit. He surrounds me on every side with His own presence and person and power. Paul put it very bluntly to the skeptics at Athens. He said: "For in him we live and move and have our very being" (see Acts 17:28 NIV).

He is here. As we open our spirits to the gentle touch of His Spirit, we derive and draw spiritual sustenance from Him. He literally becomes our life. As we allow His Spirit to actually enter our spirits in quiet, still receptivity, He comes in to share life with us (Revelation 3:20).

It is as we give time and opportunity and exposure of our spirits to Him that we become "alive" to Him. We have transmitted to us life of a caliber and a quality other than either physical (bodily) life or moral, intellectual (soulish) life. We actually are given the life of God—life from above—the eternal life of Christ Himself.

This is to know God. This is to be born anew in spirit. (WG)

12 —— Beauty Restored

The Lord is near to all who call on him, to all who call on him in truth. He fulfills the desires of those who fear him; he hears their cry and saves them.

Psalm 145:18–19 NIV

The sound of the surf storming against the shoreline can be heard like a distant roll of drums in the distance. . . .

The thunderous action of the combers clawing at the beach will strip away the sand, laying bare the shore bed of rock and rubble. The howling of the wind, the churning of the sea, the tangle of driftwood and shattered seaweed tossed up by the tides, the bleak, gaunt barrenness of the coast during such a storm, leaves the impression of utter desolation.

Those not familiar with my bit of sea edge are often dismayed by the spectacle of damage during a heavy "blow." Yet, always I am reassured that the beach will not long remain battered and bruised. Its beauty will be restored. The ocean will bring back the sand. The silt and mud and debris will be borne away into the ocean's canyon deeps. The sun will break through the clouds again. And in the place of winter's turmoil, there will be repose and rest once more.

Walking with God is like that. Always lurking behind the gloom of our darkest days is the presence of the Savior, waiting for us to recognize and respond to Him. Lord, make me aware of Your presence no matter how dark the day.

13 —— Giving Yourself to God

*The Lord is near to all who call upon him, to all who call upon him
in truth. He fulfills the desire of all who fear him,
he also hears their cry, and saves them.*

Psalm 145:18–19 RSV; read Psalm 145:13–21

In our hectic, hedonistic society, we give ourselves freely to every
new fad or freakish thing that comes along. We give our energy, time,
strength, and resources to searching, striving, and struggling to attain all
sorts of transient things that tarnish with time.

Give yourself as enthusiastically to God! What powerful, potent
people we would be if He really held prior place in our interests. Society
would be startled and shaken if it could see men and women as much
given to God as most are given to gold.

Really put Christ first. Consult Him about all of your interests and
activities. Be acutely conscious that your bodily well-being and behavior
affect Him as much as they do you. It will sober you up no end as to what
you eat, what you drink, what you wear, where you go, how you behave.
Get serious with God about your body. It is as much His residence as
yours. Respect His rights in it. Put His requirements first. Recognize that
He really owns it, not you, so you do have a responsibility to put His
desires first.

As you do, you will discover that He, not the world around you, will
become your preoccupation. You will be startled to see that your entire
perspective on life alters. Your chief center of interest will shift from
yourself to Him.

(WG)

14 —— The Strand of My Life

*The Lord watches over all who love him,
but all the wicked he will destroy.*

Psalm 145:20 NIV

As eternal as the surge of the sea, so is the ever-moving melody of
the love of God my Father flowing over me. As soothing as the sound of
the surf, so is the quiet assurance that sweeps over my soul that Christ is
my constant companion, speaking peace to my spirit. As inspiring and
thrilling as the thunder of the breakers on the beach, so is the strong
surge of God's Spirit breaking in upon my life. In a hundred places, in a

score of ways, He is ever pressing in to inspire me with great joy in songs of praise.

Yes, yes! There are grand and splendid sounds on the shore of my sea edge. But there can be music and melodies just as glorious and wondrous played on the strand of my life. It is freely available if I will but give Him the time.

15 —— Thoughts on a Mountain

Blessed is he whose help is the God of Jacob, whose hope is in the Lord his God, the Maker of heaven and earth, the sea and everything in them —the Lord who remains faithful forever.

Psalm 146:5, 6 NIV; read Psalm 146

A special interlude lingers in my memory. I had climbed carefully to the very summit of the yawning crater of Mount Haleakala on Maui. The lower slopes, as is often the case, had been wrapped in dense veils of mist and fog. As I broke out from beneath these, into the golden sunlight at the summit, I could see the highest points of the other islands, looking like a small flotilla of ships sailing in a sunlit area.

Completely entranced by the splendor of my surroundings, I strolled quietly about the summit of the barren, desertlike volcano until sundown. Gradually the sun, sinking down toward the ocean to the west, bathed my whole island world in golden radiance. It glistened from the huge expanse of moving sea waves all around. It glanced from the cumulus clouds above the leeward slopes of the island chain. It glowed from the landscape of rocks and trees and meadowlands below, as the mists rolled away. All the earth was alight with an incandescent light—bright and glorious.

It is not often one is so utterly overwhelmed with an outer glory that he finds a response within his spirit, which becomes stilled and silent before the Lord from whom it came. To be there, completely alone on that remote island mountain in mid-ocean at that precise moment of sublime splendor, was an honor of special significance. It was as though I had been allowed to stand briefly within the inner sanctuary of the Most High. It was a humbling hour.

That evening I cared not whether my tongue tasted food or my lips felt the touch of water. I had been nourished and refreshed from a source of inspiration that far transcended any ordinary human comprehension. (OG)

16 —— The "High Tides" of Life

Great is our Lord, and abundant in power;
his understanding is beyond measure.

Psalm 147:5 RSV; *read Psalm 147:1–11*

The ocean is everywhere. It flows with smooth swells over the rocks, over the inlets, over the accumulated debris deposited here by a thousand storms. The sea is bright, shining like quicksilver running into every tiny crevice or rivulet that lies upon the shore.

All the ugliness of flotsam and jetsam cast up here by stormy gales is covered by the incoming sweep of the high tide. Every deformity, every gaunt and grimy bit of junk that may have been deposited on this strand by the careless hand of man is hidden from view.

In its place there pulses back and forth the stirring sight of sparkling waves that break against the shore in a flashing spray of green and white water. Everywhere the ocean is moving logs, shifting stones, rearranging the contours of its edge. It will never be quite the same as it was before. This is when, beneath the water's impact, eternal endless changes are wrought in wondrous ways.

This thrust and change brought to the beach by extreme high tides has always thrilled me. The apparent enlargement of the ocean and corresponding contraction of the coast have portrayed to me a profound lesson in my life before God.

There just have to be times, when in His own gracious, irresistible concern, He comes flooding over my little life. There are occasions when the "high tide" of His powerful presence inundates my soiled and shabby soul. There are days when more than anything else I must have that sublime sense of His Spirit sweeping into every secret cove and inlet of my life.

17 —— Walking Humbly on the High Road

Praise the Lord from the heavens, praise him in the heights above.

Psalm 148:1 NIV; *read Psalm 148*

To have been anywhere in high country is to bring back good news of glorious days. The exciting adventures of the high country are amongst the most precious moments any man or woman can possess. They are gold bullion stored in the vaults of memory.

The prophet Isaiah shouted this word to his own contemporaries: "How beautiful upon the mountains are the feet of him that bringeth good tidings, that publisheth peace; that bringeth good tidings of good, that publisheth salvation; that saith unto Zion, Thy God reigneth!" (Isaiah 52:7 KJV).

As we walk humbly with our Lord on the high road of holiness and wholesomeness, our lives make an impact for Him far beyond our most sanguine hopes. It is the man who knows firsthand what it is to walk quietly, intimately, serenely with Christ, whose life carries a special compulsion.

Not only does he bear a unique message of good news from God, but even his own life and conduct and character are an impersonation of that message. He knows God.

As with the disciples it was said: "They had been with Jesus." So it can be with you. (WG)

18 —— Quiet Waters

> *But whoever listens to me will dwell safely,*
> *and will be secure, without fear of evil.*
>
> Proverbs 1:33 NKJV

> *. . . he leads me beside quiet waters, he restores my soul.*
>
> Psalm 23:2, 3 NIV

All of us need to find some quiet waters in life. As refreshing as the oasis for the caravan crossing the sun-scorched desert, so still waters are for the soul seared by the anguish of sorrow. We need moments of respite when in utter tranquility of spirit our Father can be given opportunity to speak to us softly to renew our spirits.

Such times often come to me in the gentle company of high mountain lakes. These small sheets of shining water are cupped in the hills, sometimes surrounded by delicate stands of birch, poplar, and willow. Others, above timberline, stand stark against the sky edge rimmed by rock and a few hardy reeds, tough enough to endure the environment of the high altitude.

The beauty and serenity of these still waters is duplicated by the incredible reflections mirrored in their shining surface. Every tree, snag, rock, distant ridge, soaring mountain peak, and fluffy cloud suspended in the sky are reproduced as if by a miracle in the gleaming water.

Here not a breath of air stirs the surface or wrinkles the water. It is as smooth as polished pewter. Sometimes on very chill mornings after a clear night of extreme cold the lake will be locked in a sheet of glare ice which serves equally as a perfect mirror.

June

When autumn colors flame in the trees, and early frost has burnished the lake or marsh edge with tints of bronze and copper, the total effect is one of majestic splendor. It is as if a painting of huge proportions has been executed on the landscape by *a master artist*.

Lord, may my life be the landscape on which You print your quiet picture.

19 —— Giving Is Getting

> *Trust in the Lord with all your heart, and do not rely on your own insight.*
>
> Proverbs 3:5 RSV; read Proverbs 3:5–8

One day many years ago God put His hand upon my land and asked me in unmistakable language: "Phillip, what is first in your affection—this magnificent property or Me? Are you prepared to give it all away to bless others? Do you really believe I can care for you without this power base, without these resources to meet your bodily needs?"

For months I was in anguish of soul and spirit. I really did not believe He could. Finally in trembling, faltering, childlike confidence, I complied with His request. I gave it all away freely to serve others of His dear people.

During the subsequent years, God in turn has poured into my life a continuous abundance. From sources unknown and unexpected He has sent all that was ever needed to meet my bodily requirements. He has filled my life full and overflowing with bodily bounties.

You see, the books I write are not theory. They are not doctrine. They come from the tough trails God and I have tramped together across the years.

Put God first and He will insure your bodily needs, whatever they be. Walk with Him in the beauty of simple trust. (WG)

20 —— Building Breakwaters

> *Above all else, guard your heart, for it is the wellspring of life.*
>
> Proverbs 4:23 NIV; read Proverbs 4:20–27

On the surface some lives appear respectable, proper and secure. Yet within, there lies the awful silt of sin, the sediment of selfishness, the sludge of a corrupt character.

There are as many ways to build breakwaters against God as human ingenuity can devise. There are scores of excuses that can be brought up to keep out Christ, to resist His Spirit.

The ultimate decision is mine as to what will be done with my bit of beach.

My life can be a bright, open expanse of beauty, joy and vigor for the honor of God. Or it can degenerate into a self-centered, constricted little character who is dead and corrupt with its own selfish preoccupation.

The former will be a joy to Christ and a blessing to every life that touches it. The latter will be a grief to God's gracious Spirit, a bane to those who seek shelter behind such artificial barriers.

21 —— Four Bears on a Mountain

Let a bear robbed of her whelps meet a man,
rather than a fool in his folly.
Proverbs 17:12 KJV; *read Hosea 13:8*

One day on a mountainside I learned a valuable lesson from a mother bear and her cubs. A half-grown black bear, his coat glistening in the rain, was stripping the last of the summer fruit from the tall and slender branches of an Olalla bush. Within moments I spied a second bear of similar size in another clump of brush, and then a third gathering the tender leaves from the tips of a hardy vine maple. Then, as if to add a special delight to the day, I saw a fourth bear, a magnificent sow (female), obviously mother to the three younger ones, turning over rocks to find ants. . . .

The obvious gentleness and cordiality with which the four bears treated one another made an enormous impression on me. . . . There simply was no pushing or shoving or angry rivalry among them. I was especially surprised at how quiet and silent every move was, every gesture, every interaction between them. There appeared to be an aura of courtesy and respect between the bears that warmed my own spirit in a strange yet wondrous way. If only human families were as cordial!

Modern people, living amid the mayhem of our giant metropolitan centers, have been cut off from the wholesome benefits of the outdoor world. Most of modern life is so conditioned and shaped by the stresses and strains of a manmade environment that in many cases the healing influence of mountains, trees, streams, birds, fields, and flowers is unknown and foreign to us.

22 —— Everything in Season

For everything there is a season,
and a time for every matter under heaven.

Ecclesiastes 3:1 RSV; read Ecclesiastes 3:1–9

As an author it is natural that I should also see life like a book. It is an unfolding tale that is being told chapter by chapter. Though it may appear superficially as one continuous whole, in reality it is not, for each of our lives is fragmented into segments. Each section has a significant beginning and a very specific end. And when that chapter is closed, it is closed! Then comes the time to move on to new adventures, to tackle new challenges, to reach for new insights, to find wider service with the Most High.

Just as summer gives way to fall, then in turn autumn is superseded by winter, so in the life of God's person there are succeeding steps by which we are led to follow Christ and pass from scene to scene in the grand pageantry of His purposes for us.

Summer is not fall. Nor is the autumn winter. Each is a season to itself. Each has a special splendor of its own. But likewise each has the fallout of wasted opportunities, squandered time, wrong choices, and willful waywardness that mar the memories of our better moments.

From time to time these demand a drastic change. There has to be a cleanup of the clutter, a renewal of the soul, a cleansing of the conscience, a fresh effulgence of Christ's life from above, and a new falling of God's Spirit upon us to bring beauty into our spirits.

Lord, renew my spirit by coming into my life in new power.

23 —— The Hollow of His Hands

Who has gathered up the wind in the hollow of his hands? Who has
wrapped up the waters in his cloak? Who has established the ends
of the earth? What is his name, and the name of his son?

Proverbs 30:4 NIV; read Proverbs 30:1–9

It has been my great privilege and long-remembered joy to spend unforgettable interludes along some of the ocean's finest beaches. The snow-white sands of the Indian Ocean on Africa's eastern seaboard, from the Cape of Good Hope to Cape Guardafui in Somalia, have cast their spell upon me. . . . I have hiked for miles along the great, open, surf-pounded beaches of Australia and New Zealand. Here the southern oceans, in their gigantic sweep around the land masses, have fashioned miles and miles of windswept sands. In the remote outreaches, a man's footprint may not be seen from one month to another.

In blazing, brilliant contrast, the beautiful beaches of Southern California, Florida, the East Coast of the United States, the Mediterranean, and the ocean islands are sometimes alive and swarming with thousands upon thousands of human visitors. Those who come by the millions to such strands are generally in search of sunshine, open vistas, and the exhilaration of ocean air. The warm weather, the blue waters, the golden sunlight, the soporific influence of wind and waves work wonders in the well-being of those who come on holiday.

But over and beyond all of this, there remains an aspect of the wave-washed strands that has moved me beyond words. It is the dimension of dynamic, ever-changing beauty, so fragile, in the details of the sand itself. It is a part of the windswept shores which cannot be seen from a distance or understood, in a remote or detached manner, from afar.

This is the intricate beauty and special splendor that wind and water work in sculpting sand. Here are three elemental materials, all in motion, each acting upon the other. Wind is moving air. Waves are moving water. Sand is moving land. As they each come under the impulse of one another, we discover patterns and designs of exquisite charm inscribed on the shore. It is the hand of my heavenly Father that fashions these. Oh, the wonder of His ways! (OG)

24 —— The Tides of Time

Again I saw that under the sun the race is not to the swift, nor the battle to the strong, nor bread to the wise, nor riches to the intelligent, nor favor to the men of skill; but time and chance happen to them all.

Ecclesiastes 9:11 RSV; read Ecclesiastes 9:11–18

If it takes fifty years to fashion a gemstone on the shore, can it not be understood that it will take a lifetime for my character to be made into the likeness of Christ?

The tides of time—the endless surf of changing circumstances, the tumbling of unexpected events, the eternal pressure of His presence, the washing of my soul as His Word sweeps over it, the stimulation and surge of His Spirit, the polish of His mercy and kindness and love—will leave me lying contented, smooth, and shining in the glory of His Sun.

This all takes time.

This all takes care.

This all occurs in the ocean of His providence for me as His person.

And because of it all, one day He will see fit to pick me up off the sands of time. He will bear me away home with Him as a special treasure. For I shall be one who has been fashioned under His watchful eye to be one of His small, smooth stones, a jewel of great worth in His estimation.

What good cheer this is for the child of God!

25 —— Open and Obedient

If you are willing and obedient, you shall eat of the good of the land.
Isaiah 1:19 RSV

The areas of my spiritual life which can be made open and available to God are my mind, my intellect, my emotions, and my will.

These all have their seat in my conscious and subconscious mind. It is perfectly possible for me to deliberately respond to the wooing of the gracious Spirit as He speaks to my innermost mind. Or, conversely, I can spurn and reject His overtures. If I do the latter He is easily grieved and quickly withdraws. He will not force an entrance or impose Himself upon me. Lord, may I be willing and obedient. May I open my life to You. (ATG)

26 —— The Winter Is Past

For, lo, the winter is past, the rain is over and gone;
The flowers appear on the earth; the time of the singing of
birds is come, and the voice of the turtle is heard in our land.
Song of Solomon 2:10, 11 KJV; read Song of Solomon 2:8–12

The deep blanket of snow draped across the high country will suckle the springs and replenish the streams that will flow from these slopes next April. The snow pack is the sure guarantee that next summer sparkling lakes will stand filled with cool, clear water to nourish a dry and thirsty land. Because these mountain slopes were buried under snow, ten thousand acres will flourish with emerald-green pastures next year—a carpet of wild flowers will be flung over the slopes. Herds of wild game will flourish on the bunch-grass ranges.

And so it was I saw clearly again the profound lessons that my Lord was imprinting indelibly upon my crushed and suffering spirit. Out of this pressure of pain, this stress of sorrow, would eventually flow streams of refreshment to others in the days to come.

Only out of the crucible of our calamities can there come the poured-out life that, though crushed, releases the fine wine of selflessness to enliven others amid their anguish. Yes, out of death comes life. Out of despair comes love. Out of darkness comes light.

It is always so with God. He is the source of all hope.

And it is He who imparts Himself to me.

27 —— Wrapped in White

Come, let's talk this over! says the Lord; no matter how deep the stain of your sins, I can take it out and make you as clean as freshly fallen snow. Even if you are stained as red as crimson, I can make you white as wool!

Isaiah 1:18 TLB; read Isaiah 1:18–20

One day I went out to walk alone in the silence that follows heavy snowfall. I climbed a remote ridge that stood sentinel above a broad upland basin of rolling hills. The whole world was wrapped in white, pensive, pure, and still unmarked by man or his machines.

It was a morning to think long thoughts—as far-reaching as the distant views that stretched fifty miles to the far horizons of the sky edge. These were precious moments to muse over the meaning of life. They provided a gentle interlude in which I could be open and receptive to the soft, still impulses of God's gracious Spirit.

It came home to me with intense clarity, equal to the brightness all about me, that just as the earth needed this great snowfall to make it utterly lovely, so, too, my life needed the unfolding purity of Christ's life to cover all my deficiencies. The ancient prophet of old, Isaiah, spoke of this in eloquent and moving language when he declared on God's behalf: "Come now, and let us reason together, saith the LORD: though your sins be as scarlet, they shall be as white as snow" (Isaiah 1:18 KJV).

28 —— On Conduct and Character

Many peoples will come and say, "Come, let us go up to the mountain of the Lord, to the house of the God of Jacob. He will teach us his ways, so that we may walk in his paths."

Isaiah 2:3 NIV; read Isaiah 2:1–4

When I was a very young man, one of my early adventures in the western mountains was to work on a fire crew in the Cascade Mountains of Washington. It was a startling and exciting introduction into the high country. The elements of danger and daring that such work demanded nourished my eager spirit of adventure. I fully believe no person has truly lived who has not, at some time, risked his or her very life in a cause greater than himself or herself.

Everything within my makeup responds energetically to the tough demands of a great challenge. My mind is quickened; my emotions are stirred; my will is set like steel to take the test, to run the risk, to overcome the obstacle.

A person's conduct in the face of danger, his character as he confronts the unknown, all reveal the stuff of which he is made. What do my conduct and character reveal about me?

29 —— Return of the Remnant

In that day the remnant of Israel, the survivors of the house of Jacob, will no longer rely on him who struck them down but will truly rely on the Lord, the Holy One of Israel. A remnant will return, a remnant of Jacob will return to the Mighty God.

Isaiah 10:20–21 NIV; read Isaiah 10:20–23

There is a warmth, an appeal, a quiet serenity in the presence of certain people. Constantly there occurs a change, a transformation, a transition from glory to glory, from character to character as the gracious Spirit of God moves upon a submissive spirit.

In the shaping of such a life others find a place of peace, an oasis of repose. It is in the work, the words, the silent influence of such a person attuned to the will of God that men and women, boys and girls, animals and even plants will thrive and flourish.

The strong people, the sturdy souls, the quietly contented characters whose impact goes on without their realizing it, are ever a benediction to both God and man in the world. Even long after they are gone, changed and transformed into the enduring dimension of eternity, their gracious, glowing endowments will remain to enrich our lives.

30 —— Undone and Unclean

Then I said, Woe is me! for I am undone; because I am a man of unclean lips, and I dwell in the midst of a people of unclean lips: for mine eyes have seen the King, the Lord of hosts.

Isaiah 6:5 KJV; read Isaiah 6:1–8

If we are sincere and searching people, in quest of ultimate truth, this "undone" condition deep within our spirits will cause us deep despair. We will know, as the British put it, that something is "seriously out of joint." And our anguish of spirit will *convince us beyond question* that something has to be put right between us and God. Seeing ourselves undone before Him, we will confess our dead and lost condition. We, in fact, mourn our plight.

This is the person who, brought to this point by the faithful inner working of Christ's Spirit, finally flings himself on God's grace and cries out, "*O God, be merciful to me, a sinner!*"

Such a one is blessed. Such a one is well on the road to reconciliation with God his Father. Such a one is on the path to peace with Christ.

For it is to this person that God's own Spirit speaks immeasurable comfort and consolation. "You are forgiven. You are cleansed. You are justified. You are set free from your sins. You are accepted into the family of God."

July

1 ——— A Welcome in a Waiting Heart

*And the spirit of the Lord shall rest upon him, the spirit of wisdom
and understanding, the spirit of counsel and might, the
spirit of knowledge and of the fear of the Lord.*

Isaiah 11:2 KJV; *read Isaiah 11:1-6*

In the providential plan of God the choice of whether or not an
individual will allow the gracious Spirit to enter is a matter of personal
cooperation. If we are warm in our affection and love and gratitude to
God we provide a welcoming climate within. Here the spirit finds it not
only easy to enter, but also conducive to the production of His own exotic
fruits.

"The Spirit, however, produces in human life fruits such as these:
love, joy, peace, patience, kindness, generosity, fidelity, tolerance and self-
control" (Galatians 5:22, Phillips).

If we would grow and produce these fruits, the one thing we must
do is draw deeply of the Spirit of Life Himself who is willing to enter the
waiting heart that is open to Him with a warm welcome.   (ATG)

2 ——— Restored to Repose

*Sing to the Lord, for he has done glorious things;
let this be known to all the world.*

Isaiah 12:5 NIV; *read Isaiah 12*

The giant sea cliffs of the ocean's edge are places of enormous
interest and beauty. There is a commingled aura of grandeur and intimacy
about them. In some places they are powerfully impressive. Their towering ramparts, standing tall and stark above the sea, give the impression of
a formidable fortress under siege from the thundering battering rams of
ocean breakers beating against their bases.

It is to such places that I have come again and again for refreshment
of mind, inspiration of spirit, and rejuvenation of body. One incident
especially stands out clearly in my memory, etched there by the excruciating events of the time.

I had been sent on an extended writing and photographic assign-
ment that took me to some twenty-nine countries around the globe. It
had been an exhausting ordeal. Arranging transportation from place to
place; living among all sorts of strange people; sleeping in nearly a hun-

dred different hostelries; eating foreign foods and sometimes drinking from unsanitary sources; trying to communicate in strange, unknown languages; and transacting my travel arrangements in unfamiliar currencies had all combined to bring me to the very verge of a total collapse. It was precisely at this point that my itinerary called for a brief halt in Tangiers, Morocco.

Fortunately for me, the family with whom I found lodging sensed immediately my utter exhaustion and need of rest. They lived near the sea, facing the wild Atlantic. In love, compassion, and deep understanding, for three days in a row, the lady of the house packed me a picnic lunch of crisp French bread, fresh cheese, and a bottle of fresh orange juice. With this in hand, camera over my shoulder, and binoculars in my pocket, she sent me off to the sea cliffs.

It saved my sanity. It restored my sense of repose and balance. It refreshed my body in a remarkable manner. . . .

There I met my Master and He ministered to me.   (OG)

3 ———— Returning and Rest

For thus saith the Lord God, the Holy One of Israel, "In returning and rest you shall be saved; in quietness and in trust shall be your strength."

Isaiah 30:15 RSV; read Isaiah 30:15–18

Too many of us are too busy; too preoccupied with the pressures upon us; too hounded and harried to call a halt and get alone with God.

In spite of this, may I urge you to do so, even if your family, friends, and other associates consider you odd, queer, and perhaps a bit "touched." Take time each day, even if only for a few fleeting moments, to get absolutely away from those around you. Get alone with God. Seek some secluded spot. Close the inner door to the inner room of your inner spirit. Be still. Be silent. Be serene.

In utter quietness open your spirit to the Spirit of God. Sigh the words that young Samuel spoke: ". . . Speak; for thy servant heareth" (1 Samuel 3:10 KJV).

There will be impressed by His Spirit, upon yours, that word; that inner conviction, that growing compulsion which can come to you only from God your Father. He will speak peace to your spirit. He will impart Himself to you. He will engulf you with His goodwill and His good cheer. He will assure you, *"I am with you always—even to the end of this noisy, high-pressure, restless age. Walk with Me in quiet confidence!"*   (WG)

July

4 ——— This Is the Way

Whether you turn to the right or to the left, your ears will hear a
voice behind you saying, "This is the way; walk in it."
Isaiah 30:21 NIV; *read Isaiah 30:15–21*

We can walk together with God. We can share life with Him. We can be acutely aware of His presence on the path. We can know His intimate friendship. We can be guided by Him in every area we enter. We can sense His gracious Spirit by our side, speaking distinctly, emphatically saying to us, "This is the way; walk in it."

This is the life to which God calls human beings. He longs for our companionship. Down through the long centuries of human history, He has come and come and come, calling men and women to walk with Him, just as today He calls to us. (WG)

5 ——— The Spirit Poured Down

. . . until at last the Spirit is poured down on us from heaven. Then
once again enormous crops will come. Then justice will rule
through the land, and out of justice, peace. Quietness
and confidence will reign forevermore.
Isaiah 32:15–17 TLB; *read Isaiah 32*

The sea wind has a special tang to it unlike any other wind found anywhere else in the world. There is a unique, stimulating pungency to ocean breezes that stirs the senses profoundly.

There are few people indeed who do not respond with an element of excitement to the invigoration of the fresh air that moves strongly at the sea edge. It stirs the blood, refreshes the lungs, and sharpens the senses. . . .

To inhale it deeply is to sense the surge of pure drafts of air entering my lungs. The high level of oxygen in the sea wind provides a powerful impulse to my whole body. My lungs pick up the oxygen rapidly to transmit it to my blood stream. It courses through my whole circulatory system, cleansing the liver, quickening the body metabolism, stimulating the brain.

The Word of the Lord is very specific, very precise, very clear about our life in His Spirit. He urges us again and again to walk in the Spirit. He emphasizes the need for us to be in the Spirit. He points out that we must open ourselves to His incoming. He must have entrance into our daily experience. He is the inspiration for our spirits, the stimulation for our souls, the quickening for our bodies. We are to be invaded and filled with His presence. So, too, I must open my spirit to the infilling of God's Spirit.

6 ——— Seeking Renewal

> *The fruit of righteousness will be peace; the effect of righteousness will be quietness and confidence forever.*
>
> Isaiah 32:17 NIV (see Lamentations 3:26)

We cannot find such assurance in the mayhem and madness of our great commercial complexes. Nor will we ever find it in the sophisticated skepticism of science and technology. Nor will it be found in our most august academic intellectualism. None of these philosophies can ever mend the soul torn with sorrow or the spirit seared with suffering. They are all cold, clinical, and cruel!

But we can find renewal in the stillness of a lake, the drift of clouds against the sky edge, the flight of a bird across the water, the reflection of a deer coming to drink, the limpid, liquid notes of a blackbird in the reeds. These things have been ever of old. They speak impressively of eternal values. They remind us that our Father is ever here; He does not change.

In their constancy we see reflected something of His continuing care and compassion for us. We comprehend, even if only dimly, in the beauty of grass and trees and sky and sun, a little of the glory and wonder of our God who continually makes all things new. In our innermost beings we grasp again the enduring truth that if He can sustain all the earth in its pristine splendor from generation to generation, He can sustain our souls as well. It is He and He alone who can regenerate us in spirit both in this life now and in that to come.

> In essence to *know Him is to know life eternal!*
> This is that which surpasses our suffering.
> It is that which overcomes even death.
> So we are set free from all fear.
> All is well. He is here.
> Thank you, Father!

7 ——— A New Day Dawning

> *O Lord, be gracious to me; we long for you. Be our strength every morning, our salvation in time of distress.*
>
> Isaiah 33:2 NIV; read Isaiah 33:1–6

July

Each dawn of each day is a new beginning in life. A fresh page has been turned and is waiting to have written upon it the passing story of my days. What imprint will be left upon this brief chapter of my all-too-short life? What impress for good and for God will be left upon the shifting sand of my brief lifespan? Each new day brings a wave-washed sheet of time, upon which something of eternal worth may or may not be etched. What am I doing with it?

Even though yesterday may have been less than truly beautiful; even though yesterday the flotsam and jetsam of my fevered day may have been flung upon the shore of my experience; even though yesterday the tracks and footprints left upon the sand of my passing hours may have been tangled, twisted, and even unsure; even in spite of all their confusion, today can be different. Today I can start again. Today, in company with my Lord, I can write a fresh chapter.

That is the graciousness of my God. It is the generosity of my heavenly Father. He who forms and fashions the sea also forms and fashions the shape of my days. He gives me new opportunity, every morning, to inscribe better today than I did either yesterday or ten thousand other yesterdays before that. (OG)

8 ———— Healing Waters

He who walks righteously and speaks uprightly . . . he will dwell on the heights; his place of defense will be the fortresses of the rocks; his bread will be given him, his water will be sure.

Isaiah 33:15–16 RSV; read Isaiah 33:13–24

From the dawn of human history men have been acutely aware of the healing properties of the seashore. . . . To use an ancient British expression, "A few weeks by the sea will put it all right again." And so because of this amazing capacity to cure so many ills, the ocean edge has always been a favorite retreat for those who sought to restore their strength.

This has been true in my own life. At the rather early age of thirty-four I was invalided and sent back from Africa with less than six months to live. It was to the sun-drenched beaches of Vancouver Island I returned. There, as I lay on the sand, swam in the sea, strolled along the cliff edge, little by little strength, healing, and vigor returned to me.

Now, well into my sixties, spared some thirty more years to serve my Master, I still refer to the seashore as "my health insurance." Few are the days that I do not spend an hour or two in solitude along the ocean edge.

The shore has an atmosphere of serenity, beauty, strength, and invigoration that stimulates the whole man. It is more, much more, than merely a balm for the body. It also has a profound impact upon our moral and spiritual lives. The sea can restore weary minds, strained emotions, flagging wills, and aching hearts. But beyond all this, it can be that strong inspiration of God to lift our spirits, cleanse our conscience, and draw us to Himself.

Thus God invades my life when I give Him time and opportunity. As Isaiah says of the righteous, they ". . . shall dwell on high. The rocks of the mountains will be their fortress of safety; food will be supplied to them and they will have all the water they need" (33:16 TLB).

9 ——— Bounty from the Sea

Who has measured the waters in the hollow of his hand,
or with the breadth of his hand marked off the heavens?

Isaiah 40:12 NIV; read Isaiah 40:12–18

An acute sense of enrichment, pleasure, and well-being has always marked life beside the sea. The ocean just does that to us. An overwhelming, upwelling stream of gratitude engulfs my entire being for the enormous privilege of being able to live in close company with the ocean. This sensation has never left me. It is as new and fresh and stimulating today as it was more than forty years ago, when for the first time I actually went to live beside the sea. It was then that the romance blossomed. Nor has my love affair with the ocean ever diminished a whit. If anything, it has grown ever more virile the more time I spend on the ocean edge.

But my first years by the Straits of Juan de Fuca still stand out as perhaps the most poignant and powerful in my long association with tides, winds, gravel beaches, rocky headlands, and mighty winter storms. I have often written about those glorious days. It was then that the ocean cast her spell upon my spirit. It was then the sea became a part of my life. It was then I learned to love her with enormous passion.

My faithful Father has walked with me down the many years since that time. I cannot measure His faithfulness, but being beside the ocean reminds me of His bounty. (OG)

10 ——— The Mind of Christ

Who has understood the [Spirit] mind of the Lord, or instructed him
as his counselor? . . . . For who has known the mind of the Lord
that he may instruct him? . . . But we have the mind of Christ.

Isaiah 40:13; 1 Corinthians 2:16 NIV

If any man or woman is to be truly converted and born again, a profound change must be made in the mind. There simply must be formed in us the very mind of Christ. We must be transformed from character to character by His gracious Spirit through His Word. Only in this way do the standards, values, and interests of Christ become ours by implicit obedience to Him.

In this way our imaginations are brought into line with His. Our thoughts are in accordance with His will. Our delight becomes the desire to please Him in positive ways.

11 —— God's Garden

[God] sits enthroned above the circle of the earth, and its people are like grasshoppers. He stretches out the heavens like a canopy, and spreads them out like a tent to live in.

Isaiah 40:22 NIV; read Isaiah 40:21–26

Hawaii has sometimes been likened to the Garden of Eden. In more than one way this is true, for here one sees new species being established in a setting of quiet beauty. Only time will determine those which survive and thrive, those which succumb.

What is true of plant life applies equally to the birds. Strange and exotic species from all over the earth have been introduced to the islands. At first it seems incongruous to see birds from South America, Africa, and Australia side by side. This man-managed invasion has been very detrimental to the native species, some of which teeter on the verge of oblivion. Only a few rare pairs remain entrenched in some of the more remote and inaccessible forests, tucked away in the toughest terrain.

All these impressions sweep over the spirit of anyone sensitive to the splendor and beauty of this ocean world. On every hand, there is constant change—endless flux—the emergence of new life forms.

As I stood alone, lost in thought, wonder, and quiet awe, overlooking an island vista, the beautiful passage from Isaiah has often come to my mind:

Yea, they shall not be planted; yea, they shall not be sown: yea, their stock shall not take root in the earth: and he shall also blow upon them, and they shall wither, and the whirlwind shall take them away as stubble. To whom then will ye liken me, or shall I be equal? saith the Holy One. Lift up your eyes on high, and behold who hath created these things, that bringeth out their host by number: he calleth them all by names by the greatness of his might, for that he is strong in power; not one faileth.   Isaiah 40:24–26 KJV   (OG)

12 —— Waiting for Renewal

. . . those who wait for the Lord—who expect, look for and hope in Him—shall change and renew their strength and power; they shall lift up their wings and mount up [close to God] as eagles [mount up to the sun]; they shall run and not be weary; they shall walk and not faint or become tired.

Isaiah 40:31 AMP; *read Isaiah 40:18–31*

"They that wait upon the Lord shall renew their strength . . ." (KJV). The words kept running through my mind time and time again. Waiting—wasn't this precisely what I had watched eagles doing so often—just sitting, resting, waiting?

All through the darkest nights, through the cold, gray gloom of morning the birds simply rested patiently, renewing their strength, waiting, perched on some dead snag or crag of rock.

The eagles know from experience that as the sunshine floods the valleys and warms the rocks and earth, gentle updrafts of air will start to rise above the surrounding ridges. It is on these thermal currents that they will soon soar with ease.

So they sit quietly, not fretting or worrying about whether they will be taken aloft. They know they will be. They renew their strength while they wait.

This is the picture of a Christian passing through the dark hours of danger and discouragement. All around him he can sense the chill down-drafts of frustration and reverses. It seems God's face is hidden from him and he cannot see ahead. Yet he need not be despondent. Rather, this is the time to wait for the Lord, to rest in the confidence that He is true to Himself in utter faithfulness.

13 —— On Eagle's Wings

But they that wait upon the Lord shall renew their strength; they shall mount up with wings as eagles; they shall run . . . and not faint.

Isaiah 40:31 KJV

I lay there on this dreamy day, a grass stem between my teeth, my head propped on a gnarled root for a pillow. But as the afternoon passed into evening I found I was not alone. High above my head two tiny specks, scarcely visible to my naked eyes, cut long spirals against the clouds. It was a pair of eagles, and I watched them circle slowly toward their tree where they would wait out the night.

The beautiful scene from Isaiah 40:31 leaped into my mind: "They that wait upon the Lord shall renew their strength; they shall mount up with wings as eagles; they shall run, and not be weary; and they shall walk, and not faint."

Entranced with the eloquent language, so simple yet so descriptive, I watched the great birds soaring on the warm air currents. Slowly there penetrated my mind and heart an acute appreciation of the precise picture that the grand old prophet, Isaiah, was trying to portray to his discouraged people. Most of his audience were simple country folk who, if they had never seen eagles, at least were familiar with the kites and vultures that are so prominent a part of rural life in the Middle East.

But for me on this summer day these two birds soaring majestically over their wilderness domain were the pristine picture of the Christian as a conqueror.

14 —— Updrafts

> *But they that wait upon the Lord shall renew their strength,*
> *they shall mount up with wings as eagles; they shall run*
> *and not be weary; and they shall walk, and not faint.*
>
> Isaiah 40:31 KJV; read Psalm 103:5

Some preachers, teachers and effervescent evangelists would lead us to believe that we can always live high in the sky, soaring against the sun. Not so. This is not God's design. Nor does He arrange our affairs that way.

We are bound to have our days of rain, our times of tears, our hours of disappointment. There are bound to be blustery storms of testing, counter air-currents of frustration, and nights of darkness.

But through them all, in them all, our Father is always there. He does not desert us. He does not abandon us. He is at work in the environment of our lives, persistent in pressing in upon us in ways we do not always see, much less understand.

In these difficult, grievous, heavy times He expects that we shall simply settle down quietly upon the shore of His great grace and wait patiently for Him. He does not call us to beat our way with flashing wings and spent bodies against the storms of life. He does not ask us to fight the adverse winds in fury.

He simply tells us that those who wait upon the Lord, who wait for the weather to change, who wait for Him to alter the environment, will mount up with wings refreshed. They shall fly and not grow weary, borne aloft on the fresh updrafts of His faithfulness.

For, our Father is true to His children. Just as the sun will shine again after the storms have swept the beach, so the rising power of Christ's presence will again warm the shore of my soul. The uplifting wind of His Spirit will once more bear up my spirit. Again I shall soar in strength and beauty.

15 —— Solace for the Soul

I will open rivers on the bare heights, and fountains in the midst of the valleys; I will make the wilderness a pool of water, and the dry land springs of water.

Isaiah 41:18 RSV; read Isaiah 41:17–20

Often, without shame or embarrassment, I have turned to the sky edge with its tumbling streams and melodious sounds to find solace for my soul, healing for my heart. There comes gentle strength and quiet assurance in the acute awareness that these upper springs have flowed undiminished, unchanged for ten thousand years. There can be renewal here at the edge of a snow-fed stream that flows from the rock with pristine purity, as clean as the wind-driven snow on the summit.

Again and again, in a long lifetime of wilderness trails and testing mountain climbs, I have stooped to bury my face in a swift-running upland stream. Long and deeply have I drunk of its cold delicious fluid. I have been refreshed, renewed, ready to push on again with the heavy pack on my back.

Besides the physical refreshment of a now-fed stream, there is a unique and special quality to the music it makes: the murmuring of its soft flow between the stones, the muted tones of its gentle laugh as it tumbles over ledges of rock, its low rumble when it rolls the boulders in its bed in full flood. Depending on the mountain breezes, these sounds rise and fall with constant variations as if played by a celestial orchestra.

Yes, there is music in the mountains. There is uplift for the weary soul. Rejuvenation awaits the spirit ready to listen and be refreshed. This is music of divine origin. Its melodies caressed the creation long before man set foot on the scene. Its harmony can heal in wondrous ways. There is deep and profound therapy in the flow of water, in the songs of a stream.

16 —— A New Song

Sing to the Lord a new song, his praise from the ends of the earth,
you who go down to the sea, and all that is in it, you
islands and all who live in them.

Isaiah 42:10 NIV; read Isaiah 42:10–13

Islands produce in me a profound upwelling of poignant gratitude to our Father for their romance and native charm. Again and again, there has risen from the depths of my innermost being a tremendous, compelling, irrepressible surge of thanksgiving to God for such beauty, such inspiration, such stimulation of soul and spirit and body as islands can provide. They are a magnificent gift of joy from our Father to His earth children.

Over and over, as constant as the breakers that used to beat on the beach a few feet from my windows overlooking the sea, there comes to my spirit this magnificent refrain from Psalm 19:1–5:

> The heavens declare the glory of God; and the firmament sheweth his handywork. Day unto day uttereth speech, and night unto night sheweth knowledge. There is no speech nor language, where their voice is not heard. Their line is gone out through all the earth, and their words to the end of the world. In them hath he set a tabernacle for the sun, Which is as a bridegroom coming out of his chamber, and rejoiceth as a strong man to run a race (KJV).

Beyond the breakers, across the sun-washed waves, lies a whole chain of islands. Like a pod of great gray whales, their backs arch out of the ocean. On clear days they are a delight to the eye. But beyond this, they beckon to me strongly. Silently but surely, they cast their spell upon me. One day soon I will set sail for their shores. Just the thought of setting foot on a fragment of land I have never trod before stirs me to the depths. It quickens my pulse, arouses my enthusiasm. I feel like singing a new song to the Lord. Indeed, He has put a song in my heart.   (OG)

17 —— The Father's Promise

But now, this is what the Lord says —he who created
you. . . . "Fear not, for I have redeemed you;
I have called you by name; you are mine."

Isaiah 43:1 NIV; read Isaiah 43:1–13

There is a joy, a spontaneity, a strange sense of challenge and adventure to making one's way along the surf's edge. It is a fine line one treads between the waves, ever expecting to be engulfed, yet finding safe footing on the seabed.

The older I become, the more apparent this principle is in life. We look back across the long years and see where a thousand waves of despair and discouragement threatened to engulf us in their overwhelming ferocity. At times, as events or circumstances came rushing in upon us, we were sure we would be caught up and crushed in their terrifying vortex. But again and again our worst fears were unfounded. The threatening menace spent itself upon the sand of time, and we were left untouched, unharmed.

This, too, is part of the gracious goodness of our Lord. Often, as I stroll on the sands between the breakers, I am reminded of those gracious words Christ shared with His disciples: ". . . In the world ye shall have tribulation: but be of good cheer; I have overcome the world" (John 16:33 KJV).

It's not that the great breaking waves of life are counteracted in some cataclysmic crisis. No, it's that in and by His own quiet arrangement of our affairs, the rushing waters simply subside into the sands of time around us, leaving us untouched and unscathed.

With refreshing joy and wonder, the words of the Lord to His ancient people come sweeping into my soul with great reassurance:

> . . . Fear not, for I have redeemed thee—I have called thee by thy name, thou art mine. When thou passest through the waters, I will be with thee; and through the rivers, they shall not overflow thee. . . . Isaiah 43:1–2 KJV   (OG)

18 —— A Touch of God

> *Thus says the Lord, who makes a way in the sea,*
> *a path in the mighty waters.*
>
> *Isaiah 43:16 RSV; read Isaiah 43:14–21*

Everywhere I look as I stand at the sea edge there is motion, life, energy. The endless vitality of its environment engulfs me. I am surrounded with the vigor of its energy. The mighty movements of its tides, waves, sea currents and ocean breezes enfold me in their irresistible embrace.

The sea edge is a special world.

At best I can do no more than stand upon its shore and sense that I am but a minute particle of humanity on the edge of an ocean stretching around the globe. Its magnitude is beyond imagination. Its power and dynamic action linked to moon, sun, stars, and all the constellations of outer space are beyond my finite understanding. It is often a realm cast in dramatic light.

So I am stilled before its majesty.

My soul is silent in its presence.

There is assurance in its might.

Few, few indeed, are the mornings when I stroll along this shore that the ocean does not impress me with its power, its glory and its majesty. I am humbled in its company. I am awed by its magnificence. Yet, wonder of wonders, I am also made glad to be with it. For me, it is a touch of God on my little life.

19 —— A Brand New Thing

For I'm going to do a brand new thing. See, I have already begun!
Don't you see it? I will make a road through the wilderness of
the world for my people to go home, and create rivers for
them in the desert!

Isaiah 43:19 TLB

The Lord is not confined to the pages of Holy Writ.

He is not to be found only in our solemn sanctuaries.

He is not restricted to liturgy or creed.

He is everywhere at work in our weary old world.

He is to be met in a thousand disguises.

His touch is to be found at every turn of the trail.

The point is I must be attuned in spirit, receptive in soul, alert in attitude, to detect the impact of His presence upon my path.

The bonuses of my Father are everywhere about me, scattered at random, freely, like shells upon the shore. But it demands time, thought, attention, and perseverance to discover their sheltered spot, their hidden secret places.

Life can be profoundly rich without being pretentious. It can be filled with overflowing vigor if we but pause to relish the fragrance of the breezes that blow across our strand. It can provide an abundance of joy and humor and goodwill if we seize the seashells scattered along the sands of our times to bear them home to be shared with others. It can be wholesome, hearty, yes, even holy, when we take the time to spend quiet interludes in company with our Father.

20 —— Daily Refreshing

For I will pour water upon him that is thirsty, and floods upon the dry ground: I will pour out my spirit upon thy seed, and my blessing upon thine offspring: and they shall spring up as among the grass, as willows by the water courses.

Isaiah 44:3–4 KJV; read Isaiah 43:1–8

The wind and ocean air which I inhaled yesterday will not do for today. The breezes which refreshed me last week will not so refresh me this morning. The surge of oxygen that cleansed and energized my body metabolism about a month ago will not suffice for my work this afternoon.

I must be refreshed, rejuvenated, requickened, yes, refilled each day. There is no other way. The supply and source is inexhaustible. The movement and flow is eternal. The dynamic energy never diminishes.

All that is required is that I expose and open myself before Him to be totally available to His personal impact upon me today. To so live—sensitive to His presence, aware of His wishes, obedient and open to His will—is to be filled and stimulated by His Spirit . . . now and on into eternity.

21 —— It Is the Lord's Doing

Shout for joy, O heavens; rejoice, O earth; burst into song, O mountains!

Isaiah 49:13 NIV; read Isaiah 49:8–13

Only the person who has spent a severe winter in a northern latitude, at comparatively high altitudes, will ever fully comprehend the true wonder of spring. There really is no other physical experience on the planet which can quite match the magic of the melting of the snow. Nothing is so designed to stimulate the entire body and quicken all the senses as the return of warm weather, stronger sunlight, and the renewal of the earth. . . .

Where there was barrenness suddenly there is exquisite beauty. Where the mountains against the sky edge were a stark white, now they are dressed in vivid green, yellow, red, and white flowers. Where there had been utter severity of scenery, now suddenly there has come softness and splendor as if painted with an artist's brush.

This total transformation of the high country from winter to spring remains one of the most magnificent spectacles upon the planet. The total transfiguration is a moving panorama that progresses with enormous power and perfect precision. It is governed by the celestial movement of the sun, moon, stars, and planets, all in orbits ordained by the meticulous mind of our Father God.

22 —— The Transforming Touch

> Hear me, you who know what is right, you people who have my law in your hearts: Do not fear the reproach of men. . . . my righteousness will last forever, my salvation through all generations.
>
> Isaiah 51:7, 8 NIV; read Isaiah 51:1–8

Like the chill winds of November, the stern events of our little lives can quickly make our days seem gaunt with grief and grim with the struggle to sustain enthusiasm. Some seasons it seems sorrow is added to sorrow until only the gray framework remains of what had once been beautiful and bright adventures. In one recent eighteen-month period my wife and I shared in the deepening gloom of no fewer than fourteen families who faced the scourge of terminal illness.

At such times of stress and distress a man needs more than sentiment or sympathy. He needs more than pious platitudes or easy pleasantries. He needs God—in all His majesty and glory and might!

Only the transforming touch of the Risen Christ upon the life can change the dark contours of the circumstances. He alone can descend upon the darkness of the soul in sorrow, bringing exuberant brightness and whiteness to dispel the doubts and gloom. He alone can transform the very outlook from one of despair to that of eager anticipation.

If this is to happen then we must be open and receptive to the presence and power of the Living Lord who gladly comes to engulf us with the wonder of His own person.

23 —— The Mission of the Meek

> For thus says the high and lofty One who inhabits eternity, whose name is Holy: "I dwell in the high and holy place, and also with him who is of a contrite and humble spirit to revive the spirit of the humble, and to revive the heart of the contrite."
>
> Isaiah 57:15 RSV; read Psalm 34:15–22

Essentially in the Scriptures where we find such phrases as: "broken-hearted"; "contrite in spirit"; "meek and lowly in heart"; this is what is meant: A man's will has been brought into subjection to the will of God. A person's powerful passions and drives and energy have been harnessed to do God's work in the world. The "meek" man is the disciplined man, trained and taught to take on great responsibilities and to discharge them without fuss and fanfare. He handles tough assignments with apparent ease.

The "meek" person is the one easily entreated of God. The Master need only speak the word and the worker will throw all of his full weight and strength into the enterprise. The "meek" man is the one under divine discipline who responds to the call of Christ and tackles the tough task without hesitation. The "meek" individual is the one who gets God's work done in the world without a lot of showmanship or theatrics.

24 —— A Soul's True Safety

The high and lofty one who inhabits eternity, the Holy One, says this:
I live in that high and holy place where those with contrite, humble
spirits dwell; and I refresh the humble and give new courage
to those with repentant hearts.

Isaiah 57:15 TLB; read Isaiah 57:15–21

During the years in which I served as a lay pastor it startled me to see how many people, even within the church, went to such great lengths to keep God out of their lives. They had built formidable breakwaters around themselves lest He come flooding into their experience.

In ignorance they had erected barriers of unbelief against Him. In fear they had fashioned bulwarks of anxiety and apprehension against Christ. In hostility and defiance they built barricades of belligerence against His Spirit.

Often these breakwaters against the incoming tides of God's grace, mercy, and compassion were erected against the church, against other Christians, against God's Good News, or against the convicting action of God's Spirit. The general attitude was: "Keep out of my life."

Somehow, strange to say, many people do not seem to mind encircling a bit of the sea of God's grace in such a way that it provides them with a so-called "safe haven." They rather enjoy having a snug little sense of security within the shelter of some formal, rigid religiosity. Even the idea of the encircling wall of a creed is enough to cut off the full impact of the incoming life of Christ. The social functions of church fellowship can be a sufficient barrier to preclude the powerful presence of God's Spirit flooding the soul with character-changing force.

Heavenly Father, break down the barriers that keep me from the center of Your will!

25 —— Close Out the Clamor

*For thus saith the high and lofty One that inhabiteth eternity, whose
name is Holy; I dwell in the high and holy place, with him also
that is of a contrite and humble spirit, to revive the spirit of
the humble, and to revive the heart of the contrite ones.*

Isaiah 57:15 KJV; read Isaiah 57:14–21

As you become increasingly aware of God's presence in your life,
you will become increasingly fond of Him. You will find that Christ really
is your favorite Friend. You will want to be alone in intimate communion.

One does not have to go into some closed room to do this. Your
special rendezvous can be anywhere, at any time, provided you take the
trouble to deliberately go to your trysting place.

Different people will have different ways of doing this. Most of my
precious moments with the Master are when I take a walk outdoors alone
or work in the garden or stroll by the sea. But by all means get alone; get
quiet; get relaxed and allow Him to share some very private, precious
moments with you.

Close out the clamor of the world all around. Only then can you
feed your inner person and grow in spirit and in truth. (WG)

26 —— A Bright Darkness

*Feed the hungry! Help those in trouble! Then your light will
shine out from the darkness, and the darkness
around you shall be as bright as day.*

Isaiah 58:10 TLB; read Isaiah 58:10–14

In a spiritual sense we must discover the meaning of darkness, especially as it relates to the formation of Christian character. The darkness of
unbelief lies all around us: the darkness of a world separated from God
who is the source of all light, and the darkness of men and women who
grope for that light, but who have not met the Man of Galilee in the light
of His own glorious life and compassion for them.

How am I to respond to such darkness around me? Will I recoil from
it? Will I withdraw from those unfortunate ones who walk in such darkness? Or will I go out into it eagerly seeking to lead some of them to my
Master? If I do, the outcome will startle me. Even that darkness will be
transformed into light and life and energy when men meet my Master.
(Read the verses of the day carefully.)

One of the tremendous personal thrills, known only to a true child of God, is the delight of introducing a soul in darkness to his own Heavenly Father and Christ Jesus his Savior, the light of the world. Such an experience energizes and vitalizes a Christian's entire life beyond the power of words to describe. It makes his inner life a bright adventure despite the darkness around him. (ATG)

27 —— The Lamb and the Law

> But your iniquities have separated you from your God;
> your sins have hidden his face from you, so that he will not hear.
>
> Isaiah 59:2 NIV; read Isaiah 59:20, 21

Somehow, somewhere, someone must build a bridge across this appalling chasm. We cannot save ourselves, try as we may. We cannot cleanse our own conscience. We cannot shrug off our own sin. There must be a sinbearer apart from ourselves.

This God has always seen and clearly understood. *Man has not!*

. . . in the wilderness at Mount Sinai, God added a bold, fresh stroke to the portrait of The Lamb of God. The two young animals before the High Priest represented another piece in the unfolding picture of God's atonement. After the lot was cast and the one was chosen for the sacrifice, its blood was carefully brought into the innermost holy place of the tabernacle to be sprinkled on the mercy seat where God met with man. Instead of suffering for their own sins, absolution and atonement were made through the death of the lamb for the entire nation.

The eternal law, the inviolate principle, that "the soul that sinneth, it shall die," had been fully exonerated. In the substitute death of another, the law was satisfied and the guilty sinners set free. (LAMB)

28 —— The Glory of God

> No longer will you need the sun or moon to give you light, for the Lord
> your God will be your everlasting light, and he will be your glory.
>
> Isaiah 60:19 TLB; read Isaiah 60:19–22

As the evening sun settled slowly over the last high ridges of the sky edge, the warm rays laid a golden glow of sheer glory over the stream. Never in all my years in the wilderness had I seen flowing water take on such wondrous beauty. Breath-taking shades of green and gold, of blue and silver, flashed in the current and gleamed from the running waters.

It seemed almost every color of the spectrum shone like light glinting from a thousand gems that sparkled in the stream. Even the intense whiteness of the tumbling rivulets turned the whole scene into a dazzling display of artistic loveliness.

And again the vivid, moving, majestic realization came to me with shining clarity: "Life does go on. Life can be beautiful. Life is touched with wonder . . . because of my Father's perpetual presence!"

My part was to look for the glory of the Lord as it was reflected to my watching gaze from day to day. Just as the sun touched the stream and turned it into a glowing scene of dazzling beauty, so the effulgence of the glory of God could transform my little life into a thing of shining beauty and gentle wonder.

29 —— Beauty for Ashes

The Spirit of the Lord God is upon me . . . to give unto them beauty for ashes, the oil of joy for mourning, the garment of praise for the spirit of heaviness. . . .

Isaiah 61:1, 3 KJV; read Isaiah 61

All of us live amid a dying world. Death dominates the planet—not just physical death, but also the death of hopes, dreams, ambitions, love, family, friends, and a hundred other human aspirations.

Yet in spite of all this decadence and despair, life can be beautiful. We can bring comfort, cheer, and consolation to our contemporaries. We can be those who weep with those who smile through their tears.

We can draw near to help people pick up the pieces and make a fresh start. We can bring beauty for ashes. We can share the Spirit of God's joy to replace the spirit of a heavy heart.

30 —— The Source and the Secret

For my people have committed two evils (says the Lord); they have forsaken me, the fountain of living waters, and hewed out cisterns for themselves, broken cisterns, that can hold no water.

Jeremiah 2:13 RSV; read Revelation 22:1–5

Throughout Scripture we have the picture given to us of Christ Himself being the true fountain of living water (Jeremiah 2:13). He is shown as the source and spring of everlasting life which is poured out continuously to thirsty men and women (Revelation 22:1). Without this invigorating flow of life I am spiritually desiccated (dried up). I live amid a world in which the mark of death and decay lies upon everything that surrounds me. I am like a tree in a desert, languishing for water.

But Christ deigned to come down into this earthly domain of death. He chose to deliberately pour out His life in His blood to deliver me from death. Now, through His resurrection power, His life eternal flows forever to those who will draw on it.

As a tree by the waters grows in spite of drought all around it, so I, by drawing upon the life of Christ, grow into His strength and beauty despite the dominion of death all around me. (ATG)

31 —— Sermons in Sand

"Should you not fear me?" declares the Lord. "Should you not tremble in my presence? I made the sand a boundary for the sea, an everlasting barrier it cannot cross. The waves may roll, but they cannot prevail; they may roar, but they cannot cross it."

Jeremiah 5:22 NIV; read Jeremiah 5:18, 19

Between a stretch of sand and a man there gently develops a beautiful intimacy which only those who have lived on a beach can understand. It is something more than the mere interaction and response to physical elements of sea, sky, sun, wind, and water. It is more than the warm caress of sunshine on the cheeks. It is beyond the stimulating sense of well-being that sweeps across human senses in contact with the ocean.

It is best defined as a spiritual response to something very much greater than ourselves: an awareness that here man is in intimate contact with an earth system which he cannot tame or control. He is in touch with tremendous forces and elemental energy, over which he has no dominion. The vast sweep of the ocean, its restless currents, its eternal movement, its never-ceasing action apart from and independent of man, humble his spirit.

This element of commingled love and respect for the sea is ever apparent, even in the hardiest of seafaring people. Though the ocean draws them to its heaving bosom with magical mysticism, they always respond to its overtures with a solemn sense of quiet, inner reverence. . . . Because their lives are bound up intimately with the sea and their homes are perched upon its windswept strand, they regard it with commingled awe and affection. They learn to read its writing on the sand. They can catch the messages it bears from the dark and distant reaches of the outer ocean. They can sense its changing moods and mighty movements, and they often know its Maker in a unique way. (OG)

August

1 ———— Songs of the Sea

Is there no balm in Gilead; is there no physician there? Why then is
not the health of the daughter of my people recovered?

Jeremiah 8:22 KJV

The sea has many sounds. It speaks in a wide range of accents to those of us who live near it and have come to love its voice. The notes played upon my strip of shore are some of the most sublime music of divine design composed in the cosmos.

The songs of the sea, the murmuring of streams, the running notes of rivers, the thundering of waterfalls, the soft melody of lakes lapping on a shore, the fine music of a fountain flowing over its rocks are all fluid sounds produced by water in motion. In this music of the ages there lies remarkable therapy for the whole of man . . . body, soul and spirit.

For me, the sound of the sea is like the balm in Gilead of which Jeremiah spoke. It soothes my restless soul; it lifts my heavy spirit. Through it, God speaks peace to my heart and assures me of His abiding presence.

2 ———— On Water and Life

Blessed is the man that trusteth in the Lord, and whose hope the Lord
is. For he shall be as a tree planted by the waters, and that spreadeth
out her roots by the river, and shall not see when heat cometh,
but her leaf shall be green; and shall not be careful in the
year of drought, neither shall cease from yielding fruit.

Jeremiah 17:7–8 KJV; read Jeremiah 17:5–8

The vital life processes of an organism are dependent on moisture in its cells. Water is essential to survival. A flourishing tree may be 80 percent moisture, which means that there must be a continuous supply available from its environment if growth is to proceed normally.

Water spells the difference between a desert and a forest. It spells the difference between a dry, shriveled, stunted tree and the splendid form of a towering cedar of Lebanon. Water is actually the essence of life within a growing tree.

Not only is moisture essential as that which combines with the air to produce carbohydrates for growth, but it is also the means of food and energy exchange within the tree. In addition, it guarantees mineral and vitamin absorption through both the leaves and roots. It determines the health and vigor of the tree.

A healthy tree's cells are turgid and charged with moisture. The sap which circulates throughout the tree is a complex combination of minerals, carbohydrates, vitamins, and proteins in suspension. The constant movement of this moisture through the tree from cell to cell conditions and controls its health.

Jesus said: ". . . whosoever will, let him take the water of life freely" (Revelation 22:17 KJV). That's the Source of my life! (ATG)

3 ——— Cleansed by Fire!

But if I say, "I will not mention him or speak any more in his name," his word is in my heart like a burning fire, shut up in my bones. . . .

Jeremiah 20:9 NIV; read Jeremiah 20:7–12

In many forests, fires burn more fiercely and with greater devastation because brush and brambles and undergrowth become established around the trees. A very clear picture of this is given in Judges 9:15 (KJV): "And the bramble said unto the trees, If in truth ye anoint me king over you, then come and put your trust in my shadow: and if not, let fire come out of the bramble, and devour the cedars of Lebanon."

Lightning also frequently strikes trees that stand out in exposed sites on ridges or open country. If a tree has dead or dry wood it may be set ablaze. Green, vigorous, luxuriant trees are not so apt to burn, though they may be scarred or split or shattered by the electrical discharge that goes to ground.

The likelihood of such a calamity befalling a strong, green vigorously growing tree is much less than for one which is dried up, diseased, or cumbered with dead wood. The rich, dense foliage of a healthy cedar, moreover, so shades the soil beneath it that it precludes brush and brambles from encircling it. So the chances of its being burned are more remote.

Is my life cluttered with the "underbrush" of the world? Lord, let Your fire cleanse me! (ATG)

4 ——— A Fire in My Bones

And I can't quit! For if I say I will never again mention the Lord—never more speak in his name—then his word in my heart is like the fire that burns in my bones, and I can't hold it in any longer.

Jeremiah 20:9 TLB

There is something profoundly primitive about man and fire. His most ancient traditions and oldest roots are shaped by fire. All the struggles to survive, the preparation of food, the shelter against the bitter wind and biting cold are bound up with fire. Beyond all this the celebration of life, the joy of comradeship, the intimacy of family ties, the offering of sacrifices and incense were entwined with fire—and still are.

Is it any wonder our Lord God sometimes refers to Himself as fire? Are we startled to see so many references in His own divine revelation to us, as His earth children, that He comes to us as fire? Is it not understandable that even of old He would choose to appear to His chosen ones in flames of fire?

It was a flame of fire that moved among the pieces of Abraham's ancient sacrifice. It was fire and smoke and a great burning that descended in power on Mount Sinai when God's presence came down upon the sacred mountain. It was a divine flame that fell upon Mount Carmel to consume Elijah's bullock as well as even the water and stones of the altar. It was prophesied by John the Baptist that when Christ came He would bring fire on earth. And visible, tangible evidence of the truth was clearly seen when flames of fire appeared upon the disciples on the Day of Pentecost in the upper room.

In the divine economy of the Most High, fire is an inescapable part of the impact of His presence on us.

5 ———— God's Word and God's Will

For I know the thoughts that I think toward you, saith the Lord, thoughts of peace, and not of evil, to give you an expected end.

Jeremiah 29:11 KJV; read Jeremiah 29:11–13

Because of the impeccable and wondrous character of God, all of His will toward both the universe as a whole, and a single soul in particular, is good, desirable, just, kind, patient, loving, gracious, gentle, strong, and generous. Above all He is faithful, sincere, honest, and totally trustworthy by virtue of the fact that this is His very makeup. He cannot be otherwise. All His intentions toward us are desirable.

Our simple responsibility is to get into God's Word, to ruminate in it, to revel in it, to rejoice and delight ourselves in discovering how great and good and generous His will is for us. We discover He has nothing but our best interests in mind. His heart is set only on our welfare. So we, too, come to want His will more than anything else. Our fiercest desire is that our wills be aligned with His will. Our joy and delight is to do His will and comply with His wishes. In all of this we show our genuine, honest love for Him. (Read John 14 and 15.) (WG)

6 ——— Create in Me a Clean Heart

The Lord hath appeared of old unto me, saying,
Yea, I have loved thee with an everlasting love:
therefore with lovingkindness have I drawn thee.

Jeremiah 31:3 KJV; read Jeremiah 31:1–14

There is enormous beauty in the transaction between breakers and the ocean, a beauty that surpasses the crashing waves flinging themselves upon the beach. There is also an eternal cleansing action in Christ's life laid down, spilled out upon my behalf to cleanse and purify me. That, too, transcends the eternal washing of the shore by the endless waves breaking over it.

The breakers make the beach beautiful both without and within. Likewise the outpouring of the love of God upon my life—the eternal, endless energy of His own person—purifies my character and beautifies my behavior.

The cleansing of the beach is one of the special secrets of the sea.

And the cleansing of my soul is one of the great mysteries of God's love for me—a love so great it stills my soul, it humbles my heart, it subdues my spirit.

"Create in me a clean heart, O God; and renew a right spirit within me" (Psalm 51:10 KJV).

7 ——— The Divine Exchange

I will cleanse them from all their iniquity, whereby they have sinned
against me; and I will pardon all their iniquities, whereby they have
sinned, and whereby they have transgressed against me [saith the Lord].

Jeremiah 33:8 KJV; read Jeremiah 33:1–9

The world is so much with me. The careless hand of man, the cruel ways of our society, the thoughtless acts and omitted courtesies of my contemporaries leave a legacy of hurts and sorrow and wreckage in my life—the black rocks of rising anger, the hard jagged reefs of dark resentment, the flotsam and jetsam of ill will that clutter my character.

Only Christ can change all this. Only He can alter the contours of my disposition. Only He can displace the debris of my soul with the surging newness of His own person. There must be an exchange of His life for mine—of His desires for my otherwise selfish impulses.

It is He, who in the high tide of His relentless patience and perseverance, presses in upon my person.

I cannot, dare not, keep Him out. It is His eternal, sure incoming, as inexorable as the rising tide, that gives hope for covering all the corruption and defilement of my days.

Those of us who wish to be utterly honest with ourselves and with our Father know full well the need of His covering. We cry from the depths: "Who can cover my iniquities? Who can enfold me in righteousness? Who can fill me with the fullness of God?"

It is He and only He who can do this for us.

There is no one else.

8 ——— New Every Morning

> . . . the Lord's . . . compassions never fail.
> They are new every morning. . . .
>
> Lamentations 3:22–23 NIV; read Lamentations 3:21–24

The art and skill of understanding the sea does not come in one day, one week, or one year. It takes a whole lifetime of learning. It calls for humility of heart, openness of spirit, and a gracious willingness to receive what the ocean can teach us earth children.

I would like to share with the reader some of the simple yet profoundly eternal principles the sea has shared with me. For I come to walk upon its shore open to its eternal wisdom, eager to discover some new and inspiring insight into life.

Each fresh dawn, as I set out to hike along the beach, I am astonished at its newness. It is the same strand I tramped along yesterday—superficially. There is still the great arching bay that runs from the broken headlands of rock in the west to the gorgeous high cliffs of orange clay on the east. There are still the same tranquil Channel Islands rising out of the Pacific to the south, like giant whales baring their backs to the sun. There are still the tall, graceful, fan palms blowing in the wind and the gorgeous Monterey pines silhouetted starkly against the red and rising sun. There is still the sturdy ice plant blanketing the sand just above high tide. There are still the alluring cries of the cormorants, pelicans, gulls, and curlews that wheel and call in the wind above the waves.

But in the face of all this apparent sameness, the ocean verge is never the same two mornings in succession. As I step upon its sand, the incredible sensation of being the first man to ever set the sole of his foot upon this particular strand overwhelms me. Never before have the uncountable millions of minute grains of sand been arranged in exactly this order. The sand lies clean—swept, polished, immaculate. Every trace of every track and footprint and mark made yesterday has been erased by the night tide. What my gaze falls upon in the early hours of the dawn is a new sheet of shifting parchment, upon which will be inscribed the passing events of a new chapter in a new day.   (OG)

9 —— In Company with Christ

The steadfast love of the Lord never ceases, his mercies never come to an end; they are new every morning; great is thy faithfulness.

Lamentations 3:23 RSV

It takes time, much time, precious time alone, in company with Christ, for the dynamic reality of His life and light and love to break through the darkness of our delusion and set us free. We do not need to seek some special services or attend some sensational staged event to witness the miracles of His power. The glory of His grace, the loveliness of His presence can be seen even in the lowly beauty of an Olalla bush. He surrounds us with new miracles every morning.

It is such an acute awareness of Christ's presence in the world of plants and trees, grass and flowers, sun and rain, clouds and earth, moon and stars, sunrise and sunset that can enable the most ordinary person "to blossom where you are planted."

10 —— He Never Fails

Because of the Lord's great love we are not consumed, for his compassions never fail. They are new every morning; great is your faithfulness. I say to myself, "The Lord is my portion; therefore I will wait for him."

Lamentations 3:22–24 NIV

Where today there is turmoil, stress and darkness, tomorrow new fields of flowers will flourish on the slopes.

In the skies so laden with heavy overcast, so charged with clouds and wind-driven snow this week, birds will soar on wing against the sun next spring. For this, too, will pass. The skies will be blue again.

All is change. Life is ever in flux. Nothing on earth remains constant. But in splendor and wonder those of us who know Christ shout with glad affirmation, "*O God, Thou changest not!*" Amid the mayhem, in calm confidence we assert boldly, "*Forever, O Lord, Thou art faithful.*"

Clouds come and go. He remains constant.

Winds blow, storms subside. He is ever by our side.

Out of it all, He alone brings comfort, consolation, and the great renewal which is such abundant compensation for all the crushing sorrow of our years—and the burning agony of our tears.

He, and He alone, makes all things new—both in this life and in the wider life yet to come beyond the skies. Bless His wondrous name forever and forever!

11 —— The Water of Life

Behold, I will liken you to a cedar in Lebanon, with fair branches and forest shade, and of great height, its top among the clouds.

Ezekiel 31:3 RSV; read Ezekiel 31:1–9

All trees, like the cedars of Lebanon, may derive water from their environment in a variety of ways. The water may be in the form of the still, silvery dew that descends during the night to settle softly on the outstretched boughs. It may be in the clouds and mists and fog that sweep in off the sea to swathe the forest in misty veils. It may be the summer showers or the winter snows. It may come through underground springs or rushing streams that cascade down the mountainside, where roots reach out to draw refreshment from the flow.

But a point to remember is that the tree does not hoard this moisture for itself. The vast network of running roots beneath the soil often exceeds the outspread canopy of trunk, branches, and leaves spread to the sky. And vast quantities of water are lifted through the framework of the tree to be transpired out into the surrounding air. This moisture, along with the discharge of oxygen, is what gives the forest atmosphere such a fresh fragrance.

Here we discover striking parallels in the life of the eager, earnest Christian who is thirsting after righteousness, eager to grow into the likeness of Christ. God's Word tells us explicitly that such shall be satisfied. "Blessed are they which do hunger and thirst after righteousness: for they shall be filled" (Matthew 5:6 KJV).

Again, in Isaiah 44:3 (KJV), "For I will pour water upon him that is thirsty, and floods upon the dry ground."

In the spiritual realm, what is the counterpart of water to a tree? It is life eternal. It is everlasting life. It is the very resurrection life of Christ

Himself imparted to mortal man. It is new life in Christ made available to me by His death and through His blood shed on Calvary. (ATG)

12 —— A Sermon from a Cedar

Behold, the Assyrian was a cedar in Lebanon with fair branches, and with a shadowing shroud, and of an high stature; and his top was among the thick boughs.

Ezekiel 31:3 KJV

The cedars of Lebanon are unique in possessing properties that make their wood resistant to insects, virtually impervious to decay, and extremely durable. This is why they are capable of growing into fine, fragrant timber suitable for the temple.

In the economy of God, He saw clearly that because death dominated the earth, the only way its power and domination could be broken was for Himself, in Christ, to enter directly into the cycle of birth, growth, life, and death upon our planet. Christ Jesus was born of a virgin, grew up among men, lived and moved among us, then died for us. But, marvel of marvels, His body did not decay (Psalm 16:10). Instead of being chained to the cycle, He shattered its power and rose directly from the dead. No wonder Christians shout, "Death is swallowed up in victory. O death, where is thy sting? O grave, where is thy victory?" (1 Corinthians 15:54–55 KJV).

What a triumph!

The shackles that had chained men to the wheel of death on this planet have been snapped. This is the magnificent overcoming life made available to man through the resurrection of Christ. (ATG)

13 —— Open to the Spirit

And I will put my Spirit within you so that you will obey my laws and do whatever I command.

Ezekiel 36:27 TLB; read Ezekiel 36:24–30

The Holy Spirit comes to us constantly from out of the very depths of the greatness of God. He is ever present with us, surrounding us on every side with the wonder of His own Person. Though invisible as the sea winds He exerts His own enormous power upon the earth. He is constantly available to us. But to enjoy the dynamic of His vitality it is essential to open ourselves fully to His influence.

This takes time. It takes time to be made wholesome. It takes time to expose ourselves to the incoming of God's Spirit. It takes time to become holy as He is, the Holy Spirit of the Most High. It takes time to be still before Him and to be sensitive to His impulses and wishes.

Just as the wind off the sea is here, moving, flowing, blowing about the beach, so the wind of God's Spirit is very much at work in the world, moving mightily around us on every side.

The essential question for the Christian is, am I aware of His presence? Do I really appreciate the fact that His energy, His power, His vitality, His influence, His benefits are freely available to me?

14 —— Healing for Crushed Spirits

I will bring healing to their crushed spirits; in free mercy I will give them back my love; my vengeance has passed them by. I will be morning dew, to make Israel grow as the lilies grow, strike roots deep as the forest of Lebanon. Those branches shall spread, it shall become fair as the olive, fragrant as Lebanon cedar.

Hosea 14:4–6, Knox Translation; read Hosea 14:4–9

Perhaps my profession, my career, my business, has become the overshadowing thing in my life. It is stifling my growth in God. It dominates my desires. I find myself becoming indifferent to Christ's claims. A falling off in correspondence with God becomes apparent in my conduct.

God in mighty mercy and jealous love for His child may bring my career tumbling down around me. My business may be blown away in the winds of adversity. Then suddenly there is space and time and opportunity for me to spread myself before Him in repentance. Only there will I sense the depth of His concern for me.

Hosea 14:4–6 puts it so clearly: Crushed spirits will be healed, love will be restored, and the still dews of His quietness will be upon my outstretched limbs. Again, the very roots of my being will lay hold afresh on Christ, they will draw their strength from God. Out of it all, my life will exude the fragrance of a revitalized and vigorous growth. (ATG)

15 —— Space to Survive

I will be like the dew to Israel; he will blossom like a lily. Like a cedar of Lebanon he will send down his roots; his young shoots will grow. . . .

Hosea 14:5–6 NIV

There were no other trees in all of Palestine to compare with the magnificent cedars of Lebanon. To those who saw them they were a thrilling sight as they grew to such grandeur on their rock-ribbed mountains. And one of the most important reasons why they attained such stature was that they had space—ample, open room—in which to flourish.

Applying this principle to the Christian life, it is interesting to observe the same law of response to space at work in human hearts.

Jesus Himself made reference to it in His parable about the sower and the seed. He emphasized how some plants were actually choked out by the competition from others (see Matthew 13:7, 22). There was simply a lack of sufficient space in which to survive.

In the Christian life, as in the life of a tree, we must face the fact that we are continually crowded and surrounded by earthly attractions, by human philosophies, by people with worldly concepts.

Now God has very definite, though at times drastic, measures for eliminating some of this competition from our lives. He literally clears away the encroaching trees and undergrowth by His fires of discipline or storms of suffering and sorrow. (ATG)

16 —— Service—or Self-gratification?

He has showed you, O man, what is good. And what does the Lord require of you? To act justly and to love mercy and to walk humbly with your God.

Micah 6:8 NIV; *read Micah 6:6–8*

We as God's people are not in this world to extract all we can from it for our own ease and selfish ends. Life is not our oyster to pry open and plunder in pride and arrogance. That is the world's gross and deplorable philosophy. But it should not be a Christian's. The world's aim is self-aggrandizement. Christ's aim is service to others.

The two are set in diametrically opposite directions. The powerful stream of our Father's will at work in the universe flows against the mindset of a society interested only in self-gratification—the so-called "me" syndrome.

Are we surprised that many moderns are so jaded? Are we taken aback by the cynicism of our age? Are we astonished by the weariness and boredom, the general discontent of our generation?

God made us for Himself, to learn to lose ourselves in the majestic grandeur of His incomprehensible greatness. He formed us to be conformed to His image in the pure joy of pouring ourselves out in the stream of His goodwill for the planet. He urges us by His Wondrous

Spirit to find our total fulfillment in complete identity with Christ and His cause in the redemption of human society. . . .

We are here to walk humbly with our Master and, working with Him, see great and wondrous changes wrought in the world around us. Not because we are great Christians, but because He is our Great God! (LOVE)

17 —— God at Work in the Whirlwind

The Lord hath his way in the whirlwind and in the storm, and the clouds are the dust of his feet.

Nahum 1:3 KJV; read Nahum 1:1–5

Just yesterday morning the phone rang. It was the wife of my next dearest friend in this area. Her strong man had suddenly been stricken with a massive stroke. Unable to speak, unable to articulate his thoughts, unable to move one side of his big sturdy frame, he now lay like a fallen tree.

This was the twenty-ninth person in our circle of friends to have the terrible threat of death descend like a dark cloud across the horizon of life. In eighteen months this tragic story had swept over us in agonizing intensity almost thirty times. O the tears, the fears, the inner anguish!

Again and again, the stabbing, searing, searching questions come through trembling lips and tear-burned eyes: "Can God be in all of this? Is He really here? Does He truly care?"

"Yes!" Again and again I affirm the truth. "He has his way in the whirlwind and in the storm. The clouds are the dust of his feet." He, the Risen One, the Living God, is here present in our pain. He is at work in the whirlwind of our despair, moving behind the scenes in the dark clouds of our chaos and confusion. Of this, I am confident!

18 —— Healing from the Sun

[The Lord says:] But for you who fear my name, the Sun of Righteousness will rise with healing in his wings. And you will go free, leaping with joy like calves let out to pasture.

Malachi 4:2 TLB; read Malachi 4:1–3

It is in the sum total of ten thousand new days—in the accumulated impact of uncounted new sunrises, in the exquisite beauty of unnumbered dawns—that my life can be changed from glory to glory, from character to character, by the pristine splendor of the Spirit of the Living Lord who surrounds me with His effulgence.

For just as my soul is stirred and stimulated by the rising of the sun, so, too, my spirit is inspired and quickened by the splendor of the Son of God, whom the psalmist calls the Sun of Glory.

He rises with great healing in His majesty. He rises amongst us bringing new hope for every day. He rises to shed over us mercies and bounties of blessings that are new every morning.

In the acute awareness of all this, life becomes much more than a mere march of time across the calendar. In company with Christ each dawn comes as the beginning of a new chapter in the pageantry of my days.

What is inscribed upon that chapter depends upon the intense sensitivity of my spirit to His. It comes from the willingness of my will to comply with my Father's wishes. It can be beautiful if He is allowed to be the author of my work.

19 —— Baptized with Fire

[John the Baptist said:] "I baptize you with water for repentance, but he who is coming after me is mightier than I, whose sandals I am not worthy to carry: he will baptize you with the Holy Spirit and with fire."

Matthew 3:11 RSV; read Matthew 3:11–17

Most of us do not take the bold, somewhat blunt statements of Scripture very seriously when they speak of fire in the life of the Christian. Too often these comments are relegated to romantic imagery or regarded as rather primitive language for conveying the idea of light, warmth, or comfort to man.

We really do not want to deal with the dire results that a genuine conflagration of celestial burning might have on our cozy culture. The modern church of the late twentieth century in North America knows virtually nothing about fire on the mountain. Our fire suppression equipment has become so sophisticated, so ready on standby, so swift to respond to the first spark that smolders, that the glorious Spirit of the Living Christ can hardly get a good blaze started in any soul!

The fierce burning that comes with shattering conviction of sin is scarcely known today. The sweeping, searing flames of fear of divine judgment and inescapable justice from a righteous God are no longer in the land. The intense inner fires of purification and cleansing and change that once swept through the souls of men like Wesley, Whitfield and Wilberforce are well-nigh a bed of ashes in the comfortable company of the contemporary church.

Lord, let Your fire fall on me—and make me clean!

20 —— A Dimension of Deliverance

Blessed are those that mourn, for they shall be comforted!
Matthew 5:4 RSV; read Isaiah 61:1–3

God keeps His promises. He will give us new life. But first we must mourn our spiritual death. The person poor in spirit, who in a spiritual dimension mourns and grieves over his or her own spiritual poverty, will best know the life of Christ made real within. The one who decries his own inner deadness will most surely be made alive with the quickening assurance and comforting presence of God Himself.

As I pen these lines, there sweeps through my spirit again the acute and painful agony of those days in my life when I realized that in truth I was "dead to God." All my life I had listened to the Word of God. For almost forty years I had been attending all sorts of churches. Yet deep down in my spirit there was no acute awareness of the living Christ.

Graciously, persistently, patiently, God's Spirit entreated me to turn from my self-assured, self-centered, self-confident conduct to seek Him. Oh, the turmoil of those times! Oh, the tears of anguish that flowed in the darkness of my despair! Oh, the melancholy mourning of a man who longed and yearned for God to quicken and make him alive in a new dimension of deliverance from death to life, from darkness to light, from despair to love.

And God did! Bless His name!
He is faithful.
He is true to Himself.

21 —— A Joyous Inheritance

Blessed are the meek, for they shall inherit the earth.
Matthew 5:5 RSV; read Matthew 5:1–16

The meek individual has found the place of peace. He no longer struggles and fights and pushes to become top man on the totem pole of society. The threat of being pushed off his little pinnacle of prestige no longer haunts him.

He is not caught up in the pettiness of the so-called "pecking order." Content to quietly serve others, he has no fear of falling. There is no need to try so desperately to impress others. His main concern is to do whatever he does to the very best of his ability to satisfy the Master and thus bring Him honor.

So for him, the earth, instead of being a battleground, becomes a happy home for the few years he is here. He is at peace with God, with others, with himself. And this indeed is a joyous inheritance.

22 —— The Purpose in Pain

Blessed are the meek, for they will inherit the earth . . . that you may be the sons of your father in heaven. He causes his sun to rise on the evil and the good, and sends rain on the righteous and the unrighteous.

Matthew 5:5, 45 NIV

The principles of creation, re-creation, and eternal duration apply equally whether they be in the natural realm of grass and sea and rock or in the supernatural realm of mind and will and stony spirits. This is a salient point which Jesus, the Living Christ, made again and again in His use of simple earthly parables to explain profound spiritual principles. The two realities of natural life and spiritual life are contagious. They cannot be separated, even though our scholars and theologians would try to deceive us into believing otherwise. Too much, far too much of modern preaching and teaching is based upon purely human philosophy spawned by so-called "thinkers" whose mindset has emerged from the chaos of our manmade urban environment.

And so as I have sought solace and strength and reassurance for my own soul and spirit in recent months, I turned away from the pious platitudes of preachers and teachers and scholars. There was no adequate explanation there for the unending stream of sorrow, the ever-flowing anguish of pain and separation which pours over the planet.

It is not enough to cry out against the agony.

It is not enough to submit sullenly to the sorrow.

It is not enough to accept the separation stoically.

If we are truly Christians, if we are in reality children of the Most High, if we are at all sensitive to God's gracious Spirit at work in this weary old world, we must be able to perceive our Father's purposes in all our pain.

23 —— Treasure between the Tides

Blessed are they which do hunger and thirst after righteousness;
for they shall be filled.

Matthew 5:6 KJV

As I pick up a shell, wash the clinging sand from its surface, and feel its form between my fingers it elicits awe and admiration from within. The special shape, the delicate designs in its surface, the smooth flow of its convolutions, the exquisite hues of its colors, the sheer loveliness of its form command my attention and draw from my spirit genuine gratitude.

All of this happens the moment I pause in mid-step to stoop down and pick up the treasure from between the tides.

It takes time to do this.

It takes some thought as well.

It takes attention to what the sea is offering.

All of life is like that. Everywhere, scattered here and there along the shore of our lives the tides of time cast up their quota of beautiful bonuses. They may not all be obvious. Some will be less than spectacular. Yet scattered along the strand of our ordinary days it is possible to find precious gifts from God.

And Jesus' promise is this: ". . . they shall be filled."

24 —— Filled with His Presence

Blessed are those who hunger and thirst for righteousness:
for they shall be satisfied.

Matthew 5:6 RSV

He actually comes into my spirit by His Spirit to reside. He is the living Christ who, very much alive, arises to become the dominant person in my experience. He fills my life.

This "filling" by God's Spirit of which Jesus spoke and about which much has been said in the New Testament appears to confuse many. It really need not be so if we understand in simple terms what is meant.

To be filled with the presence of God is to enjoy His company and companionship in all of life. It is to know Him as our life mate, exactly as in a beautiful marriage. Two people never really "know" each other until they become fully open and available to each other. It is only when each has invited the other to come into his or her life and fully share all their experience that their days are "filled" with the other's presence and person.

This is why Jesus referred to Himself as the groom, and His church (you and me) as His bride. He comes into our lives to fill them continuously with His own person, His own presence, His own influence.

25 —— A Measure of Mercy

> *Blessed are the merciful: for they shall obtain mercy.*
> *Matthew 5:7* KJV

In my own life I am acutely aware that I am a roughhewn man. Because of my rather tough, rough upbringing in a frontier environment, I simply do not possess the polish of the "man about town." There are characteristics in my makeup which may seem harsh and unyielding. But, despite this, my life has been deeply touched by the mercy of those who took the time to try and understand me—who cared enough to forgive so many faults and who in mercy made me their friend.

Often these were people to whom I had shown no special kindness. Their bestowal of mercy on me was something totally unexpected and undeserved. Because of this, it has been a double delight. More than that, it has been an enormous inspiration that lifted and challenged me to respond in a measure beyond my wildest dreams.

Mercy does just that to people. It excites and stimulates their hope. It reassures them that life can be beautiful. It convinces them that there is good reason to carry on and push for better things if others care that much.

This all implies that if someone has extended mercy to me, surely I, in turn, can and must extend mercy to others.

But, to really find the true source of inner inspiration for this sort of conduct, the Christian simply must look beyond his fellow man. He must look away to the mercy of God our Father. Nothing else in all the world will so humble us. Nothing else will so move our stony spirits to extend mercy. Nothing else will so powerfully induce us to do the proper thing in extending genuine mercy to our contemporaries.

26 —— The Path of Peace Exemplified

> *Blessed are the peacemakers: for they shall be called the children of God.*
> *Matthew 5:9* KJV

We live in an atmosphere of antagonism, and an environment of enmity. Yet amid such adversity Christ calls us to produce peace.

This peace is love quietly, strongly, persistently meeting every on-slaught against it with goodwill. It is that inner attitude of tranquility and tolerance in the face of angry attacks. It is the willingness to accept the assaults of others even at the price of personal humiliation. It implies that even though my enemies and detractors may be at war with me I can be at peace with them.

This principle of producing peace was of course best exemplified in the life of our Lord. For though He did nothing but good amongst men, His jealous opponents were determined to destroy Him. When they had done their very worst and He hung in burning shame and agony upon the cross, a tough Roman centurion looked upon His bruised and broken body to exclaim: "Surely, this man was the son of God!"

For though Christ had been reviled, He did not revile in return. Though He had been falsely accused, He did not react in flaming anger. Instead, He was silent before His assailants, asking only in quiet tones, "Why do you do this to me?" Of course they really did not know. Steeped in their own sin and selfishness it was impossible for them to see the enormity of their evil. It is always thus with men at war with others. So from the depths of His Spirit, Christ cried out, "Father, forgive them, for they know not what they do!"

We must do the same. There can be no other path to peace.

27 —— Salt for Society

[Jesus said:] "You are the salt of the earth. . . ."
Matthew 5:13 RSV

Have we allowed human ideology, human philosophy, human values to superimpose themselves upon our way of thinking, our standard of behavior, our lifestyle?

Is it true to say that we as Christians are an element in society that is as distinct as salt to food, or light to darkness? Or is the reverse true? Has society actually succeeded in impinging itself upon us to the extent we are no different than the world?

A great uneasiness is beginning to be felt amongst God's people everywhere. It is no longer a case where the church is vigorously pene-trating the world with God's message of salvation. It is now a case of the world penetrating the church with humanistic philosophies, cultural pride, business techniques, and contemporary conduct.

Because of this the church probably stands in its greatest hour of peril, despite its apparent popularity and prominence in Western society. For arrogance always comes before a terrible fall.

It is imperative, therefore, that we see clearly what our Lord said our role should be as "salt for society."

28 —— Loving My Neighbor

> *[Jesus said:] "You have heard that it was said,*
> *'You shall love your neighbor and hate your enemy.'"*
>
> *Matthew 5:43 RSV; read Matthew 5:43–48*

In the world, amid a cynical society apart from God, social relationships are so often pursued for selfish, often sordid ends. Men and women play false and cruel games with one another in the name of love, friendship, or camaraderie. Yet all the time they are actually exploiting, impoverishing, and bewildering one another in lust, greed, and cruel cynicism.

The person who is walking with God in his emotions simply dares not indulge in such duplicity. We are God's people. We are governed by His behavior standards. We are sincere, honest, open, and genuine. If we are Christ's friends we do not fool around with the feelings of others. We do not capitalize on their capacity to reciprocate our advances. We simply do not take advantage of them. We do not give, in order to get.

If I am walking with God's Spirit as my constant companion and counselor, I shall have compassion, concern, and a genuine care for others as He does. This is to love my neighbor (anyone who crosses my path in life) as I love myself. I shall make no emotional move that adds to his load in life. Instead I shall endeavor to help him bear his burden with greater joy and a lighter step. (WG)

29 —— Consider the Lilies

> *And why are you anxious about clothing? Consider the lilies of the field, how they grow; they neither toil nor spin; yet I tell you, even Solomon in all his glory was not arrayed like one of these.*
>
> *Matthew 6:28, 29 RSV; read Matthew 6:25–34*

Often as I have been out on the mountains, hiking hard on a remote ridge at the edge of the sky, it has startled me to come across a lone Olalla bush, bursting with blossoms or laden with delicious fruit. By the superb miracle of my Father's loving arrangement, beauty of bloom and a banquet of fruit have been distilled from the tough raw materials of stony soil, burning sunlight, and hidden underground seeps of moisture.

On the gaunt granite He has laid out some of the most beautiful bouquets in all the earth. And there, too, He has turned rain, sunshine and gravel into the most delectable fruit and juice for the gentle refreshment of all who pass by.

Our modern preachers and hyper-evangelists urge us to demand our "miracles" from God. They rant at us to claim our rights and receive some sort of dramatic demonstration from the divine. They insist that only by special signs and wonders will the world ever come to acknowledge Christ as God very God.

He Himself told us no such spectacular displays were necessary to demonstrate His deity!

Instead He urged us to look around and quietly notice the lily of the field, the fledgling sparrow fallen from its nest, the Olalla bush blowing in the breeze. There in the ordinary events of the natural world around us lay a thousand miracles of His making, the lovely touch of our Father's care.

30 —— Of Wood and Wind

Though the rain comes in torrents, and the floods rise and the storm winds beat against his house, it won't collapse, for it is built on rock.

Matthew 7:25 TLB; *read Matthew 7:21–29*

Looking at the trees at timberline we see a dimension to their growth not often recognized by the casual passerby.

It is the rare and elegant quality of the actual wood produced within the wind-tossed trees. Its grain is of exquisite texture interspersed with whorls and curving lines of unusual gracefulness. The stresses and strains of being tossed and twisted by the wind and sleet and deep snows of winter produce an extra flow of resins in the tree. Not only does this give the fibers a remarkable tight-grained texture but it gives off also an exquisite fragrance.

An expert violin maker, who is a master craftsman, tells me that he spends weeks each summer searching for special trees above timberline. From these he takes his choicest material to create musical instruments of the finest quality and tone.

Wood produced in the high and tough terrain above the usual timber bears within it a rare timbre and lovely resonance not found in ordinary lumber cut at lower elevations. The fury of storms, the shortness of the growing season, the wrenching of the winds, the strain of survival in such an austere setting—all these combine to produce some of the toughest, choicest, most wondrous wood in all the world.

Lord, make of me the kind of wood You can use!

31 —— Sea Walls and Sand Castles

. . . Every one who hears these words of mine and does not do them
will be like a foolish man who built his house upon the sand . . .
Every one who hears . . . and does them will be like a
wise man who built his house upon the rock.

Matthew 7:26, 24 RSV

All of us build our sand castles on the sands of time. All of us dream our little dreams of what we shall do with our lives. We dig our deep moats around those very private ambitions. We carefully erect our walls of self-protection to surround our elaborate aspirations. We shape and mold our decisions and personal choices into castles of self-interest and self-gratification.

Most of us do this happily, blithely in our youth. We behave as though there were only time, lots of time, and us. There seem to be so many years ahead, so many seasons to carry out our schemes, so many days to do our thing. We forget so soon that God is even there; and though He is, He seems as remote as the moon that turns the beach to silver at night.

Yes, not only do we plan and build and scheme and work to erect our sand castles, we also forget that the tides of time and the power of God's presence are as inexorable as the ocean tides rising in response to the gravitational pull of the moon.

For in the full flood of high tide—under the rising surge of the incoming wave, beneath the sweeping course of the ocean currents the castle—the walls, the moats, the work of our dreams—will disappear . . . lost in oblivion.

Such is the end of those aims and ambitions built in thoughtless, careless abandon without reckoning on the power of God. Beautiful but for a day, they are swept away into nothing. Lord, help me to build on the Rock!

September

1 ——— Broken or Brash?

> *Come to me, all who labor and are heavy laden, and*
> *I will give you rest. Take my yoke upon you, and learn from me. . . .*
>
> Matthew 11:28–29 RSV; read Matthew 11:25–30

The one "broken" to the Master's yoke is the one who at last has stepped into stride with God. He acknowledges that Christ is in control. He accepts the load laid on him as matched to his strength. He admits that all is well and finds ease and rest therein.

The Master stated without hesitation that it was these who would inherit the earth. Of course most of us do not really believe this. Everything in our civilized culture cries out against such a concept. We who have been totally conditioned by our sophisticated Western society are sure that to be big, bold, brash and brazen is still best. We insist that one must simply get ahead on his own by grim determination and fierce fighting. . . .

It is the meek person who finds that faith in God begins to flourish in his/her life. The self-made, self-sufficient individual sees no need to trust another, let alone Christ, as his Master.

But men and women broken to serve Christ come quickly to the place where they must trust Him for guidance and supervision and the supply of all their needs.

It is no longer a case of carrying on in one's own way. It is not a matter of doing one's own thing. It is not a question of realizing only one's own ambitions. Instead, life is seen from God's perspective. And to achieve the grand purposes of God, simple trust and quiet faith are needed. These He bestows in ample abundance upon the meek. And great results take place.

2 ——— The Joyous Journey

> *For whosoever shall do the will of my Father which is in heaven,*
> *the same is my brother, and sister, and mother.*
>
> Matthew 12:50 KJV; read Matthew 12:46–50

Refuse to let reverses, frustrations, discouragements, or seeming disasters distract your attention from God's will for you. Pursue His purposes. Set your sights on His loftiest ideals and aspirations for you. Let nothing intrude between Him and you.

You can be a great achiever with God. You can climb the heights and reach otherwise impossible pinnacles. His inspiration, His companionship, His goodwill, His cheer, and hope are all there for you to revel in. But it is up to you to want to do this. It is up to you to choose with your will to reach the high country of noble living in company with Christ. These are your decisions. They are a definite, deliberate act of your will.

Invite God Himself by His Spirit to share your traveling days through this life's tangled trails. He will be glad to come. And your journey will be joyous. (WG)

3 ——— A Solace of Solitude

> *And after he had dismissed the crowds,*
> *he went up on the mountain by himself to pray.*
> Matthew 14:23 RSV; *read Matthew 14:13–27*

It is noteworthy that even Christ Himself, when He was here among us, continually separated Himself from the clamor of the crowds. He simply had to detach Himself from the pressure of people and the crush of the cities to find solitude on the mountain slopes. Nor is it mere accident that we are told this again and again by those who were closest to Him.

Finding stillness was an essential part of His life.

He did not neglect this exercise.

It was something He did continually at personal cost and the risk of gross misunderstanding.

It was the sure guarantee that His character would not be compressed or deformed by His contemporaries.

It was in the stillness of the night that He gave Himself to prayer, to meditation, and to quiet spiritual communication with His Father. These were interludes of inspiration, uplift, and restoration for His spirit.

If such moments were precious to Him, how much more so it must be true for us! It is in these quiet times that we can be open and receptive to the still, small voice of the Most High.

4 ——— The Lost Lamb

> *What do you think? If a man owns a hundred sheep, and one of them*
> *wanders away, will he not leave the ninety-nine on the hills*
> *and go to look for the one that wandered off?*
> Matthew 18:12 NIV; *read Matthew 18:10–14*

September

Wherever Jesus went, the impact of His person and the dynamic of His teaching attracted enormous public interest. Men and women by the multitudes came to Him for healing of body, for cleansing from disease, for delivery from demons, for restoration of sight, for uplift of spirit, for refreshment of soul, for forgiveness of sins.

The lives He touched were turned around. The eyes He looked into, with such enormous love, beheld the beauty of God in this One, yet most of them knew Him not. He was the Lamb of God moving amongst the lost sheep of the nation of Israel, bringing back a few strays from their self-willed wandering.

Repeatedly and emphatically He stated that He had come to seek and to save the lost sheep that had strayed. . . . It was for the cross that He had come! The horrible hounding of His footsteps; the cruel, relentless attacks on His person and teaching; the final explosive confrontations with the ecclesiastical hierarchy of the day; the stirring triumphal entry into Jerusalem; the moving last supper with His men; the agony of Gethsemane; the bestial betrayal; the mock trial by those in power—these were all but a dramatic prelude to the cataclysm at Golgotha.

In all of this anguish, Christ moved with quiet strength and calm serenity. Nothing, nothing, took Him by surprise. Though He was "the Man of Sorrows," acquainted with grief—both ours and His—He was also "The Lamb of God," moving in might and majesty. (LAMB)

5 ———— Walking in Harmony

[Jesus said:] "Where two or three come together in my name, there am I with them."

Matthew 18:20 NIV; read Matthew 18:19–20

Walking together with God means harmony. It is virtually impossible for two people to walk together, unless they are in agreement. You will notice that if there is the least discord, one or the other will quickly move ahead, while the other deliberately falls behind. They immediately separate.

Amos, the ancient prophet of old, called by God from caring for cattle to the lofty role of a prophet to his people, put it this way: "Can two walk together, except they be agreed?" (Amos 3:3 KJV).

So the sharp, stabbing, startling question comes to all of us. Are you in agreement with God? Are you in accord with Christ? Are you in sympathy with and sensitive to the overtures of His Spirit? Unless you are, to speak of walking with God is sheer self-delusion.

It is noteworthy that the people who walk together are those who are extremely fond of each other. Parent and child, sweethearts, lovers, chums, intimates, husbands and wives—the list is long and the life a blessed one. (WG)

6 —————— He Is Ever with Us

> *Jesus saith unto her, Mary. She turned herself and saith unto him, Rabboni, which is to say, Master.*
>
> John 20:16 KJV; read Matthew 20:1–16

The cooling breeze picked up strength as the quiet hours passed. It moved through the trees as surely as the breath of a master musician drawing lovely notes from his woodwind instrument. There was music in the wind, celestial music of the Master's making. It brought solace, comfort, and healing to my aching heart. There was divine therapy in the gentle movement of the air that cooled my fevered face and dried my tear-stained cheeks.

When I first came to this still spot, it seemed I was so much, so very much alone. In the agony of my anguish, like Mary on the resurrection morn, it seemed no one else was there. Through her tear-blinded eyes she saw only dimly the outline of the empty tomb, the grave shapes of the gaunt, gray olive trees.

But in that grim garden there was also the Lord of Glory—her Master—Rabboni. He spoke her name and she knew Him. In ecstasy she fell at His feet. And so, too, did I on this sparse mountainside.

There broke through again into my awareness the acute revelation: "O Christ, You never leave us; You never abandon us to the vagaries of life's constant changes; You never let us tramp the trail of tears alone. You are ever near, ever dear, ever here."

7 —————— Daily Decisions

> *Then they will reply, "Lord, when did we ever see you hungry or thirsty or a stranger or naked or sick or in prison, and not help you?" And I will answer, "When you refused to help the least of these my brothers, you were refusing to help me."*
>
> Matthew 25:44, 45 TLB; read Matthew 25:31–45

The daily decisions we make to devote ourselves to Christ and to His interests in the earth are evidence of His love in us. John, the dearly beloved old Apostle, wrote with such impact, "My little children, let us not love in word or in tongue; but in deed [action] and in truth [integrity]" (1 John 3:18 NKJV).

As we learn to love both Christ and His own children in the earth, that devotion will be much more than mere rhetoric. It will be shown in tears, in toil, in sharing, in giving, in earnest intercession—in a thousand little ways in which we do God's will in this weary world. As this love is learned in the crucible of life, it is demonstrated with joy and whole-hearted delight.

To love with the love of God is not martyrdom. It is not to feel put upon or exploited. It is not to be deprived of joy. Quite the opposite! For the person who has found that which is much greater than himself, in which to invest all of life, has found the secret to serenity.

The greatest good to which any individual can give his entire being is God Himself, in Christ. And God is love. So to give ourselves to Him is to give ourselves to loving Him, in person and in His people.

Where do we find God? We find Him in Christ. We find Him in the poor, the needy, the lost, the people whom He brings across our path. For by His own definite declaration He has said, "Inasmuch as you did not do it to one of the least of these, you did not do it to Me" (Matthew 25:45 NKJV).

(LOVE)

8 ———— Challenged by Christ

. . . surely I will be with you always, to the very end of the age.
Matthew 28:20 b NIV; read Matthew 28:16–20

Anyone who does much walking or hiking soon discovers that much of its pleasure comes from the challenge of climbing. We are not content to just loaf along on the level; to dawdle in the lowlands becomes a bore. Something stirs within us to scale the heights, to tackle the ridges, to gain the summit, to get onto high ground.

It is precisely the same in walking together with God. Let me assure you that Christ is no ordinary hiking companion. He is not content to let you linger too long in the valleys of ease and lethargy. Instead, He calls us to a challenging walk. We don't dawdle in the ditch of despair or side roads of worldly skepticism.

There is far, far too often a tendency on the part of Christians, both amongst leaders and laypeople, to try and make their people feel comfortable, cozy, and contented in their padded pews. The church can become a community of emotional cripples, leaning upon each other for mutual comfort and consolation, without meeting the crying needs of a broken world all around.

Christ challenges us to go out and face the fury of the storm. He bids us climb the cliff and search the mountainside for the lost and straying. He compels us with His own compassion to accompany Him along the highways and hedgerows in search of stragglers and self-willed sinners.   (WG)

9 ——— Growing Christlike

*Then he called his disciples and the crowds to come over and listen.
"If any of you want to be my follower," he told them, "you must
put aside your own pleasures and shoulder your cross,
and follow me closely."*

Mark 8:34 TLB; read Mark 8:31–38

Jesus told His disciples, "Let . . . [a man] deny himself [die to his own desires], and take up his cross [that will cut him from his claim to himself], and follow me" (Mark 8:34 KJV).

How do I do this in actual practice? I simply recognize that as a Christian there are some desires of the old life to which I must die. Most of these are selfish and self-centered attractions. Paul tells us to reckon ourselves dead to them.

For instance, my natural inclination may be to love exaggerating and telling tall stories. All that this achieves is the inflation of my ego. As a Christian I have to take the position that this tendency simply does not have a place in my conduct. I positively reject it. I count (reckon) myself estranged from it, as having no place for it in me. Immediately at that point it drops off like a falling leaf or dead branch and I become more Christlike on that characteristic.

But many of us are not resolute enough nor earnest enough in our dealings with God to live this way. Then for our own good He steps in and prunes us in what sometimes can be a painful process.   (ATG)

10 ——— Through the Eyes of a Child

*Verily I say unto you, Whosoever shall not receive the kingdom of
God as a little child, he shall not enter therein.*

Mark 10:15 KJV; read Mark 10:13–16

As my grandson and I sat munching our food, casting our glances across the sparkling waters of the lake, three black bears suddenly burst out of the trees and rushed up the bank across the little bay from us. At last we had caught up with the little characters whose tracks we had followed all morning.

It was as if a ghost of the imagination had suddenly taken concrete shape in bone, muscle, and shining black fur before our eyes. Like three phantoms come to life they hurried across a clearing and vanished into the timber.

For both of us it had been a day of joyous high adventure. The hours had been touched with awe at the unexpected. We had been inspired, stimulated with the wonder of the world. Fresh enthusiasm had mingled with vivid memories to lend a special splendor to our tramp.

Again I had looked, with warm excitement, through the eyes of a small boy, my grandson, Den. With the sense of fresh discovery I had tasted the sweet wine of wild berries. In that special sense of well-being, contentment, and spontaneous delight of a lad, I again reveled in the flight of birds, the antics of an untamed squirrel, the smooth motion of a jewel-like snake.

Awe, wonder, enthusiasm were being reborn, rekindled, regenerated in an elderly gentleman who hiked in company with a small lad across the high hills against the sky edge.

11 —— Living in Love

Love the Lord your God with all your heart and with all your soul and with all your mind and with all your strength . . .
(and) your neighbor as yourself.
Mark 12:30 NIV; read Mark 12:28–34

Life is a series of choices. Am I going to accept the challenge, count the cost and move out of my comfortable lifestyle to tramp the trail of testing and self-discipline with Him? Am I willing to be "wrung out," exposed to hardship, and exercised to the limit to gain ground with God?

Do I truly love Him with all my mind, soul, strength, and heart? "To truly love God with all one's heart" is perhaps the most maligned and least understood phrase in the church today. Its counterpart, "and love your neighbor as yourself," is equally obscure and distorted by our soft society.

From God's perspective, "to love" is to entertain and express good-will toward another. It is to set the will to seek the best for all concerned. It is abandoning every element of selfish self-indulgence to expend one's self fully for the well-being of all others.

This is the high calling to which Christ challenges His followers. Not until we walk this noble way do we know anything of living the lofty life to which He summons us.

12 —— The Caring Christ

> But the chief priests stirred up the crowd to
> have Pilate release Barrabas instead.
>
> Mark 15:11 NIV; read Mark 15:6–15

In utter blindness, ignorance, and folly the society of the day laid cruel hands upon the Lamb of God, offering Him as a substitute for subversive Barabbas, a man given to violence and intrigue. The mob thought it a joke of sorts. They screamed for the innocent blood of an innocent man, little knowing how desperately their depraved souls needed that blood to cleanse and purge them from their own poisonous iniquity. . . .

As Christ hung on the cross, the crowds clapped their hands in glee. They jeered at His plight and pain. They scoffed as though He were nothing more than a scarecrow suspended on a hill between heaven and earth. Little did they know that as His Spirit was given up, He entered the hell of separation from His own righteousness so that they might be clothed in His own holiness. . . .

Only the rough, battle-hardened Roman Centurion and his elite guard looked upon the Lamb of God in brokenness of heart and contrition of spirit. They cried out from the depths of their spirits:

"Surely this was the Son of God!"

Only God could lay down His life with such royal dignity for such contemptible humanity.

Such amazing condescension is almost beyond my puny ability to grasp. Such incredible humility is beyond my capacity to understand. Such awesome compassion for lost sheep like myself is beyond my hard heart to resist. From out of the depths of my innermost being there is wrung the cry, "You came, Christ, You came because You cared!" (LAMB)

13 —— Governed by God

> And the multitudes asked him, "What then shall we do?" And he
> answered them, "He who has two coats, let him share with him
> who has none; and he who has food, let him do likewise."
>
> Luke 3:10, 11 RSV; read Luke 3:7–14

To walk with God in my emotions is to be governed by God in my behavior. It is an unmistakable mark of men and women moving in close communion with Christ that their emotions are governed not by self-interest, but by God. In their actions and reactions with others, the over-riding desire and consideration is for the benefit and welfare of others. They have passed the point where they feel they were put on the planet just to please themselves.

Their relationships with other people, whether in a group or singly, is motivated not by self-indulgence but rather with the desire to enrich and bless others. They do not participate in emotional experiences at the expense of others in order to enhance their own egos. They do not exploit another person to promote their own ends. This is the mark of the mature Christian.

(WG)

14 —— God's Last Word

He is like a man which built a house, and digged deep, and laid the
foundation on a rock; and when the flood arose, the stream
beat vehemently upon that house, and could not shake it:
for it was founded on a rock.

Luke 6:48 KJV; read Luke 6:46–49

For years and years I was building a strong sea wall of self-defense against God. It was not shaped from concrete and reinforcing steel. Instead it was fashioned from the formidable, tough, unyielding rigidity of my own self-will. It was so stubborn and determined it withstood the stresses and strains of countless storms.

I was very sure my strong will was as secure as any sea wall. It would keep the incoming tides of my Father's pervasive presence from invading my privacy. It would restrain the waves of His love and concern from washing into my life. It would exclude the impact of His Spirit upon the inner sanctum of my spirit.

For some of us it takes years for the eternal tides of Christ's coming, and coming, and coming again, to finally break down the last tough barrier of our resistance. It takes the eternal perseverance of our Father to demolish the hardness of our hearts. It takes the sweeping waves of His Spirit to finally surge over the strong bulwarks of our souls.

Then and only then, lying broken before Him—contrite in spirit, shattered in soul, repentant in genuine remorse—do we see clearly how we built our lives oblivious to His power, patience, and perseverance.

Often, all there remains of our best laid schemes is wreckage. All of it is a grim reminder: "Let your life, your character, your career be built always in the intense awareness, 'O God, *You are here, I cannot keep You out.'"

Ultimately, always, He will have the last word!

15 —— Death Is a Doorway

> . . . *when they entered, they did not find the body of the Lord Jesus. . . . In their fright the women bowed down . . . but the men said to them, "Why do you look for the living among the dead? He is not here; he has risen!"*
>
> Luke 24:3–6 NIV; *read Luke 24:1–12*

This One whom His friends thought they had interred in such a beautiful tomb was not wrapped in death. "He is not here!" the angel declared. "He has risen!" He whom men had treated with such violence and deceit had broken the bands of death. He had destroyed the fear of death. And now all men could pass through it . . . and beyond it, into the glorious realm of our God.

Surely, death was now but the doorway through which men could step into that new dimension of life with Christ.

He, the Lamb of God, had come; He had tasted death for every man; He had conquered; He had finished His earth work.

The resurrection of Christ has been an oft-neglected theme in the church. Yet at the time it happened, it transformed and galvanized a cringing, fearful little band as no other event could. The sudden, unmistakable, undeniable presence of the Risen Lord was the tremendous thrust and divine dynamic of the early church. (LAMB)

16 —— Heated Hearts

> *And they said one to another, Did not our heart burn within us, while he talked with us by the way, and while he opened to us the scriptures?*
>
> Luke 24:32 KJV; *read Luke 24:28–35*

A vital requirement for growth is heat. A tree may be flooded with light but unless the temperature is above 40 degrees F. there will be little or no growth.

When trees grow at very high altitudes on mountains or on the fringe of the true Arctic zones they are dwarfed and stunted by cold. . . .

September

But the cedars of Lebanon have the benefit of being native to a warm and sunny climate. They enjoy a long growing season during which the weather is balmy and conducive to growth most of the year.

As in the case of light, the tree or its leaves are incapable of growth, even in the summer, unless there is a proper internal response to the warmth around them. Only a healthy tree is sensitive to the stimulus of heat . . . thus producing maximum growth.

Turning to the Christian life, it is a sad but true observation that there are innumerable Christians with stunted, dwarfed characters like a tree at timberline. They may have been exposed to a tremendous amount of light all their lives but there has been virtually no growth. In fact, some have literally stood still, unmoving and unchanged, from the time of their beginning a new life in Christ. They are really not more than seedlings or spindly saplings from which little timber can come to fashion a temple for the Most High.

This lack of maturity in Christian character brings contempt upon the church. Many who claim to have known the Lord for twenty, thirty, or forty years, have characters which are a mockery because there has been no growth, nor change, no transformation into the likeness of Christ. Lord, may that not be true of me. (ATG)

17 —— Of Light and Life

All things were made by him; and without him was not any thing made that was made. In him was life; and the life was the light of men. And the light shineth in darkness; and the darkness comprehended it not.

John 1:3–5 KJV

The majestic cedars of Lebanon, their great, widespread limbs reaching into the sunny skies of northern Palestine, are in reality stretching toward the sun. Every live twig and needle they possess turns to the precise position where it will benefit most from the sunlight streaming down upon it.

Response to sunlight year after year is part of the secret of their stature.

In the realm of the supernatural (spiritual) life the same identical principle of growth holds true. We are told emphatically in the verses at the head of this meditation that God is life and this life was the light of men. (ATG)

18 —— The Nature of Believing

He (John) came as a witness to . . . that light, so that through
him all men might believe. He himself was not the light;
he came only as a witness to the light.

John 1:7, 8 NIV; read John 1:1–14

What does the word "believe" as used in Scripture really mean? Giving mental assent? Accepting an idea as true? Giving credence to the concept of an historical Christ?

To simply accept that He was born in Bethlehem, lived and ministered among men for thirty-three years, then died a dreadful death on a cruel Roman gibbet is not *believing*, in the spiritual dimension of the word. Even millions of Moslems believe in Jesus Christ this way.

Our Lord Himself when He was here on earth had trouble getting people to really believe. He decried the fact that though He spoke to them about Himself, though He taught them truth clearly, though He performed mighty miracles, they still did not truly believe (John 10:24–38).

To believe means that one has a deep inner passion (thirst) for Jesus Christ which can be satisfied only by partaking of His own life and Spirit. "Jesus said unto them, I am the bread of life; he that cometh to me shall never hunger; and he that believeth on me shall never thirst" (John 6:35–36 KJV). In the next chapter of John, on the last day of the great feast, "Jesus stood and cried, saying, If any man thirst, let him come unto me, and drink. He that *believeth* on me, as the scripture hath said, out of his belly shall flow rivers of living water" (John 7:37–38 KJV). (LAMB)

19 —— The God of All Grace

The next day John saw Jesus coming toward him and said,
"Look, the Lamb of God, who takes away the sin of the world!"

John 1:29 NIV; read John 1:29–36

The world as a whole does not honor or esteem Christ as someone special or worthy of acclaim. He is regarded with disdain as someone meek and weak. He is put down as someone pathetic. He is made of no account with ridicule, jests, and cruel jeers.

His name is bandied about by millions in profuse profanity and loathsome oaths. His dignity is dragged in the dust by thousands who think it great sport and very cunning to hold Him in contempt and scorn. Blatant books and scandalous films are produced to portray Him as a pervert or false pretender.

No other god in all the world is attacked with such vehemence or vituperation. He is the object of an ongoing lampoon by those whose own lives are sordid and sunk in debauchery. The assaults of man against this One have never abated. He is not esteemed except by those few who have learned to know Him and love Him.

Yet, let me remind you that though men have done such dreadful despite to the Lamb of God, He in turn has never turned against us. He has never returned railing for railing. He has never reciprocated in anger against those who rejected Him.

Rather, His response has ever been, "Father, forgive them, for they know not what they do." What an incredible attitude of generous grace! What a great God!

(LAMB)

20 —— Stillborn?

Jesus answered and said unto him, verily, verily, I say unto thee, except a man be born again, he cannot see the kingdom of God.

John 3:3 KJV; read John 3:3–8

The church is full of "stillborn" babes. There may have been a time of delivery. But the new life came to nothing. There has been no "aliveness," no "growth," no walking with God, no maturing.

The "born again" person soon discovers that if he or she is in Christ, old things (former things) are passed away. All things become new and changed because of the process of re-creation that goes on in the presence of and under the impulse of God's Word and God's Spirit (2 Corinthians 5:17).

The daily diet of feeding on God's Word, the steady exposure to His Spirit in that Word, in prayer, in quiet meditation, in compliance with His commands, brings about enormous changes in the newborn Christian.

The old worldly ways; the flashy, fleshly lifestyle; the old, loose standards of morality; the self-indulgence, selfish self-interest; the duplicity and deception; the rivalry, bitterness, and hostility all begin to be patterns of the past. In their place the wind of God's Spirit and the presence of Christ's person bring about goodwill, good cheer, honesty, compassion . . . and all the fruits of the Spirit.

(WG)

21 —— What Kind of Spring Am I?

Jesus said to her, "Every one who drinks of this water will thirst again, but whoever drinks of the water that I shall give him will never thirst; the water that I shall give him will become in him a spring of water welling up to eternal life."

John 4:13–14 RSV

As men and women search us out in the dry and barren hills of our times will they discover a quiet, gentle, hidden spring through which there pulses the very life of Christ? It is of Him they must drink, not of us! It is of His life and energy they must imbibe, not of our human personality. It is by His vitality they will be quickened, made alive, fully refreshed, not by our fallible human nature.

Jesus was very explicit when He stated categorically, "He that believeth on me, as the scripture hath said, out of his belly shall flow rivers of living water" (John 7:38 KJV). To believe in Christ is to open one's life to Him completely. It is actually to allow Him unobstructed access into our souls and spirits. It is literally to permit Him to fill us with His presence. It is to take of His very life and imbibe of it fully. It is utterly to assimilate Him until our whole being is saturated, revitalized, and overflowing with His life.

When this takes place we become the hidden springs through which the renewal and refreshment of God's very life flows to others. He it is, then, who touches and transforms all around us. It is He who brings life out of death, love out of despair, and His joy out of our mourning.

22 —— Water from Within

[Jesus said:] ". . . whosoever drinketh of this water that I shall give him shall never thirst; but the water that I shall give him shall be in him a well of water springing up into everlasting life."

John 4:14 KJV; read John 4:1–26

Just as water is lifted high in the tallest cedar against all the downward pull of gravity, so the triumphant life of Christ is uplifted in me through the upwelling life of His Spirit within. He it is who counteracts all the downward drag of sin and death in the decadent world around me (see Romans 8:2).

To live thus, cleansed and enlivened by the water of life which flows continually from Christ for thirsty men, is to live and grow up in Him.

173

What is more, it is to have springing up from within my innermost being a surge of life that flows out (is transpired) to those around me in refreshment and benediction.

"The man who believes in me, as the scripture said, will have rivers of living water flowing from his inmost heart" (John 7:38, Phillips).   (ATG)

23 —— The Living Water

> *Whoever drinks the water I give him will never thirst. Indeed,*
> *the water I give him will become in him a spring*
> *of water welling up to eternal life.*
>
> John 4:14 NIV

In the realm of our physical well-being, if we thirst, we must drink water. Our bodies are roughly 70 percent liquid. To maintain cell turgidity and for body metabolism to proceed normally in good health, water must be assimilated into our systems daily; water is essential in order to sustain the chemical and physical exchanges of nutrition as planned. Likewise, in the spiritual sense, to believe implies that the very life of God in Christ must be assimilated into our spirits, into our souls. We must actually open our innermost being to receive Him. We then become partakers of the very nature of God himself.

The result of this kind of *believing* will be a diametric change in us. We are no longer just men and women who know about the historical Jesus. We are no longer those who merely discuss a doctrinal Christ in a casual, clinical way. We will no longer regard God as a distant deity, detached and far away from us in the immensity of outer space. Christ becomes the very source of our life, our constant companion. His presence by His Spirit is a living, dynamic reality. His will, His wishes, His intentions, His purposes become ours. He is the confidante for all our decisions. We know Him, and we are acutely and serenely aware that He knows us.   (LAMB)

24 —— A Reason for Living

> *God is a Spirit: and they that worship him [i.e., commune with him]*
> *must worship him in spirit and in truth.*
>
> John 4:24 KJV

Happily for us, the gracious, solicitous Spirit of our God does not leave us alone in our arrogant self-assurance. He does pursue us. He is

"The Hound of Heaven." He is the Counselor who counsels us to seek and search for God. He is the One who tenderly, yet tenaciously turns us from our humanistic preoccupations to a longing for the living Lord. He is the Divine Suitor who woos our wandering spirits from the world to see the wonder of Christ's own superb character. It is He who shows us the indefatigable love of our Father God.

In all of His gracious and generous concern for us, we begin to discern, "Yes, indeed, I am poor in spirit. I am empty. I do need God. I am missing the mark in life. I must have this spiritual quickening of my spirit. I have to be aroused, awakened from my spiritual sleep. I must come alive to Christ, lest I die."

Such a person is blessed.

Such a person is favored.

Such a person is bound to find the reality, the very reason for all of life and the incoming of God's kingdom—His presence and power in the everyday affairs of life.

25 —— The Cost of Climbing

When Jesus therefore perceived that they would come and take him by force, to make him a king, he departed again into a mountain himself alone.

John 6:15 KJV

Getting onto "higher ground" with God is hard work. There is a cost in climbing. Too many Christians think they can attain the summit of spiritual experience with a single startling surge of energy. It is almost as if they thought the lofty life of communing with Christ could be achieved with one bold leap of faith, or some single session at a weekend retreat.

This simply is not so.

Our Father invites us to walk with Him steadily and surely, day by day, taking one step of faith after another in calm succession. There will be interludes in which the trail may seem very tedious. It may even appear to go up, then down, back and forth, in rather boring switchbacks. There will be times when nothing thrilling excites our view. Yet we can still be gaining ground. . . . There are going to be obstacles to surmount, deep waters to ford, before we get out of the woods. Christ never guaranteed that the going would all be easy.

Even when we do break out into the open alpine meadows above timberline there will be miry stretches along the trail. The chill, upland atmosphere can cut to one's bones. The experience of wide horizons and awesome vistas can be tempered by biting winds and driving sleet. It is worth them all.

When we keep company with Christ in the lofty life of separation from the common crowd, we find there is a high cost. That cost is one of accepting the challenge daily to do His will and comply with His wishes. It might seem much easier just to settle down in a soft spot. It may entail the criticism of others around us.

But He calls us to push on with Him steadily. Our Lord wants us to take the upward view of the sky edge. He calls us to live dangerously with Him in the full and abundant joy of His hearty companionship in the high country.

26 —— Life-Giving Water

Then Jesus declared: "I am the bread of life. He who comes to me will never go hungry, and he who believes in me will never be thirsty."

John 6:35 NIV; *read John 6:35–40*

The flow of life surging and pulsing through me to refresh this weary old world must be from God Himself. It must be the continuous outpouring of His Presence by His Spirit which touches and transforms all around me. Any person naive enough, arrogant enough, stupid enough to believe that it is his or her own charm, charisma, or capabilities that change and enliven others, lives in utter self-delusion.

One of the terrible tragedies of human behavior is for people to turn to other human beings in an effort to find sustenance for their spirits. They are always deluded, ever disappointed. Our spirits can only find life in the Living Spirit of the Living Lord. Our eternal quest for life-giving water can only be quenched by the eternal life of God Himself coming to us through the hidden springs of His own person who indwells those who are open channels for His life.

27 —— Taking Time for God

The Spirit gives life; the flesh counts for nothing.
The words I have spoken to you are spirit and they are life.

John 6:63 NIV; *read John 6:60–66*

Our Lord Himself, when He was here amongst us as a man, made the stunning, stabbing statement, "It is the spirit that quickeneth; the flesh profiteth nothing: the words that I speak unto you, they are spirit, and they are life" (John 6:63 KJV).

God, very God, articulates Himself in language we can understand. He does communicate His will and wishes to us. He does reveal His character to us. He does disclose His conduct. He throws the illuminating light of His truth on the path we are to take in life.

This is why the Scriptures must be taken seriously. They must be studied. They must be read and reread. They are His love letters to us. They should elicit a profound, compelling response from us. (Read all of Psalm 119 prayerfully.)

It takes time, a lot of time, precious time, to listen, to hear, to understand, "to see" what He is saying. Most of us are slow of spirit, preoccupied with our petty pursuits and petty pride. We are not sensitive to His Spirit speaking to us in His Word. Too often we are preoccupied with the workaday world and whirl of pleasure around us.   (WG)

28 —— Hidden Springs

> [Jesus said:] "If any one thirst, let him come to me and drink.
> He who believes in me, as the scripture has said, "Out
> of his heart shall flow rivers of living water."
>
> John 7:37–38 RSV

The hidden springs are special spots of unusual beauty. In more open locations they are often encircled with a green sward of grass. I love to lie in the sun and listen to the soft sounds of the clear water running between the rocks. Often the surrounding stones are sheathed in deep soft moss. Ferns and flowers grow among the rocks and nature shapes a bit of pristine paradise in this spot.

What is the secret of the hidden springs? How is it possible for so much life and vigor and beauty to be sustained in these austere surroundings? Whence the clear, pure-flowing streamlet that turns a waste of rock and sand and blasted mountain slope into a vale of refreshments?

The source lies in the great skies that arch over the lofty, shining peaks. It is the weather systems of cloud and mist and snow and rain that swathe these heights in veils of moisture. It is the shining snowfields on the summit of the ranges and crest of the high ridges. It is the gentle, persistent percolation of moisture through rock and soil and forest duff to emerge in this spot.

The mountain spring is not its own source of origin. Its story does not begin where it is born and come to light in the shining sun. The energy of its flow, the quickening of its waters are not inherent in the spring itself. Rather, the spring, amid so much desolation and desert dryness, gives life from a source outside itself, of eternal duration far beyond its own tiny boundaries.

So it is with the Christian: his source is the Holy Spirit who fills his life and permeates his being.

29 —— Free Indeed . . .

[Jesus said:] "If you continue in my word, you are truly my disciples, and you will know the truth, and the truth will make you free. . . . So if the Son makes you free, you will be free indeed."

John 7:32, 36 RSV

As adaptable as man may be, the long winter nights, the deep freeze of unrelenting cold, the unmerciful winds bearing blizzards, tend to shrink one's soul and shrivel the spirit as if constricted in a prison. It is the coming of spring that sets one free. The gentle advent of strong, warm sunshine liberates one's locked-in life to wander at will once more. . . .

There is nothing haphazard about spring. It is not a fickle affair that happens some years and not others. Its advent is sure; its impact is enormous. Its coming produces incredible changes. It ushers in a wondrous regeneration of life.

For those of us sensitive in soul to the changes around us, spring spells liberty, freedom, and stimulation. Our spirits, attuned to the world around us, surge with new life. The urge to go out and explore, to hike, to climb a cliff, to roam at random, to wander free in the wind is a heady impulse that cannot be denied. Our hearts are set to singing. A bright light of excitement fills our eyes. Our muscles must move. Our strength must be spent in splendid exhilaration.

Though we scarcely seem to realize it, we too are being remade, quickened, reborn in resurrection life. The winter is past, the darkness is gone, the cold has vanished under the warming sun. And we are free, free, free!

30 —— Living Water

[Jesus said:] "If anyone is thirsty, let him come to me and drink. For the Scriptures declare that rivers of living water shall flow from the inmost being of anyone who believes in me."

John 7:37–38 TLB

The best of us have lives that, like mountain springs, are often plugged with debris and muddied with fallen earth and rock. The supply of live water is almost cut off because of the trampling of hooves, the accumulation of dead wood and leaves.

Most of us as God's people are really not vibrant springs through which there surges the very life of the eternal God. The hard knocks of life, the rocks of rank unbelief, the mud of trampled hopes and broken dreams, the silt of sorrow and sadness, the dead wood of death and despair, the fallen leaves of frustration often choke off Christ's life in us.

People come to us searching for strength, uplift, solace, and refreshment. Instead, they find despair, defeat, and dark bitterness. Too often our characters are choked up with the cares of life, the calamities of our corrupt society, the ennui of a cynical culture. We claim to be Christians, the children of the Most High, when in reality we are a reproach to our Father, a despair to His Spirit.

What we need, and need desperately, is to be renewed ourselves. We need a sudden cleansing, pulsing surge of God's Own Life to flush away the debris. We need His grace to scour away the silt and mud of a wrong mindset, to flow freely through us without hindrance.

October

1 ——— Springtime to Our Souls

*Jesus replied, "You are slaves of sin. . . . And slaves don't
have rights, but the Son has every right there is! So if the
Son sets you free, you will indeed be free—"*

John 8:34–36 TLB; *read John 8:31–59*

Only the total availability of our souls to the impinging presence of
the Living Lord can set them free. Just as the sun of spring rising ever
higher in the sky releases the earth from its winter bondage, so the new
life of the Risen Sun, the Christ of God, sets our spirits free. Jesus
Himself said without apology, "If the Son [Sun] therefore shall make
you free, ye shall be free indeed" (John 8:36 KJV). Free to follow Him.
Free to revel in His love. Free to find abundant energy, hope, and life
in Him.

All of us have our summer days of strength and bright assurance. All
of us, too, have our autumn days when the shadows lengthen across our
years. All of us will have our winters of deep despair and the dark pain of
death. And all of us can know again the powerful resurgence of Christ's
triumphant, overcoming life made real in our experience by His presence
and resurrection power.

We must find our life, our strength, our love, our hope, our ultimate
healing, and wholeness in Christ. All other human philosophies will
cheat us of the best. All other false religions, mysticism, or spiritism of any
sort, are but a delusion that leads to darkness, despair, and death.

But glory of glories, wonder of wonders, Christ brings His light
amid our darkness. He brings His love into our despair. He brings His life
to replace our death. *He is springtime to our souls!*

2 ——— Pastures of Plenty

By me if any man enter in, he shall . . . find pasture.

John 10:9 KJV; *read John 10:7–18*

In the Christian life many of the places we may be led into will
appear to us as dark, dangerous, and somewhat disagreeable. But it
simply must be remembered that He is there with us in it. He is very
much at work in the situation. His energy, effort, and strength expended
on my behalf, even in this deep, dark place, are bound to produce a
benefit for me.

3 ———— The Abundant Life

I came that they may have life, and have it abundantly. . . . My sheep hear my voice, and I know them, and they follow me; and I give them eternal life, and they shall never perish, and no one shall snatch them out of my hand.

John 10:10, 27–28 RSV; read John 10:22–30

It is the constant coming, coming, coming of His life which enables us to understand that thus He truly transcends death. And this life comes to us in many forms and diverse ways that are much more than mere words or vague ideas.

That life comes to us in the integrity of His commitments to us as His people. He carries out His promises. His Spirit does actually bring us comfort. He does console us in the chaos. He does compensate us for our loss.

In the stream of His life that flows to us there may well be the sand and gravel of grievous events that grind us down. But they are the abrasive agents used in His purposes to shape us to His divine design. Just because we are Christians, there are no guarantees given to us by our Father that we shall be exempted or spared from the cutting circumstances of life.

It is often the individuals who have borne the greatest grief and endured the longest abuse who emerge beautiful in character, strong in spirit, unflinching in faith. It is they to whom we turn in our moments of despair. For it is they who have withstood the deep waters of suffering to become lovely in life.

4 ———— On Gifts and Gratitude

He that loveth me shall be loved of my Father, and I will love him, and will manifest myself to him. If a man loves me, he will keep my words: . . . and my Father will love him, and we will come unto him, and make our abode with him.

John 14:21, 23 KJV; read John 14:15–24

Just as a tree surrounded with summer sunlight grows rapidly in response to light and warmth, so can I grow as a Christian the moment I respond to the love of God which surrounds me on every side.

The love of God to men is a continuous outpouring just as are the warm rays of sunlight from the sun. This outpouring finds expression in a myriad of forms. It is the food I eat, the heat for my home, the air I breathe, the water I drink, my friends and my family, my faculties of sight, sound, and sense. In fact, "every good gift and every perfect gift is from above, and cometh down from the Father of lights" (James 1:17 KJV).

God's love to us, however, found its most poignant and sublime expression in His own Son who came to live among men, then die and rise again, to make it possible for us to share his eternal life.

How then do I respond to this love? How do I react so that it will produce growth in my character?

As with light, so with love, I must hold myself open to allow it to enter—for love begets love.

This is done by deliberately maintaining what I call "an attitude of gratitude."

If I determine, by God's help, to discover something good from Him for which to be genuinely grateful in every event and circumstance of life, it will surprise me to feel my heart warmed toward Him. This will result in an inner glow of gratitude.

Instead of complaining I will find myself thanking Him for His kindness and mercy and love each day. (ATG)

5 —— Peace, Power, and Praise

Jesus answered and said unto him, if a man love me, he will keep my words: and my Father will love him, and we will come unto him, and make our abode with him.

John 14:23 KJV

A true life of praise to God implies three salient things:

1) I acknowledge He is God, very God, and that He arranges all my affairs with only my best interests in mind because He loves me. This applies even when things appear to my view to be awry.

2) I accept everything that happens along life's path as His provision. This is the path of peace. I do not fight life, trying to change everything or everyone. They, instead, are accepted and allowed to modify and mature me.

3) I approve of what God has done and how He does it. This sets His Spirit free to do abundantly more than I can ever hope or imagine. I praise Him that it is He who is at work in me both to will and to do His good pleasure (Ephesians 3:16-21; Philippians 2:12-15). This is to walk with God in peace, power, and praise. (WG)

6 ———— Of Roots and Fruit

> [Jesus said:] "Yes, I am the Vine; you are the branches.
> Whoever lives in me and I in him shall produce a large
> crop of fruit. For apart from me you can't do a thing."
>
> John 15:5 TLB; read John 15:1–8

One warm summer day I went in search of a special Ollala bush that I had marked carefully on one of my hikes. It stood all alone on a steep, stony slope far removed from any other bushes of its kind. It was laden with beautiful berries of unusual size. So when they were fully ripe I was determined to return and harvest the wild bounty. . . .

Before I had come that morning the wild ones had been there before me. The lower limbs, easily reached by cunning coyotes, had been stripped. The upper clusters had been picked over by the birds. So I was fortunate to find an abundance still remained for me to harvest.

As I picked my share I marveled at such bounty coming from an uncultivated, untended tree in such an unlikely spot. Here the soil was thin, stony, riddled with rocks, and baked by the relentless sun. The seasonal winds whipped the bush back and forth without mercy, lashing its limbs with every savage blow. And the heavy loads of winter snows fell upon the branches, bending some to the ground, drifting over its base with ice and frost.

In spite of all the adversities of its environment, all the abuse of rough weather, all the stresses of its stern and tough location, the Olalla bush flowered and fruited in this spot with joyous abandon because of its deep roots.

It was a vivid, living demonstration of that ancient adage—"*Just bloom where you are planted!*" It sounds so simple. Sometimes it has an almost romantic touch to it. Like so many spiritual concepts it is often spoken too swiftly and glibly by someone who has never faced the fierce, formidable challenges of living a truly productive life in a most desolate and desperate environment. To do so takes deep roots!

7 ———— The Ground of Our Joy

> I have told you this so that my joy may be in you
> and that your joy may be complete.
>
> John 15:11 NIV; read John 15:9–17

October

The love of God as seen in the life of Christ makes no attempt whatever to find its fulfillment in loving the passing pleasures of the earth scene. It does not, *cannot*, rejoice in the iniquity of deception and disillusionment perpetrated on the planet by the "god of this world" and the gross folly of human philosophy.

The character of Christ is grounded in the unchangeable goodness of God. It is founded on the eternal faithfulness of our Father. It is based on the enduring reliability of His mercy, love and justice.

These indestructible, unshakeable qualities in the life of God Himself are the eternal ground of all joy. The tremendous truth which seems to escape most Christians completely is that this unique disclosure comes only from Christ. It simply cannot come from man, the world, or any other spirit beings.

He and only He is truth. Without apology he stated emphatically, "I am the way, the truth, and the life. No man cometh unto the Father, but by me" (John 14:6 KJV).

And that quality of joy which transcends the turmoil of our times, which stands calm and sure when all else is shaken around us, which reposes in strength and surety amid the disasters of our days, is founded in our Father's love. The eternal truth that He is ever with us, enfolding us in His wondrous care, is the ground of our joy. (LOVE)

8 ———— The Companionship of Christ

No longer do I call you servants, for the servant does not know what his master is doing; but I have called you friends, for all that I have heard from my Father I have made known to you.

John 15:15 RSV

Jesus told His twelve companions, "In the world ye shall have tribulation: but be of good cheer; I have overcome the world" (see John 16:33 KJV). He also declared, "I am with you always, even to the end of this age" (see Matthew 28:20).

Deliberately, with a strong will, cultivate the companionship of Christ as you walk through this weary old world. "O Christ, You are here. I shall take the tough trails of life as You take them. I shall triumph and overcome obstacles as You do!"

How? What is the secret?

By daily denying my own selfish desires, whims, and petty pride.

Let the same principle of death to self, crossing out the little petty priorities of my own person, put an end to my peevishness and petulance. This is the crossing out of my self-centered will in all its daily decisions.

This is to have the "cross" of Christ, who is my Companion, become a powerful principle in the daily, hourly events of my life.

"Not my will, but Yours, O Lord, be done here." Or, put another way, "Yes, Master, if that is the best way for us to go, then let's go!"

Walking this way with God in a submissive will is to have His power released in our experiences. God is set free to lead us along difficult but challenging trails. His Spirit is thrilled to take us over places we otherwise would have refused to go. (WG)

9 ——— The Character of the Cedar

[Jesus said:] "If the world hates you,
know that it has hated me before it hated you."

John 15:18 RSV; read John 15:18–27

One of the faulty concepts that has crept into the church is that if a man becomes a Christian, then everything in life's garden will suddenly become agreeable and delightful; that there will be nothing but blessing and prosperity and peacefulness.

This simply is not so, and more especially for the man or woman courageous enough to take an open stand, set apart from the crowd, where the blasts of criticism, scorn, and ridicule of a cynical world will be felt at their fiercest.

But exactly as in the case of the cedar that clings alone to its rocky cliff, there will be incorporated into that character a strength, a hardiness, a toughness, and a rugged vitality matched only by its beauty and attractiveness that sets it apart from its fellows. Outwardly a Christian's life may appear the worse for wear and tear, as does the cedar. Even our Master was a man of sorrows and acquainted with grief. But oh, what a figure set apart He was—sinners were drawn to Him and children loved Him. (ATG)

10 ——— Advanced by Adversity

[Jesus said:] "I have told you all this so that you will have peace of
heart and mind. Here on earth you will have many trials and
sorrows; but cheer up, for I have overcome the world."

John 16:33 TLB; read John 14:1–12

Well above the thick forest stands, where individual trees stood exposed on some rugged ridge, I have found trees of exquisite beauty and matchless character. There they stood, their forms twisted and battered into striking shapes. Here was the stuff to delight an artist, the beauty to challenge a photographer.

But beside this, all the fury of sleet and wind and snow and sun had fashioned an inner beauty beyond belief. Here was wood with grain of luster and lovely lines. Wood with whirls and curves that would delight the heart of a wood carver—even those old craftsmen who carved the flowers and fruits that were to adorn the inner sanctuary of Solomon's temple.

Turning to the normal life of the Christian we are confronted with the simple fact that in this life we are going to have troubles. Jesus said, "In the world ye shall have tribulation: but be of good cheer; I have overcome the world" (John 16:33 KJV).

The life of our Lord Himself was, outwardly, a continuous series of testings and turmoil. He was a virtual storm center about which there raged relentlessly all the fury of his enemies and detractors. Yet within there was the quiet acceptance of every adversity as a part of the Father's will.   (ATG)

11 —— Salt and Light

As You sent Me into the world, I also have sent them into the world.
John 17:18 NKJV; *read John 17:6–19*

The eternal hope and optimism of our God still remains. He will not permit darkness to overcome light. He will see to it that life prevails over death. And He assures us that His love can surpass our despair. In all this divine activity we as His people are to be active agents.

Jesus stated categorically that we who belong to Him are "The light of the world." He said also, "You are the salt of the earth." Yet most of us do not clearly grasp how that can be—probably because we do not truly realize the deepening darkness of the society in which we live, nor the illness of which we are in integral part.

After all, most of us are products of the Western world. We have been conditioned by our culture to conform to certain standards. In our sophistication we assume our culture is the most advanced and desirable ever to appear on the planet.

Perhaps we are wrong in all of this.

Perhaps we have been led to believe a lie.

Perhaps in ignorance we of the Western world have been deluded by false gods, yet knew them not.

In our pride as the most enlightened society on earth we have become stricken with a terminal illness. It appears to be benign when in truth it is malignant. What is it? Could it be our arrogance as a society?

12 —— The Great Illuminator

But when he, the Spirit of truth, comes, he will guide you into all truth. He will not speak on his own; he will speak only what he hears, and he will tell you what is yet to come.

John 16:13 NIV; read John 16:5–16

During the past thirty years a large segment of Christendom has suddenly awakened to the presence of the Person of God the Holy Spirit. This acute awareness has enlivened many who formerly were enmeshed in rigid ritual or formal orthodoxy. Unfortunately, too, there has come with this renewal some spurious teaching and counterfeit experiences which have misled some who truly longed to walk with God in truth.

God's Spirit is the Spirit of Truth. He is the great Illuminator. He does not draw attention to Himself. He focuses our affection on Christ and on our Father. (WG)

13 —— The Life of Christ

[Jesus said:] Now this is eternal life: that they may know you, the only true God, and Jesus Christ, whom you have sent.

John 17:3 NIV; read John 17:1–5

Beneath the giant, outstretched limbs of the parent cedar there may be thousands of seeds scattered upon the earth. Yet out of these only a few dozen may be viable (possessing life). All were produced by the tree, but not all will become new trees. Some lack *life.*

The same is true of people. God makes it very clear that, though He is the Father of all men by creation, only those to whom *the life of Christ* has been vitally imparted are spiritually alive. All others are dead. This sobering truth confronts every individual. (ATG)

14 —— The Path to Freedom

When Jesus therefore had received the vinegar, he said, It is finished. . . .

John 19:30 KJV; read John 17:4

From the instant He declared triumphantly, "It is finished!" and volitionally freed His own Spirit from its imprisonment in human flesh and form, a path of utter freedom was fashioned for all men to follow.

For death could not hold Him!

For decay could not touch Him!

From birth up to His death, He had been subject to the terrible degradation of our human condition. But at the moment of His resurrection He took to Himself again all the splendor, power, majesty, dominion, glory, and dignity of the Godhead.

When His friends wrapped His body in fine linen and special spices, these gestures were but a human screen for the majestic movements of God in the unseen world.

He was alive! He was active. He was ministering to the multitudes of human spirits imprisoned prior to this hour. He was setting them free to follow Him, just as in subsequent centuries other imprisoned spirits, including yours and mine, could be freed to follow the Lamb of God, no longer bound by the shackles of death which He shattered for all time. (See 1 Peter 3:18–20). (LAMB)

15 —— Many Convincing Proofs

After his suffering, he showed himself to these men and gave many convincing proofs that he was alive. He appeared to them over a period of forty days and spoke about the kingdom of God.

Acts 1:3 NIV; *read Acts 1:1–11*

For forty days and nights Jesus moved among His friends and followers in His wonderful glorified body. Eventually more than 500 people saw Him. Here was the Lamb of God slain from before the foundation of the earth now appearing in resplendent resurrection form, understandable to human senses yet not restrained by the human condition.

"I am the resurrection and the life," He told Martha. The resurrection life which transformed His own body was the final stamp which validated and vindicated His life and death. This transformation more than any other single event brought His followers to a belief in Him that they had never had before.

One look into the empty grave, one moment's recognition of Rabboni's voice, one touch of His nail-pierced hands, one instant's breaking of bread, one breakfast by the beloved Galilee, and they all knew "it is the Master." . . .

This was the beginning of a new age, a new dimension of responsibility. From now on the Lamb of God would entrust to His brethren on earth the care and concern of other lost sheep. "As the Father sent me into the world, so send I you!" (LAMB)

16 —— The Gift of the Spirit

And we are witnesses to these things, and so is the Holy Spirit whom God has given to those who obey him.

Acts 5:32 RSV; read Acts 5:29–32

The Spirit of God is just that! He is the One who transmits to me not only truth about God but actually conveys to me the very life of the risen, living Christ as well. He is the One who is my constant Companion. He is my Counselor. He is my Comrade-in-Arms on the trail of life we tramp together. He is the One who says to me in the depths of my spirit, "This is the way, walk in it." (Read John 14, 15, 16, and 17 prayerfully.)

It is the Spirit of God who will enter your spirit and share life with you, touch you, inspire you, enliven you, as you make yourself available to His own purposes for you. This is not meant to be passive and phlegmatic, open to subversive, counterfeit (evil) spirits which proliferate on every side. Rather it is to be alert, awake, available, eager to act in prompt obedience to His inner urging—*His own presence. He is God resident within.*

He speaks to us, touches us, teaches us truth through God's own Word, which He Himself inspired. He lays upon our spirits a profound inner conviction that "I ought, or I ought not," in our walk with Him. He gives Himself to us in generous measure. He transforms and leads us in the path of right living. (WG)

17 —— The Generosity of a Gracious God

Therefore, my brothers, I want you to know that through Jesus the forgiveness of sins is proclaimed to you.

Acts 13:38 NIV; read Acts 26:15–18

Instead of wreaking vengeance upon us for our vile behavior, God absorbs the gross injustice of our conduct and extends to us the generosity of His own gracious forgiveness.

This is the One who, in the person of Christ, came among us, laying aside the power, splendor, and authority of His divine position, to make Himself of no reputation, to stand all the abuse heaped upon Him, to absorb all the insults and degradation hurled at Him, to extend forgiveness to us fallen men.

189

October

Someone had to accept the death sentence for fallen man. That One was God our Father Himself, Judge of all the earth, Savior of all lost men, who saw there was no other way to deliver us.

In the person of His own Son, in the guise of human form, having set aside His glory in the eternal dimension of the heavenlies, the suffering Savior stripped Himself, stepped down to our place, and as the Suffering Substitute paid the price of the sin charged against us in order to deliver us.

No wonder we have been granted total forgiveness.

No wonder complete reparation has been made for our wrongs. No wonder utter reconciliation has been accomplished for us in the overwhelming, loving generosity of our Gracious God . . . our Father in Heaven. (LAMB)

18 —— Bonus Thoughts from Birds

[Paul said:] "He made the world and everything in it, and since he is Lord of heaven and earth, he doesn't live in man-made temples; and human hands can't minister to his needs—for he has no needs! He himself gives life and breath to everything, and satisfies every need there is. . . . For in him we live and move and are! As one of your own poets says it, 'We are the sons of God!"

Acts 17:24–25, 28 TLB

No two species of birds have precisely the same life pattern. Their movements on the sand, their search for sustenance from the sea, their flight formation, their form and rate of wingbeat, their cries in the ocean wind are all different and engaging. Each has found its own niche here in the complex pattern of ocean life. Each brings to the beach its own unique beauty and inspiration. Each enlivens and enriches my days along the shore.

Often as I watch the birds I am deeply impressed with the concept that they are as much an integral part of the shore as sand or sea or shell or stone. It may be at times they are only transients, visitors, moving up and down the Pacific flyway from the Arctic to South America. Still they are a part of the pulsing ebb and flow of the sea life that surrounds me. They are in constant motion as much as the surge of the surf or the wind over the water.

They are in truth one of the beautiful bonuses so richly bequeathed upon all of us who love the shore and spend a part of our lives there.

It is exactly the same in our life with the Lord. Often, so often, I am profoundly impressed by the beauty of the bountiful bonuses He brings to my days. I can never be sure what sudden shining surprises He will inject into my experience.

Lord, help me to see with the eyes of my soul those lessons from life You have for me. Help me to appreciate those "bonuses" that come quietly at Your hand into my life.

19 —— The Normal Christian Life

"For in him we live and move and have our being."
As some of your own poets have said, "we are his offspring."

Acts 17:28 NIV; read Acts 17:24–31

The new, inner life of the reborn Christian is in reality the very Spirit of Christ Himself imparted to mortal man. This is what is meant by "receiving Christ" into the heart. It is achieved through the invasion of man's spirit by the Spirit of the living God. Only the Spirit of God occupying and controlling the spirit of a man makes that man capable of responding to the stimuli which, surrounding him on every side, emanate from God. This correspondence with God is the normal Christian life. It is what Scripture calls walking with God or "fellowship . . . with the Father" or being "alive unto God."

A genuine Christian moves and lives and has his being in God (Acts 17:28). God becomes his very environment. And it is only in this atmosphere that he grows in Christ. (ATG)

20 —— The Rainbow of Promise

Against all hope, Abraham . . . believed . . . being fully persuaded that God had power to do what he had promised.

Romans 4:18, 21 NIV; read Romans 4:16–25

God's promises often come to us like a beautiful rainbow. I recall vividly one evening going down to walk on the storm-battered beach. It had been a most difficult day, dark not only because of the howling storm, but also dreary because of painful reverses in other areas of life. It seemed I had never seen the beach in such disarray, stripped of its lovely sand, strewn with storm wreckage. It exactly matched the melancholy mood of my own inner spirit, grieved and torn with trouble.

I stumbled over the wet stones, hunching my back against the gale. Grimly I pulled the big wool sweater tight around my chest; I uttered a silent prayer of relief and respite: "O Father, reassure me You are here!"

In a matter of moments an exquisite, brilliant, glowing rainbow began to arch over the beach. One end was anchored on the dark brooding bluffs. The other stood strongly amid the surging black and white breakers in the sea. Arched over the agony of a storm-stripped beach with its broken piles of shattered driftwood and scattered flotsam shone the wondrous colors of the most beautiful rainbow I had ever seen. . . .

Wave upon wave of enormous emotion swept through my soul. Impulse upon impulse of powerful reassurance inundated my spirit. In the splendor of the rainbow I sensed again the eternal, enduring goodness of my God. In the blaze of light from the setting sun I saw acutely the changeless character of Christ. Like Noah of old, after the dreadful ordeal of the flood, I sensed again the presence and promise of the almighty Spirit of the Eternal God: *"I am here. All is well. Fear not."*

21 —— Melodies of the Spirit

And hope does not disappoint us, because God has poured out his love into our hearts by the Holy Spirit, whom he has given us.

Romans 5:5 NIV; *read Romans 5:1–5*

On some occasions God's Spirit, through His Word, comes to me with great force and profound conviction. He speaks loudly, clearly. As pervasive and powerful as the ocean is upon my bit of beach, so equally is the presence and power of Christ in the life of His intimate companions. There come times in the life of the earnest Christian when all of his experiences are under the influence and touch of the Master. It is God, the very God, who, at work upon his life, produces music not of his making.

The shore does not compose the melodies played out upon its strand. The sea does! The shore does not shape the sounds of the surf. The ocean does! The beach is but the amplifier from which there emerges the score of the Maestro.

So it is with me. If there is to emerge from my brief and fleeting sojourn here any music of eternal worth, it must be of my Master's making. My spirit attuned to His can reverberate with the rhythms of eternity. My soul in resonant response to His voice can reflect the joyous music of my God. Out of the innermost depths of my being can come melodies arranged and scored in the sanctuary of The Most High.

22 —— The Breezes of the Spirit

. . . hope does not disappoint us, because God's love has been poured into our hearts through the Holy Spirit which has been given to us.

Romans 5:5 RSV

To breathe deeply of the ocean breezes is to be tremendously invigorated. It is to be fully alive, to sense the strength and vitality of the ocean itself entering my whole being.

There is something very arresting about these air movements which is reassuring. They come fresh every day. They are inexhaustible. Though not visible, they are enormously apparent. They exert a constant impact on anyone or anything exposed to them . . . they do not diminish!

Most important, not only does the sea wind surround me on every side, it actually fills my whole being within as I open myself to receive its rejuvenation. It runs its fingers through my hair; it kisses my cheek with its touch; it caresses me in tenderness; it stirs me with energy and vitality as it surges into my body.

It makes me strong and fit, alive and energetic.

Little wonder that I love to walk in the wind.

Little marvel that I relish its touch on my senses.

Little surprise that I open myself to breathe it deeply.

All of which is a vigorous response to the wind's gentle, yet persistent impress on my life. I come to love it. I relish its vitality. I revel in its invisible presence.

It is exactly the same with the wind of the gracious Spirit of God. He is everywhere present around me, though unseen to my physical eyes. His power and energy pervade the earth. His benefits enfold me on every side. His mercy and compassion come to me fresh and new every day. And if allowed to, He will enter my life, there to do His own dramatic work as surely as the sea breezes that blow along my beach.

23 —— From Death Comes Life

For if we have been planted together in the likeness of his death, we shall be also in the likeness of his resurrection.

Romans 6:5 KJV; *read Romans 6:1–5*

Humus represents the critical link in the so-called energy conversion cycle which is made up of birth, growth, death, decay, and rebirth. All of life is dependent upon this complex process. It explains why we say there can be no life or growth without there first being death. In fact, the entire biota (living world) is conditioned by death. Life can only come from preexisting life which is made available through death. For example, in a forest a tree takes root, runs its life course, comes to the end of its growth, then one day under a fierce storm crashes back to the earth. Immediately the agents of decay go to work on the mass of splintered wood, reducing it to humus. Soon other tree seedlings take root in the decomposing material and a new array of life emerges from the dead form. Through the death of one, new life has been imparted to many others.

It is startling to discover this same principle running throughout the Bible. From beginning to end we find the theme that spiritual life is dependent upon sacrificial death. The supreme and universal application of this principle came at Calvary. God saw that it was imperative He Himself should die in the form of His own Son in order that there might be made available to all men of all time the opportunity for them to be born anew into His life. Or as the verse above puts it, "planted together in the likeness of his death." This then enables us to grow up into the life of His resurrection. For it is on the very life of Christ that we draw our sustenance, exactly as the young cedar derives new life from the prostrate form of its predecessor. (ATG)

24 —— Freed from Debris

So you also must consider yourselves dead to sin and alive to God in Christ Jesus.

Romans 6:11 RSV; read Romans 6:6–11

Often after a terrible storm one can walk under a cedar tree and see a veritable carpet of limbs, leaves, twigs, and other debris lying beneath it. Debris must fall in my spiritual life as well.

It may not always be that I am in the wrong. Sometimes it happens that I am accused without a cause. Still it is right for me to accept this cross with gladness. My Lord did when there was no fault found in Him. To do this is to be made one with Him, to be identified with Him, to grow in *Him*. Thus from death come resurrection life and newness of character.

As a Christian progresses along this path, over his life steals that ineffable glow resembling the rich foliage of a tree growing in soil charged with humus. The world has less and less claim on his character; he discovers that the old desires are losing their attraction. He is set free from the world. *He is alive unto God.* (ATG)

25 —— Praying in the Spirit

> *In the same way, the Spirit helps us in our weakness.*
> *We do not know what we ought to pray for, but the Spirit*
> *himself intercedes for us with groans that words cannot express.*
>
> Romans 8:26 NIV; *read Romans 8:22–27*

The most profound prayer any person ever engages in seldom finds expression in human syllables. It is the stirring of our spirits by God's Spirit in such a way that we long with enormous inner longing. We are still, silent, subdued, yearning, knowing, seeing Him whom to know is life eternal.

Our Lord made it abundantly clear that much of our praying, done either in public or in private, was really pagan. (Read Matthew 6:5–15.) The repetitive, thoughtless, mouthing of tired old phrases, or ritualistic rhetoric, is not the manner in which a man consciously communes with his Creator.

It is God's Spirit who impresses upon our spirits what we are to pray about. Seeing clearly what His concerns are, we proceed in faith to respond by placing these petitions before Him. This is the prayer of faith. He then honors and answers those prayers in the profound way which is most appropriate both to His will and our needs.

This is what is meant by Christ being both the Author and the Finisher of our faith. Our prayers are conceived in our spirits by Him. They are consummated in His own good time in His own best way. And for all of this we give Him our genuine gratitude.

Communing with Christ this way, we come to walk with God in quiet strength, serene stability, and constant assurance.   (WG)

26 —— A Living Sacrifice

> *I appeal to you therefore, brethren, by the mercies of God,*
> *to present your bodies as a living sacrifice, holy and*
> *acceptable to God, which is your spiritual worship.*
>
> Romans 12:1 RSV; *read Romans 12:1–8*

The incoming of Christ's presence in power and great glory is a burning, scorching, searing experience that utterly changes the contours of our characters. Once we have been exposed to the fire of God's own purifying presence the old debris and detrius are destroyed, wiped out, purged from our lives. We are never, ever, the same again. . . .

The time has come when the fierce up-drafts of the wind of His Spirit need to sweep through our comfortable churches and compel people to fall on their faces in humble contrition. The day is long overdo when the fire from above flashes across the skies of our times to come crashing with lightning bolts into the stony ground of our rock-hard hearts. The hour is here when as a rotten society of overindulgent people we again hear the roar and rumble of the majestic voice of our Father calling us to be a cleansed and, respectfully, separate church.

Often as I hike alone in these high hills I cry out to the Most High to descend upon us in great power. I beseech Him to "break out" upon us with a fierce burning. I implore Him to release His Sovereign Spirit to sweep freely and fiercely across the earth convincing men of sin, righteousness and judgment to come.

Unless this happens there can be no renewal.

Only the purifying presence of the Lord God Himself will ever deliver us from our decadence. He alone can bring us new life, new vitality, new beauty.

There has to be fire on the mountains again.

27 —— Love at Its Loftiest

Don't just pretend that you love others: really love them. Hate what is wrong. Stand on the side of the good. Love each other with brotherly affection and take delight in honoring one another.

Romans 12:9, 10 TLB; read Romans 12:9–21

Christ calls us, as His followers, to live our lives on a lofty plane. He sheds His great love abroad in our characters to keep us from getting mired in the cruel criticism and mud-slinging that is all too common in some Christian circles. Too many are envious of the success or blessings or benefits bestowed on their brothers and sisters in God's family.

Instead we should be glad and cheer for those who are doing well. We should rejoice for any ground gained by those who love the Lord. We should thank our Father for every inch of territory taken by any Christian in his contest with the enemy.

Our Master calls us to be large in spirit. He is delighted to see us become generous and great-hearted toward others engaged in the same work we are doing. He is more impressed with our gracious goodwill, expressed in mercy and kindness, than any other impressive sacrifice we may make. "But go and learn what this means: 'I desire mercy and not sacrifice.' For I did not come to call the righteous, but sinners, to repentance" (Matthew 9:13, NKJV).

Why? Simply because the greatest personal sacrifice one can offer to Him or to one's fellowmen is selfless love—a love that smiles when others succeed; a love that cheers when others triumph; a generous love that does no envy or become jealous. (LOVE)

28 —— Planted in Christ

And by a miracle God sent them food to eat and water to drink there in the desert; they drank the water that Christ gave them. He was there with them as a mighty Rock of spiritual refreshment.

1 Corinthians 10:3, 4 TLB; read 1 Corinthians 10:1–5

Christ Jesus offers Himself as a sure rock upon which a man can establish his character. I am told clearly and concisely that the very roots of my being have been *planted in him* just as God chose to plant the cedars in the high hills of Lebanon. "For if we have been planted together in the likeness of his death, we shall also be in the likeness of his resurrection" (Romans 6:5 KJV).

Having been established in such a setting with all the resources of Christ made available to me, there is no reason why I shouldn't grow except for my own indolence, my reluctance to put out an effort to search for the riches in Him just as the tree roots search the soil. (ATG)

29 —— Life from Above

For whenever you eat this bread and drink this cup, you proclaim the Lord's death until he comes.

1 Corinthians 11:26 NIV; read 1 Corinthians 11:23–32

Eternal life—everlasting life, endless life—is not some single, sterile, gift-wrapped package dropped down into my soul at a single point in time. This is a false and dreadful concept held by uncounted hosts of ill-informed Christians. Little wonder their experience of Christ is so sterile, so fossilized, so dead.

Life is a dynamic, daily interaction between an organism and its environment. As the organism enters directly into its life-giving surroundings, the energy of the biota, in turn, enters into it. Only then is there perpetuation of life.

This explains why our Lord, Jesus Christ, continually emphasized that for man to have life from above it was imperative to "eat of Him" and "drink of Him" daily! To "eat of Christ" is to come to Him every day in a deliberate act of faith, exercising our wills to expose and open our lives fully to the impulses of His Word and His Spirit. It is the entrance of His Word that gives us His life. For the words which He speaks to us, they become spirit and they become life to us as they are ingested and accepted.

"To drink of Christ" is to believe in Him implicitly. It is to assimilate His truth, His life, His spirit, His person by a deliberate function of quiet faith. We then proceed to comply with His commands, carry out His wishes, and cooperate with His intentions for us.

The net result is to find His very life surging in us and through us. We are in Christ. He is in us. We are energized by His Word, enlivened by His Spirit, and so made abundantly productive through our Father's bountiful grace.

30 —— A More Excellent Way

Yet I show you a more excellent way, Though I speak with the tongues of men and of angels, but have not love, I have become as sounding brass or a clanging cymbal.

1 Corinthians 12:31; 13:1 NKJV; read 1 Corinthians 13

God Himself has given us a remarkable revelation of His own love in Scripture. It comes with startling significance in the very center of the Spirit's most detailed discourse on God's special "gifts" to the church. It stands there with towering grandeur as a call to all Christians: the more excellent way in which the church can know Christ and live for Him in this world is through His love and by His life.

This thirteenth chapter of the first letter to the carnal church at Corinth is a compelling description of Christ's character. Here is the divine declaration of Christian attitude and behavior, the way in which Christ Himself calls us to conduct ourselves as His followers—His people, His Bride. It is the great central theme around which all other considerations in the church are of secondary consequence and peripheral importance.

This dazzling revelation of Christ's divine love, like a diamond, outshines with burning brilliance all the other precious gems of God's gifts. With enormous power and value it transcends all other unique capacities given to the church for service. It is Christ Himself—His love—His life that is "the more excellent way." (LOVE)

31 —— A Quality of Kindness

Charity suffereth long, and is kind. . . .

1 Corinthians 13:4 KJV

The truly kind person is one who does not flinch at the cost of extending kindness. He forgets his own personal preferences to proffer help and healing to another. At the price of inconvenience, labor, and personal privation he goes out quietly and without fanfare to bring pleasure to another. Sensitive to the sorrow and suffering of a struggling society, he undertakes to do what he can to alleviate this suffering. He tries to make the world a better and brighter place for those enmeshed in its pain and pathos.

This is the quality of kindness that characterizes God our Father. He does care. He does suffer for us. Our heavenly Father does come to us in absolute honesty and openness. He lays down His life for us, and He expends Himself without hesitation to enrich us. He identifies Himself with us in our dilemma. Utterly merciful, totally compassionate, incredibly self-giving, He has our welfare and well-being ever in mind—always.

November

1 ——— True Love

> *Love does not demand its own way.*
>
> 1 Corinthians 13:5 TLB; *read 1 John 3:11–24*

Love does not demand its own way!

What an astounding statement! So simple to say. So difficult for us to do. So characteristic of Christ!

This concept diametrically cuts across all our self-centered concepts of what constitutes complete and full achievement. It smashes into atoms all our vaunted human vanity of total self-realization. It is the spear plunged into the heart of our egocentric preoccupation.

These words embody the true meaning of the cross in the life of the Christian.

Unless we clearly understand this idea, there will be a never-ending controversy in our relationship to God our Father. We will conflict with Christ Himself. There will be inner subversion against the Spirit of God who endeavors to guide us.

In our arrogance most of us are very sure we know what is best for us. We too often choose our own tangled way through life. We insist on achieving our own ends.

Then we wonder why our lives become snarls from which only God Himself can extricate us. Oh, such awful agony we endure because of our own self-willed behavior! What wasted years we forfeit chasing rainbows of our own devising, goals that have no end but an emptiness that mocks us!

(LOVE)

2 ——— The Greatest of These Is Love

> *So faith, hope, love abide, these three; but the greatest of these is love.*
>
> 1 Corinthians 13:13 RSV; *read Psalm 42*

If we are to find complete satisfaction in Christ, there is no other way than to submerge ourselves in the stream of His life. We need to come to Him and drink deeply of His love. We must find our refreshment, our constant reinvigoration, in His consistent character. Here lies the secret to quiet serenity, confident strength, and sure stability amid all the changing circumstances which face a Christian in today's world.

In Psalm 42 we are given a beautiful word picture of a deer in distress. It is being pursued by the hunters and their hounds in the hills. For safety and survival it rushes down the slopes and into the stream.

There in the cooling, refreshing current that flows from the snow-mantled mountains its thirst is slaked; its safety is assured; its survival is guaranteed. This dramatic poem, written under the inspiration of God's Spirit, portrays precisely the elements inherent in the picture of a man or woman plunging fully into the refreshing, protecting fullness of God's life and love, finding total salvation amid life's strains and stresses. . . .

This is a vivid picture of what it means to come to Christ, to drink of Him, to know Him, to relish Him. (LOVE)

3 ———— Conscience for the Christian

> For our boast is this, the testimony of our conscience that we
> have behaved in the world, and still more toward you,
> with holiness and godly sincerity, not by earthly
> wisdom but by the grace of God.
>
> 2 Corinthians 1:12 RSV; read 2 Corinthians 1:8–14

In the Word of God, three words are always used to describe a healthy conscience. It is called either "good" or "pure" or "clear," depending on the translation.

In contradistinction it is also referred to as "evil" or "seared" when not functioning properly. Sometimes the word "dead" is also used.

Put another way we might say that our spiritual eyesight is either clear or blurred. It is either excellent or impaired. It is wholesome and healthy or it is damaged and blinded.

And how we see God and His will determines very largely how we live and walk with Him.

The interesting and surprising thing about conscience is that it is almost always discussed in God's Word together with faith. Our faith is dependent upon and determined by the condition of our conscience (1 Timothy 1:5–19; Hebrews 9:12–15; 10:16–22).

Faith is my positive response to God Himself and to His Word to the point where I will act in confidence. The more clearly I see Him, the more intimately I perceive His will with a clear conscience, the more readily I respond in rugged, fearless faith. If my conscience is clouded, my sight of Him is impaired. Then my faith falters and I cannot walk with Him in happy light.

Conscience is to my spirit,
What sight is to my body, and mind is
To my soul. (WG)

November

4 ——— Daily Dying

For as by a man came death, by a man has come also the
resurrection of the dead. For as in Adam all die,
so also in Christ shall all be made alive.

1 Corinthians 15:21–22 RSV; read 1 Corinthians 15:20–28

Just as new seedlings strike root and grow luxuriantly upon the fallen trunk of a former forest monarch, so there is life and growth available to me through the sacrificial death of the Lord of Glory. Young Christians are sometimes bewildered by this principle, yet we are told plainly, "For since by man came death, by man came also the resurrection of the dead. For as in Adam all die, even so in Christ shall all be made alive" (1 Corinthians 15:21–22 KJV).

Actually from the time of birth or even germination, every living thing is dying. If we stand long enough under one of the giant cedars we will notice a continual dropping of cast-off limbs, twigs, bark, needles, and ripened cones. This material falls in a steady rain beneath the tree, adding to the humus of the soil in which it is growing. Not only does it contribute to its own good but also that of all the lesser trees and shrubs growing about its base. Still another benefit is that this removes what would otherwise become diseased.

This daily dying, though it might appear a painful process to the tree, is one of its most wholesome growth activities. Likewise in my daily spiritual life I have to discover that there are areas of my character which can be improved only by severe pruning, either through outright death or by God's cutting hand. (ATG)

5 ——— Growing through Adversity

Blessed be the God and Father of our Lord Jesus Christ . . . who
comforts us in all our affliction, so that we may be able to
comfort those who are in any affliction, with the comfort
with which we . . . are comforted by God.

2 Corinthians 1:3 RSV; read 2 Corinthians 1:3–7

The growth of character is possible only under adversity. It is something that can be produced only under the inexorable stress and strain of stormy weather. The tree which responds vigorously to the wrenching winds and bending snow grows tough and strong and durable. Inwardly there is the continuous, quiet, unspectacular growth in godliness. The inner life becomes rich, lustrous, and mellow. Built into the very fiber and grain of the soul are a charm and beauty that only blustery weather could possibly produce.

Most of us want to avoid the hard things, the adverse winds, the testing times. Let us not. They are God's method of making special timber for adorning His sanctuary. (ATG)

6 ——— The Fire of God

> *If any man's work is burned up, he will suffer loss, though he himself will be saved, but only as through fire.*
>
> 2 Corinthians 3:15 RSV; read 2 Corinthians 3:11–15

As Christians we are inclined to forget that our heavenly Father who is all love and mercy and compassion to us is at the same time altogether righteous, holy, just, and severe in disciplining those who disobey.

In a very real sense one of the most serious difficulties an earnest Christian faces in his conduct on earth is found in the area of his intimate contact with non-Christians.

In this realm lies the ever-present temptation to become too closely involved with the life, enterprise, and interests of the world. Many of these associations may appear perfectly legitimate and even worthwhile, but they may not necessarily be of merit in God's mind. Like the brambles and underbrush entwining themselves around the trunks of the cedars, they slowly but inexorably enmesh us in an apparently harmless though potentially flammable association.

The Christian who is keen for God and growing in Christ should not allow the entanglements of the world to wrap themselves around him. This is precisely what happened to "righteous Lot," who, when fire fell on Sodom and Gomorrah, was stripped of everything and came within a hairs breadth of losing his own life. It was only the angels' direct intervention and Abraham's prayers for his survival that saved him from disaster. (ATG)

7 ——— The Transforming Power of Light

> *And we all, with unveiled face, beholding the glory of the Lord, are being changed into his likeness from one degree of glory to another; for this comes from the Lord who is the Spirit.*
>
> 2 Corinthians 3:18 RSV; read 2 Corinthians 3:12–18

November

The remarkable truth about exposure to light, whether in the natural or supernatural, is that the growth produced by it is the actual transmutation of light. The tree itself is transformed into a light-storing, light-giving body. This is shown when we burn a slab of wood and see its flames give off light energy accumulated through many summers of patient growth.

Likewise, my character is changed and transformed into the very character of God when continually exposed to Him. Paul stated this clearly when he said, "And all of us, with unveiled faces, reflecting like bright mirrors the glory [character] of the Lord, are being transformed into the same likeness, from one degree of holiness to another, even as derived from the Lord the Spirit" (2 Corinthians 3:18, Weymouth N.T.). (ATG)

8 —— A Glory in It All

For our light and momentary troubles are achieving
for an eternal glory that far outweighs them all.

2 Corinthians 4:17 NIV

Choice characters, fragrant lives, rare quality of life are not produced without the strain of sorrow and the suffering of adversity. Some of us will have to endure privation in personal isolation and more than likely without any public acclaim. Most of our inner anguish of soul is borne alone in the solitude of our own lives. We are not public performers, playing to a rapt but fickle audience.

Our greatest griefs are more often than not those of the spirit. Our stresses come most painfully within the very fibers of our souls. The agonizing separation within that attends the onslaught of suffering, the agony of losing loved ones, the betrayal of friends can be healed only by the gracious ministrations of God's own Gracious Spirit. But He does bind us up. He does inject His own presence into our lives. He does enable us to grow more beautiful, more gracious, more resonant with His compassion.

The end result is that our own characters do become more desirable. We do mature into men and women of wondrous warmth. We do, little by little, develop into fit material for the Master's use.

And out of it all, one day, there will emerge celestial music and glorious melodies that can enrich and uplift others clear around the earth because we grew at the sky edge.

9 ——— Designed for Perfection

And we, who with unveiled faces all reflect the Lord's glory, are being transformed into his likeness with ever-increasing glory, which comes from the Lord, who is the Spirit.

2 Corinthians 3:18 NIV

He is at work in us changing us from glory to glory. He is re-creating us to be conformed to the character of Christ. He is actively leading us to follow in His footsteps.

All this is part of growing up into the maturity which He has purposed for us, a progressive process. It is a life of moving into the godliness of our Father.

This is His best intention for us. This is His great love for us. This is His life in us.

Many Christians are alarmed and dismayed by the idea of perfection. They need not be. It is an inspiring and wondrous design intended by our loving Father for our completion as His people.

It was never His intention that we should remain as mere infants, tiny tots, our nourishment only in milk, barely able to crawl around in a cradle. His profound longing, as with a human parent, is that we should grow up in Him. We should become strong in His Spirit. We should mature into men and women who have His mind, His will, His life, delighting to walk with Him. (LOVE)

10 ——— Discoveries in the Darkness

For it is the God who said, "Let light shine out of darkness," who has shone in our hearts to give the light of the knowledge of the glory of God in the face of Christ.

2 Corinthians 4:6 RSV; *read 2 Corinthians 4:1–6*

Christians at times are so caught up in being busy about many things that God deliberately lets darkness descend around them just so He can have a chance to take a quiet walk with them alone for a change. There in the coolness and stillness, frustrated souls are refreshed, the fever of life is forgotten, and men become "like a watered garden."

In the darkness lies part of the secret to a character that is wholesome, fruitful, radiant, yet balanced in its godly behavior. For some of us it is only in the darkness we dare draw so close to Christ that we later come away with the myrrh and frankincense of His own presence upon us.

November

It is only in the darkness that I discover something of the sweet fellowship of His suffering—taste a little of the awesome agony He endured for me in the darkness of Gethsemane.

In the darkness I understand at last something of those wondrous words, "not my will, but thine be done." (ATG)

11 —— Soaring with Serenity

We are troubled on every side, yet not distressed; we are perplexed, but not in despair; Persecuted, but not forsaken; cast down, but not destroyed; Always bearing about in the body the dying of the Lord Jesus, that the life also of Jesus might be made manifest in our body.

2 Corinthians 4:8–11 KJV; *read 2 Corinthians 4:7–18*

Probably the thing that impresses anyone who has watched eagles soaring the most is the apparent ease and utter serenity with which they fly. Of course this would be impossible without the skill that comes from long practice.

The demands made upon the Christian who would lead a triumphant and serene life are no less exacting. The believer will often grow weary. He or she will be tempted to relax vigilance. One will be impulsive and prone to a faltering up-and-down experience. Like a young eagle, one will do a good deal of flapping and flopping around before he or she has mastered the art of continuous soaring. In fact, one might become quite exhausted and downcast on occasion from trying so hard to fly on one's own strength instead of just resting on God's faithfulness. . . .

12 —— The Strength of Stillness

That is why we never give up. Though our bodies are dying, our inner strength in the Lord is growing every day.

2 Corinthians 4:16 TLB

One simply cannot get through life without excruciating experiences of one kind or another. It is absolutely inevitable that there will be days when it seems we are going to be driven into destruction. People or events just do gang up on us. The irony of life is that calamities, like crows, come in bunches of unexpected, rapid sequence, one rushing in upon another.

Often our first impulse is to flee or take flight. Somehow we want to take to the trees. We lash out left and right hoping to keep the destruction at bay. But we seldom succeed.

The more prudent move is to settle down in stillness, waiting quietly for the crisis to pass. This is not an easy decision to make. It often seems much more heroic to try to fight our way out of the fray. Yet that is not the best way.

The longer I live, the more often I discover that to wait patiently is the secret to power and peace. Standing quietly, serene in the strength that comes from knowing Christ, one can overcome. Wait upon the Most High. Trust in His remarkable wisdom. Let the strength of His Spirit support us. All will be well!

13 —— Power over Perils

For we know that if the worldly tent we live in is destroyed,
we have a building from God, a house not made
with hands, eternal in the heavens.

2 Corinthians 5:1 RSV; read 2 Corinthians 5:1–10

The Christian life is a perilous one; it is threatened with danger and destruction on every hand. "We are troubled on every side, yet not distressed; we are perplexed, but not in despair; Persecuted, but not forsaken; cast down, but not destroyed; always bearing about in the body the dying of the Lord Jesus, that the life [resurrection] also of Jesus might be made manifest in our body" (2 Corinthians 4:8–10 KJV).

This is the exact picture of how a virile Christian responds to the stimuli of perils which encircle him.

How do I realize this resurrection life within?

How do I acquire this vitality to counteract all the forces of evil and sin and despair that surround me in a dying and despairing world?

By calmly claiming and acting on God's own declaration: "Ye are of God, little children, and have overcome them: because greater is he [Christ] that is in you, than he [Satan] that is in the world" (1 John 4:4 KJV).

This takes trust, simple faith, implicit confidence in God. Faith is more than mere belief; it is an absolute conviction, an implicit confidence that gives me the grit *to act on* and *respond to* the declarations of divine truth.

(ATG)

207

14 —— In Good Conscience

Therefore, knowing the fear of the Lord, we persuade men; but what we are is known to God, and I hope it is known also to your conscience.

2 Corinthians 5:11 RSV; read 2 Corinthians 5:1–11

Put in very plain language we can say that conscience is the eyesight of the spirit. With it a person perceives and holds in view whatever may be shown to the spirit as being either of God's character or God's intentions.

Depending upon whatever is presented to it, a person's conscience will determine not only what he believes but also what he does.

For example, the Hindu widow's conscience convinces her that she should fling herself on the funeral pyre of her deceased husband. She has been brought to "see" this as the most noble act she can perform to appease her gods.

A pagan African woman will, if she gives birth to twin girls, bury both alive. Her conscience is convinced that this is proper. Her pagan conscience constrains her to commit this act because it is the finest, most self-sacrificing step she can take.

A Muslim, in good conscience, without any compunction, will slay an infidel. It is his guarantee of glory. He has done the will of Allah. He has acted with a clear Muslim conscience.

Paul, formerly the petulant, self-righteous Pharisee, persecuted the early Christians with intense hatred. In all good conscience he hounded and harried them all across the country from city to city, sure he was doing God's will. Then he "saw" the bright light on the Damascus road and was given a new conscience. (WG)

15 —— Who Is Your God?

What agreement is there between the temple of God and idols? For we are the temple of the living God. As God has said: "I will live with them and walk among them, and I will be their God, and they will be my people."

2 Corinthians 6:16 NIV; read 2 Corinthians 2:16–18; see Ephesians 2:20

There is something very refreshing, very beneficial in getting clear away from the same old, familiar surroundings into the fresh air, sunshine, and brisk breezes out-of-doors. It does us a world of good.

Christ calls us in the same special way. He called the fishermen from their familiar nets, boats, and beloved Lake of Galilee. He called Matthew from his tax collector's post. He called Mary from plying her "profession" as a prostitute.

God calls us to walk with Him away from the old garrulous gang, away from the cozy comfort of our conventional little circle of companions, away from the sometimes tired and worn-out, weary old world that has enclosed us and cramped us within its confines for so long.

Are you jaded with life? Is your little round of living a bore and a drag? God calls you to come out of it, get clear of it, break away from your old behavior patterns. Part company with your former companions who only contributed to your skepticism and cynicism. Leave the wretched old world with its hopeless ways and despairing days. Allow God's gracious Spirit to separate you from the staleness of a sinking society. (WG)

16 —— No Solution in Sea Walls

Since we have these promises, dear friends, let us purify ourselves
from everything that contaminates body and spirit,
perfecting holiness out of reverence for God.

2 Corinthians 7:1 NIV; read 2 Corinthians 6:16–7:1

All sorts of elaborate sea walls have been erected to try to provide people with protection from the ocean. Yet the sea will not be held back. Year after year it presses in upon the ocean edge, its coming as persistent as the tides.

Several years ago I used to live a short distance from a harbor. It was about a mile away, as the pelicans fly in a direct line along the water's edge. The annual ritual of dredging the harbor was regarded with disgust and revulsion by local residents. The pollution was appalling—the stench overpowering. The desecration of the beaches was disgusting.

Yet no lasting remedy has ever been found for the evils caused by this breakwater. No permanent solution has been devised for overcoming the defilement of this harbor. Nor will there be any—for in simple fact, man has shut out the sea! He has closed off the cleansing action of the ocean currents. He has excluded the healing, life-giving touch of the changing tides.

Often the powerful parallel so apparent in the hopeless quandary of the harbor has come home to my own spirit with tremendous force. For we human beings build our "breakwaters" against God. We erect our barriers to keep out the strong currents of Christ's life that come flowing toward us. We devise elaborate schemes and structures to hold back the impact of His Holy Spirit upon our souls.

The tragic, terrible truth is that most men and women do not want their lives left open, exposed, vulnerable to the impact of God's life upon them. They much prefer to build their snug little harbors of selfish self-interest where, they imagine, they are safe and secure in the storms of life.

The double tragedy is that what on the surface may appear to be so serene, below the surface is dark with defilement. What at first glance looks so desirable and successful, on closer examination proves to be rotten and corrupt with unspeakable pollution and insoluble problems.

Lord, help me to open my life to Your cleansing!

17 —— Faith That Doesn't Fail

> *. . . a man is not justified by works of the law but through faith in Jesus Christ, even we have believed in Christ Jesus, in order to be justified by faith in Christ, and not by works of the law, because by works of the law shall no one be justified.*
>
> Galatians 2:16 RSV; *read Romans 3:21–26*

Christ and He alone is the object of our faith. He is the bedrock of our hope. He is the epicenter of our own love. We are in Him. He is in us. Therein lies our endurance amid all the changing scenes and circumstances of this unpredictable life scene.

Down to the very last day that we tread the tangled trails of our earthly sojourn we will find that "*faithful is he that calleth you, who also will do it*" (1 Thessalonians 5:24 KJV).

Then when the call comes to us "to come home," even through the door of death and beyond the grave, our sure and serene confidence will be in Him. For then, and only then, will our faith be turned to spiritual sight, for we shall see Him face to face. And then our hope shall be turned to the living reality of heaven and home for we shall be in His visible presence forever and ever.

Such stirring and thrilling expectations set before us as His people are but a part of His gracious, generous love for us. Not only for all of this life does He supply us with faith, hope, and love, but also far beyond. Into the endless avenues of eternity His love never fails us.

Praise His wonderful name!   (LOVE)

18 —— Filled to Bear Fruit

> . . . *the fruit of the Spirit is love, joy, peace, longsuffering,*
> *kindness, goodness, faithfulness, gentleness, self-control.*
> *Against such there is no law.*
>
> Galatians 5:22–23 NKJV; *read Galatians 5:22–26, Matthew 12:33–37*

The fruits of God's Spirit—love, joy, peace, longsuffering, kindness, goodness, faithfulness, gentleness, self-control—are each a dynamic, living function of the very love of God. Each is active, growing, benefiting the life of the believer in whom Christ resides, as well as all those whose lives He touches through that believer.

We only have the fruits of God's Spirit to the extent we have the presence and person of Christ's life within. The degree to which we allow Christ to control all of our character, conduct and conversation will determine the abundance or scarcity of the fruit of His life produced in us.

To put it in the plainest possible terms, *the fruits of the Spirit are the character of Christ made visible in me by His presence at work in me.* It is literally the life of God governing my character, the love of God shown to others through my conduct and conversation.

The actual expression of these fruits in our daily lives stands as the supreme test of whether or not Christ lives in us, filling us for fruit-bearing by His Spirit. (LOVE)

19 —— The Gift of Life

> *And he made known to us the mystery of his will according to his*
> *good pleasure, which he purposed in Christ, to be put into effect when*
> *the times will have reached their fulfillment—to bring all things in*
> *heaven and on earth together under one head, even Christ.*
>
> Ephesians 1:9, 10 NIV; *read Ephesians 1:3–10*

We stand in amazement before the realization that God the Father purposes, desires, and wills that we should develop our inherent capacity to become like Himself. Yet this is only possible if first we have His life in us. He yearns to give us the *gift of life.* Nothing thrills Him more than to see us accept Christ who becomes our *new life.*

This remains one of the moving mysteries of human history (see Ephesians 1). The realization that the all-wise, all-loving, all-righteous, all-powerful One should choose to impart to man not only His own divine life but also the capacity to mature into His own likeness overwhelms the human heart. (ATG)

20 —— Community with God

But God, who is rich in mercy, for his great love wherewith he loved us, even when we were dead in sins, hath quickened us together with Christ, (by grace ye are saved) . . . and made us sit together in heavenly places in Christ Jesus.

Ephesians 2:4–6 KJV; read Ephesians 2:4–10

When two people are in harmony with one another they are said to be in communion. There is a oneness between them. There is open, unclouded interaction. This sort of clear communication brings enormous pleasure and benefit to both parties. It generates goodwill, develops deep, abiding friendship, and fosters powerful faith between the two people.

It can be exactly the same with us and God. In fact, a part of the original motivation that moved God to create man in the beginning was His desire to have sons and daughters with whom He could commune in spirit. We are told this very clearly in Ephesians 1:

For consider what he has done—before the foundation of the world he chose us to be, in Christ, his children, holy and blameless in his sight. He planned, in his love, that we should be adopted as his own children through Jesus Christ—this was his will and pleasure that we might praise that glorious generosity of his which he granted to us in his Beloved.   Ephesians 1:4–6 PHILLIPS

This is a sublime picture portrayed for us under the inspiration of God's own gracious Spirit. We see ourselves brought into the family of our Heavenly Father. We see our complete acceptance as His children because of the great generosity He shows toward us. We see God yearning and longing for us to learn to commune with Him at the intimate and profound level of child with parent. Hand in hand we walk with God our Father. (WG)

21 —— True Beauty

For we are his workmanship, created in Christ Jesus for good works, which God prepared beforehand, that we should walk in them.

Ephesians 2:10 RSV

It is the compassion of Christ's love, the incoming waves of His wondrous grace that flood over me day upon day to submerge my spirit in Himself.

There, often unseen by the world, unrecognized by my contemporaries, unnoticed, even by my most intimate associates, He fashions me to the unique pattern of His special design for me. No two of us are exactly the same. Each is a "one-of-a-kind" creation shaped by the Master's hand.

In Christian circles it becomes increasingly common to hear the remark, "He is a beautiful person" or "She is a beautiful soul." It is really a carryover into the church from a crass culture which exalts so-called "beautiful people"—a synonym for the sophisticated, wealthy, upper set of society.

Amongst God's people the definition of true beauty is not in terms of charm, charisma or the subtle flatteries of fashion, outward appearance, or pride. It is, rather, beauty of behavior, loyalty of life, serenity of spirit.

These attributes of character and perfection of personality are seldom the sort to attract public acclaim. They are hardly the hallmark of those men and women adored by the world.

For, even of our Lord it was said, "He hath no form nor comeliness; and when we shall see him, there is no beauty that we should desire him. He is despised and rejected of men; a man of sorrows, and acquainted with grief . . ." (Isaiah 53:2–3).

The world's estimation of "beauty," and God's evaluation of beauty in His people are sometimes poles apart. And we must recognize that often the rugged character and sterling soul shaped under the formidable fashioning of the hand of God, beautiful to His eyes, may indeed be despised by our contemporaries.

22 —— Rested and Rooted

> . . . *that Christ may dwell in your hearts through faith; that you, being rooted and grounded in love, may have power to comprehend with all the saints what is the breadth and length and height and depth, and to know the love of Christ which surpasses knowledge, that you may be filled with all the fulness of God.*
>
> *Ephesians 3:17–18* RSV; *read Ephesians 3:14–21*

The tireless roots of the cedars of Lebanon penetrated and honeycombed the soil that lay upon those mountains, drawing from it minerals which would be built up into the very tissues and fibers of the timber. It is not just happenstance that these cedars have towering trunks which stand like tall spires upon the mountainside. Their roots are bound up with the very soil upon which they grow.

What a sublime picture this is of the Christian whose life is rooted and grounded in Christ Jesus!

November

Again and again throughout Scripture the inspired writers have used the metaphor of our God as a rock. For example: "I will publish the name of the Lord: ascribe ye greatness unto our God. He is the rock, his work is perfect". (Deuteronomy 32:2–4 KJV).

In the spiritual realm the strength and stamina of my character will depend upon the sort of material from which it is built. It will be conditioned by the source from which I draw spiritual sustenance. The decision as to where I choose to sink my spiritual roots and on what I prefer to feed my mind and heart and soul rests with me.   (ATG)

23 —— Going to God

> Then we will no longer be infants, tossed back and forth by the
> waves, and blown here and there by every wind of teaching and
> by the cunning and craftiness of men in their deceitful scheming.
>
> Ephesians 4:14 NIV; read Ephesians 4:1–16

We live in a busy, bustling world. Our society is the product of a clamorous culture. Life is noisy. It is often rude, increasingly crude. Enormous pressures of a hundred sorts exert a profound impact upon us. The tensions of our technology have been transmitted to our lifestyle. We are, for the most part, people driven by enormous desires; aroused by insatiable appetites; tantalized by tempting tastes; inflamed by passing pursuits and passions.

So we rush to and fro. We are people on the go. And amid all the mayhem God calls to us softly, persistently, patiently, and says: "Be still, and know that I am God . . ." (Psalm 46:10 KJV).   (WG)

24 —— Growing in Gratitude and Graciousness

> Rather, speaking the truth in love, we are to grow up
> in every way into him who is the head, into Christ. . . .
>
> Ephesians 4:15 RSV; read Luke 23:13–35

To do this is to grow in love and affection and warmth, not only to Christ but also to those around me.

True appreciation is one certain way to give great pleasure and love back to my Heavenly Father.

What is more, in this sort of inner climate, compounded of love and appreciation, the gracious Holy Spirit comes into my being, eager to produce His own fruits of a sunnier clime.

This is to know what it is to have our hearts burn within us, moved by a warm, compelling affection for Christ—growing in gratitude and graciousness. (ATG)

25 —— Equipped for Action

> *Put on the whole armor of God,*
> *that you may be able to stand against the wiles of the devil.*
>
> Ephesians 6:11 RSV; *read Ephesians 6*

Fortunately for me, long years of wilderness experience had taught me the basic behavior essential to survival in the high country. One went properly attired in heavy bush pants, high-laced hiking boots, warm clothing, and above all, with alert senses. Reflexes must be swift and smooth and silent.

So it is, too, in the Christian experience. Our walk with God through the tangled trails of this brief earthly sojourn is not without its perils. There are abroad in the wilderness of our days not only high adventures with Christ but also some severe risks. The Word of God alerts us to these.

In passages such as the sixth chapter of Ephesians we are given explicit instructions as to what antagonists we can and will encounter. We are supplied with specific information on how to equip and garb ourselves so that we can survive unexpected emergencies.

Sometimes we are startled by the sudden appearance of the enemy, no matter what guise he assumes. But this does not mean we need to fall prey to his devices. If we are properly equipped in soul and spirit against his attack it will come to nothing. When we are fully alert with the Word of God active in our lives, we survive unscathed.

26 —— The Immortal Made Mortal

> *[Christ Jesus] made himself nothing, taking the very*
> *nature of a servant, being made in human likeness.*
>
> Philippians 2:7 NIV; *read Isaiah 53*

Despite the most concerted attempts of human society, human philosophy, human governments and human ignorance to obliterate Christ's presence and power, He has become the dearest person in all of life to a hundred million hearts from centuries past to the present. His deity goes unchallenged by those who know Him as Savior and Redeemer.

215

Isaiah declared that He would be taken from prison and from judgment—that He would be cut off out of the land of the living, stricken for the transgression of His people. Here was His remarkable willingness—even beyond that, His *intention*—to be made captive in our human condition, to be humiliated and falsely accused, incarcerated in the narrow confines of our humanity. This He did, not by compulsion or constraint from without, but by His own choice: "It *pleased* the Lord to bruise him . . ."

Jesus Christ was not a martyr. He who was subjected to such gross humiliation by His contemporaries was not merely caught in the toils and terror of fickle fate. He was, rather, God deliberately setting aside His honor, prestige, and splendor. The Eternal One quietly stripped Himself of His own power to take upon Himself the mantle of a man in human flesh and form. The everlasting *I Am* set aside His endless immortality to enter the captivity of an earth-bound body subject to death. The Supreme Sovereign of the universe *made Himself* of no reputation to become a suffering servant, The Lamb slain for our sins (Philippians 2:1–8). *He* is the One I worship! (LAMB)

27 —— Do It!

> *For it is God which worketh in you both to will*
> *and to do of his good pleasure.*
> Philippians 2:13 KJV; *read Philippians 2:12–18*

The will of God streams and flows like a colossal, cosmic current through the seas of time. Only the person who also moves in accord with it finds purpose and direction in a divine destiny of utter fulfillment.

If you would walk with God in your will, discover what it is. Then do it! Step out in simple faith, your attention centered in Christ to go where He asks you to go; to live as He instructs you to live; to be what He asks you to be; to do what he asks you to do.

As you set your will to so live, you are taking the first giant step of faith which He will honor. He in turn will be faithful to you and empower you to walk with Him in joy. (WG)

28 —— The Spirit-Controlled Mind

> . . . *For God is at work in you, both to will and*
> *to work for his good pleasure.*
> Philippians 2:13 RSV; *read Philippians 2:12–18*

If I wish to have a Christian mind marked by the qualities of the mind of Christ, it is proper for the production of such a mind to come about by the inner working of the gracious Spirit in my mind. My appetites, my desires, my ambitions, my motives, will be molded and made up of impulses which had their origin with Him. The degree to which this is done daily in my life is proportional to the degree to which I deliberately allow Him to enter and control my mind, emotions, and will.

Not only will this result in my thinking upon those things which are pure and lovely and of good report, but it will mean my entire life exudes a wholesome aura of decency and uplift and integrity. To be with me will be akin to walking amid the cedars of Lebanon—which are both noble and fragrant—trees of the high places. This is to know something of the secret growth in godliness.

The question is, have I ever sincerely and earnestly invited the Holy Spirit to occupy and take control of my mind in this manner? He awaits my invitation to enter and begin His own winsome work of growth. It is He who will give me a godly disposition.

"For it is God which worketh in you both to will and to do of his good pleasure" (Philippians 2:13 KJV).　　　　　　　　　　(ATG)

29 —— To Know Him

Now I have given up everything else —I have found it to be the only way to really know Christ and to experience the mighty power that brought him back to life again, and to find out what it means to suffer and to die with him.

Philippians 3:10 TLB; *read Philippians 3:1–11*

The great cycle of the seasons goes on year upon year, enacted against the giant backdrop of the sky edge. We watch in humble awe and spellbound wonder as moon after moon the pageantry of the planet is played out upon the earth. The siblimely orchestrated script of the Divine Director is acted out in incredible detail by ten thousand participants. Each is directed by His will, guided by His genesis, moved by His inspiration.

If this can be true for lesser life forms, such as birds and bees and bears and balsam broom or bunch grass, then surely it can be equally true for us human beings created in Christ's own image. The utter tragedy and terrible truth is it seldom does happen. For horror upon horror, most men's hearts (wills) have been deliberately set, and very purposely hardened, against the gracious good will of our loving Father.

This need not be so. There can be harmony between us and Him. It is not impossible for a person to come to *truly know Christ*, whom to know is life everlasting. It is absolutely true that if men and women welcome Christ as wholeheartedly as they welcome the warmth of spring, new life, abundant life, the very life of the risen Lord, can pour into their beings.

30 ——— Focusing on Christ

Not as though I had already attained, either were already perfect;
but I follow after, if that I may apprehend that for which
also I am apprehended of Christ Jesus.
Philippians 3:12 KJV; read Philippians 3:12–14

When an ardent hiker heads for the high country, he keeps his eyes fastened on the far ridges and shining summmit. He stimulates himself and steels his resolve to reach the top by focusing his attention on the ultimate goal.

If he has a traveling companion, a hiking partner, he will also give him much of his thought, time, and interest. By doing this, the obstacles and hardships and strain of the climb are scarcely noticed. The tough, rough spots are taken in stride without undue stress or strain. His eyes and interest are not centered on the immediate problems along the path, but on reaching the mountaintop.

It is precisely the same in our walk with God. Where is your focal point of interest? Are you completely preoccupied with the petty pressures and problems of the immediate moment? Are you so taken up with self-interest that you can't see the shining heights of God's purposes and plan for the world? Is your gaze only on the ground of your grinding, grumbling grievances, or does God Himself fill your view?

Learn to refocus your attention on Christ. Make Him your confidante. Keep Him always in view. Set your will deliberately to see Him; then press on toward the destination of the high country and lofty life to which He has called you. (WG)

1 ——— Climbing above the Clouds

I press on toward the goal to win the prize for which God has called me heavenward in Christ Jesus.

Philippians 3:14 NIV

One winter day I left my comfortable hearth to climb a nearby mountain. After hours of climbing I finally broke out above the clouds into the bright winter sunshine at the summit. As I gazed down at the vast panorama around me, I felt it had been worth climbing the challenging heights.

Rare interludes like this are precious moments a man can store in the vault of his memory. They are beautiful bonuses given from my Father's generous hand. They are gifts of pure pleasure bestowed by His bounty.

But they would never have been mine had I chosen instead just to sit softly by my hearth. They would have been missed had I preferred just to stay at home, refusing to risk the storm or tackle the trail.

2 ——— Think about These Things

Finally, brethren, whatever is true, whatever is honorable, whatever is just . . . pure . . . lovely . . . gracious, if there is any excellence, if there is anything worthy of praise, think about these things. And the peace of God, which passes all understanding, will keep your hearts and minds in Christ Jesus.

Philippians 4:8, 7 RSV; read Philippians 4:1–9

There is an old hymn that used to be sung in our sanctuaries much more than it is today. Entitled "Take Time to Be Holy," its theme is that a person who would be whole and wholesome in life has to take the time to be alone with the Lord. There have to be intimate interludes with Christ in which He can convey His life and character to us.

It takes time to look for the special little gifts His gracious Spirit sees fit to bestow upon us in the common round of our daily lives. Like shells upon the sand, they may not always be obvious. They may not be so large we just stumble over them. It may take time and effort and thought to find them. But it can become a habit for us to be constantly on the lookout for bits of divine loveliness and natural beauty all about. There is such a thing as God's child learning to look for the exquisite touch of his Father's hand and heart in the world around him.

This is what the apostle Paul was admonishing us to do in Philippians, ". . . think about these things."

December

3 ——— The Supremacy of Christ

> *He [Christ] is the image of the invisible God,*
> *the firstborn over all creation.*
>
> Colossians 1:15 NIV; *read Colossians 1:15–21*

No one can do anything better with his time than give special attention to Jesus Christ. He is not just another historical figure who set foot briefly on the stage of human history. He is not just another religious teacher who founded another world religion. He is not just another deity amongst many strange gods devised by man's imagination. He is not just a divine, superb idea expressing supernatural doctrine.

Jesus Christ is God, very God. He always is! He existed before planet earth was ever formed for human habitation. He brought it into being. He is present all through its agonizing ongoing. He breaks through from the supernatural realm to be born amongst us as a man—*God incognito*—*God in mufti*—God in human guise.

He lives amongst us, works amongst us, ministers amongst us, teaches truth amongst us, suffers amongst us, dies in our stead amongst us, rises amongst us, ascends back to His former splendor amongst us, He is alive amongst us!

He is God, very God, revealing God to us. He is, as Paul put it, ". . . the visible expression of the invisible God . . . (Colossians 1:15 Phillips).

Jesus Christ communicates to us the very character of God. He conveys to us the conduct of God. He assures our questing spirits that through Himself, God very God speaks to us, touches us, in unmistakable terms.

(WG)

4 ——— Growing in the Lord

> *Let your roots grow down into him and draw up nourishment from*
> *him. See that you go on growing in the Lord, and become strong*
> *and vigorous in the truth you were taught. Let your lives*
> *overflow with joy and thanksgiving for all he has done.*
>
> Colossians 2:7 TLB; *read Colossians 2:6–10*

One of the interesting things about the root system of a tree is that very often it actually exceeds in size and scale the total mass of the trunk, limbs, and leaves which can be seen above the ground. It is not unusual for a tree to have miles of roots and rootlets.

The great tasks of this underground network are not only to anchor the tree to the ground but—much more importantly—to search out and absorb the available nutrients in the soil. By a very complex process the minerals are absorbed through the root hairs at the tips of the rootlets which are always growing rapidly. This material is then taken up into the tree and built into the very fibers and tissues of the trunk and branches. This is what gives strength and sturdiness to the entire tree. Yet it must be remembered that all this goes on below ground in silence and without fanfare.

Similarly, if we would grow up into Christ, if we would be built up in Him, there must be a quiet searching of His Word; there must be an assimilation of the riches available to us in secret, diligent study.   (ATG)

5 ——— Love from the Lamb

Since then, you have been raised with Christ, set your hearts on things above, where Christ is seated at the right hand of God.

Colossians 3:1 NIV; read Colossians 3:1–3

For all He has borne on my behalf, Christ asks only that I reach out my hands in faith and lay them in quiet trust upon His person. Just as the priest in faith placed his hands on the living animal which would be led away into the wilderness, so now I can rely upon my divine Sinbearer to act for me. Christ's assurance to me is that if I do so, my sins will be borne away, nevermore to be remembered against me. "I will put my laws into their hearts, and in their minds will I write them; and their sins and iniquities *will I remember no more*" (Hebrews 10:16–17). What deliverance! What freedom!

Even beyond His wonderful forgiveness and acceptance, the Father invites us to enter now *with boldness* into the holiest by the blood of Jesus. A child of God can have this confidence because of the ministry of the divine Scapegoat. Under the protection of God's divine forgetfulness, we can in turn forgive and accept others; and we can even forgive ourselves. We then know what it is to walk in the light, the wondrous brightness of His presence. Our days have meaning. Our years have purpose. Our despair has turned into the laughter of a joyous love—love for God; love for other followers of the Lamb; love for the lost.   (LAMB)

December

6 ———— Peace from the Most High

> *Now the Lord of peace himself give you peace*
> *always by all means. The Lord be with you all.*
>
> 2 Thessalonians 3:16 KJV; *read Romans 15:33 and Ruth 2:4*

There are encounters in which Christ communes with me in the very depths of my being. Through His Word and by His Spirit His presence becomes every bit as tangible to my soul and spirit as the touch of the sun on my cheek, the caress of the sea wind on my face, the refreshment of the ocean on my body.

Most of us know very little indeed about opening ourselves to the incoming peace of the presence of The Most High. Rarely do we expose our minds, our emotions, our wills fully to the influence of His Holy Person. We seldom dare to invite the living Lord to search our spirits, cleanse our conscience, enliven our intuition, so bringing us into close communion with Himself—the Christ of eternity, the One who loves us so profoundly. But when we do, we find peace—His peace—for He speaks peace to us.

7 ———— On Meekness and Weakness

> *Put them in mind to be subject to principalities and powers, to obey*
> *magistrates, to be ready to every good work, to speak evil of no man,*
> *to be no brawlers, but gentle, showing all meekness unto all men.*
>
> Titus 3:1–2 KJV; *read Titus 3:1–8*

Meek men are not weak men. The meek are gracious, congenial individuals who are easy to get along with. These genial, good-natured souls win friends on every side because they refuse to shove, push, and throw their weight around. They do not win their wars with brutal battles and fierce fights. They win their way into a hundred hearts and homes with the passport of a lowly, loving spirit.

Their unique genius is their gentleness. This quality of life does not come from a position of feeble impotence, but rather from a tremendous inner strength and serenity. Only the strong, stable spirit can afford to be gentle. It is the sublime Spirit of the living God who bestows upon us the capacity to express genuine concern and compassion for others. His self-less self-giving enables us to treat others with courtesy and consideration. This quality is much more than a thin veneer of proper propriety or superficial politeness. . . . Rather, it is the epitome of a laid-down life, poured out, laid out, lived out on behalf of others.

8 —————— Listen for God's Voice

And since Christ is so much superior [as a High Priest], the Holy Spirit warns us to listen to him, to be careful to hear his voice today and not let our hearts become set against him, as the people of Israel did . . .

Hebrews 3:7, 8 TLB; *read Hebrews 3:1–9*

We live in a noisy, crowded, busy world. At least most people do. Jammed and crushed into the "pressure-cooker" crucibles of our contemporary cities and towns, millions of human beings know little about solitude and stillness.

The thunder of traffic twenty-four hours a day, the rumble and roar of aircraft overhead, the cacophony of loud music, blatant advertising and high-powered programs in the media invade the sanctuary of our homes.

Relentlessly the presence and pressures of other people make their impact upon us. Our bodies grow weary from the constant assault of noise, commotion, and tension. Heart attacks, insomnia, ulcers, and irritability are part of the price paid for such physical abuse.

Often men and women suffer enormous anxieties and stress in mind and emotions because of the constant tensions of our twentieth-century society. Without realizing it their nervous systems and mental stability are strained to the breaking point. Some eventually do succumb. Mental institutions, psychiatric hospitals, and offices that claim to cure the condition are crowded with pathetic patients. . . .

Man was made for a greater good than all of these. He was made for God. And he will never find rest of soul, serenity of spirit, until he finds that repose in stillness and quietness in company with Christ.

9 —————— Of Love and Obedience

Though He was a Son, yet He learned obedience by the things which He suffered. And having been perfected, He became the author of eternal salvation to all who obey Him.

Hebrews 5:8, 9 NKJV; *read Hebrews 5:5–11*

Many modern Christians deeply resist the idea that love and obedience are intertwined in our relationship to both God and men. The assertion that these attitudes so inherent in Christ's character should also be a hallmark of a Christian raises inner resistance in the Western mind used to democratic ideas of "freedom" and "doing our own thing." They retort that to so live is to be "under the law," to be legalistic, to be bound.

Yet the answer to all of these charges is simply to read quietly Christ's last great discourse with His disciples in John, chapters 14, 15, and 16. He iterates and reiterates that "if you love me, you will keep my commandments—you will abide in my word—you will do what I direct you to do."

In layman's language, we will learn to love God and man, just as Christ learned it, by obedience and suffering and patient perseverance. We will begin to "go by the book," the Book of Life that contains all the rules necessary for successful loving.   (LOVE)

10 —— Covered by the Most High

[God said:] "I will be merciful to them in their wrongdoings, and I will remember their sins no more."

Hebrews 8:12 TLB; *read Hebrews 8:10–13*

The beach does not cover itself.
It is covered by the sea.
The shore does not change itself.
It is shaped by the tides.
The sea edge does not diminish its own size.
The ocean does this as it sweeps in upon it.
The alterations and rearrangements of the coast are the eternal work of the eternal tides.

And in my life as one who lies open, exposed and receptive to the action of The Most High, it is He who will cover and conform me to His own pattern of ultimate perfection. He does not relent, He does not rest. He neither slumbers nor sleeps. It is He who is at work upon my soul and within my spirit both to will and to do according to His own grand designs.

The incoming of Christ by His sublime Spirit always changes the contours of our lives. Once we have been filled with all the fullness of His grace and goodness we are never the same again. His presence can inundate every crevice, can fill every corner of our convoluted lives.

11 —— A Better Sacrifice

By faith Abel offered God a better sacrifice than Cain did. By faith he was commended as a righteous man, when God spoke well of his offerings. And by faith he still speaks, even though he is dead.

Hebrews 11:4 NIV; *read Genesis 4:1–16*

This is the first record of a human being's deliberate choice of God's appointed way for making appropriate atonement between himself and his God. It was not the slaying of the lamb which somehow earned God's favor, but it was the *One* whom that slain lamb represented which made this an action of implicit faith. Abel was saying, "O God, just as I have seen this little lamb's life laid down on my behalf, so I realize it represents Your life laid down in my stead." This simple shepherd offered the lamb to his loving God, confident it would be accepted because it portrayed in flesh and blood the divine life of the Eternal Lamb Himself.

God looked on in love. He accepted the sacrifice. He was satisfied. Abel depended on God's generosity, not on his own good conduct. Here was the pattern for proper reparation for all men for all time. Their total dependence must be upon divine intervention, not on their own human effort. (LAMB)

12 —— New Promise in Each New Day

Let us fix our eyes on Jesus, the author and perfecter of our faith, who for the joy set before him endured the cross, scorning its shame, and sat down at the right hand of the throne of God.

Hebrews 12:2 NIV; *read Hebrews 12:1–11*

Every dawn breaks anew upon my soul with the promise that today can be cherished. It is a special treasure of time entrusted to me for the Master's use. It is not bestowed to be squandered in languid living; rather, it is received to be emblazoned with impulses and actions of His design.

He is the author and originator of those lasting impressions of divine love, which through my humble hands and lowly heart can decorate this day. Under the gentle stimulus of His winsome Spirit, the spotless scroll of this strand of time can be embroidered with blessings as beautiful as the lacework of white foam on the beach at break of day.

It may be but a fleeting smile, a gracious gesture, a tender thought, yet it leaves an imprint for all of eternity. For in every action there lies a shaping power that changes character for all of time. So in the dawn of each new day comes the chance to be conformed ever more closely to the character of Christ.

13 —— The Cross and the Throne

> *Let us fix our eyes on Jesus, the author and perfecter of our faith, who for the joy set before him endured the cross, scorning its shame, and sat down at the right hand of the throne of God.*
>
> Hebrews 12:2 NIV

The cross in the life of God's person is more than a symbol of Calvary on the church steeple. It is more than an ornate crucifix on the church altar. It is more than a sentimental symbol of our Lord's awful agony.

The cross represents the judgment of divine justice upon sin and selfishness. It stands for the wide forgiveness of God's love and mercy extended to us in our pollution, declaring the depths to which Christ descended to restore, redeem and make us whole as His own people. This He achieved by laying down His life for us—pouring Himself out that we might be preserved and not perish in our own defilement.

This same purifying, redeeming, mighty work must proceed within my own life. Daily, in a discipline of total obedience to His will and wishes, my old, selfish life must be crossed out in conformity to His character. His Spirit must so submerge mine in counteracting power and purity that my soul shall be set free from selfishness exactly as the beach is cleared of its corruption.

This healing action brings an inner holiness—a knowledge of the wholeness within a wholesome spirit and a righteous soul at peace with God and with good will to men.

14 —— The Constancy of Christ

> *Jesus Christ is the same yesterday and today and forever.*
>
> Hebrews 13:8 NIV; read Hebrews 1:10–12

No other quality in the character of Christ elicits our awe or stablizes our souls in the same way as His constancy. It is the remarkable consistency of His conduct that makes Him stand out as a symbol of strength and integrity above the chaos of human history (see 2 Cor. 4:18; Malachi 3:6; Hebrews 1:10–12; 13:8).

All around us the earth scene is one of never-ending confusion, change, and calamity. Civilizations emerge, rise and then collapse. Human society stumbles along from failure to failure. The best-laid plans of governments fail. The sophisticated schemes of economic well-being fail. The hopes of nations and people fail. All is change, all is in flux, all is in transition and turmoil.

Amid the ruins, in great, unchanging consistency, Christ stands serene and sure and unfailing. Oh, the majesty of The Monarch of the Universe! Oh, the grandeur of Our Lord! Oh, the splendor of heaven's royal Sovereign!

What assurance He brings to our spirits. What calm repose He bestows upon our souls. What sure strength He injects into our puny lives. He does not fail! He cannot fail! He *will not* fail His followers!

This basic truth should put steel in our spines. It should put fire in our faith. It should put peace in our hearts. (LOVE)

15 —— Tongues on Fire

> *The tongue is a fire . . . an unrighteous world among our members. . . .*
>
> James 3:6 RSV; *read James 3:1–12*

How does one respond to spiritual light so that its entrance will produce growth of character?

Here is a simple illustration. Suppose my character is continually marred by my caustic tongue. Not only can it carve up my acquaintances but it continually brings reproach on my Master.

Then one day the light of God's Word on this matter suddenly streams into my aroused consciousness from James 3.

I am faced with two choices. Either I can turn away from this light, spurn it, ignore it, excuse myself by saying, "Oh well, that's just a weakness of mine." Or I can turn toward God on this point in repentance. I can allow the light to penetrate to the bottom of my being about this matter. I reach out in genuine repentance (an absolute, sincere decision to quit) and embrace the light. At the same time I ask that the gracious Holy Spirit empower me to control my conduct.

This is faith in action. Faith in action is the Christian's response to light. And the moment I respond thus, God gives power (for light is energy) to grow on this point.

Merely to feel sorry for having offended someone with my tongue and then to return and do the same again is neither to repent, nor to respond to light, nor to grow in this area of my life.

It is in fact to fold up and wilt just as a leaf does which refuses sunlight. This denotes that I am sick and weak. (ATG)

December

16 —— Surviving the Strain

As an example of suffering and patience . . .
take the prophets who spoke in the name of the Lord.

James 5:10 RSV; *read James 5:7–11*

The individual whose life has been exposed to stormy weather and survived the strain is most often the one with a quiet inner calm, a sweet serenity of spirit.

Beyond and above this, the picturesque trees above timberline—the battered, beaten, bent, and beautiful trees of the high country—possess the finest aroma. Their wood is impregnated with pitch and resins that act as lubricants between the flexing fibers of their wind-tossed timber. When this wood is sawn and planed and shaped under the master craftsman's cutting tools, its fragrance fills the air and all the building.

Such perfume is produced only by adversity.

God, give me grace to thank You for hardship.

When I do, my life and spirit will grow beautifully winsome—not bitter or cynical. (ATG)

17 —— Signs of the New Life

Being born again, not of corruptible seed, but of incorruptible,
by the word of God, which liveth and abideth forever.

1 Peter 1:23 NIV; *read 1 Peter 1:17–25*

A newborn infant soon lets the whole world know in unmistakable terms that it has new life in its new environment. Very much alive, it breathes deeply. It cries and calls out. It develops an enormous appetite that demands frequent feedings. It gurgles contentedly in the comfort and reassurance of its family. It rests and sleeps soundly. It moves its legs and arms, rolls about, and soon tries to learn how to walk.

We look for the same signs in a newborn child of God. His inspiration (in-breathing) should start to come from God. He should be willing to give voice and witness to the new life within, vigorously, vehemently. A keen appetite and hunger should develop for the milk of God's Word. The Scriptures should become a new and strengthening source of stamina—something that is drawn upon eagerly, daily. There should be a sense of gaiety and joy and contentment in the company and fellowship of God's family. There should be quiet rest in God. By degrees we should see the newborn one exercising faith, beginning to try and take the first faltering steps to walk with God.

If these simple signs are missing, we have every reason to question the authenticity of the claim to being "born again," of *knowing God*, or having eternal life in fellowship with *His Spirit*.   (WG)

18 —— In the World, but Not of It

For it is time for judgment to begin with the family of God;
and if it begins with us, what will the outcome be for
those who do not obey the gospel of God?

1 Peter 4:17 NIV; read 1 Peter 4:12–19

When we become too closely identified with the world in which we live, disaster may stalk us and even engulf us in its rushing fury, just the way fire sweeps through the underbrush to set the cedars alight.

God makes it very clear that judgment must first begin with His own people. And we must consistently remind ourselves that though He is longsuffering, and patient in His dealing with us, there are times when a Christian who compromises with the world will be punished promptly and with awesome severity. On occasion, like a bolt of lightning flashing from a thundercloud, death may even descend to consume the living tree. This is what happened to Ananias and Sapphira, who dropped dead when they tried to deceive God over a real estate transaction (Acts 5:1–11).

Jesus entreated His Father that though we are in the world, we would not be of it (John 17:14–17). We can do no better than pray the same prayer ourselves. Moreover, God expects us to use the discretion He has given us to detect dangerous situations when they present themselves. He expects us to have the simple courage to refuse unnecessary entanglements. This is best assured when we are growing steadily in him.   (ATG)

19 —— The Crucible of Suffering

After you have suffered a little while, our God, who is full of kindness
through Jesus Christ, will give you his eternal glory. He personally will
come and pick you up . . . and make you stronger than ever.

1 Peter 5:10 TLB

I am always stirred by the solitary trees that find footing and flourish in the harsh and rugged upland realm. Occasionally these trees grow utterly alone, clinging tenaciously to some crack in a cliff or standing sturdily on a rock outcrop where wind and weather lash them mercilessly. More often they grow in little clusters, a few unyielding individuals giving mutual support to each other in the exposed and perilous paths of hail, sleet, snow, and roaring winds.

Unlike animals, birds, or men, trees simply cannot shift or move about to protect themselves from the adverse vagaries of weather. Rooted to one spot they must stand there and survive the onslaught of sun, wind, snow, storms, blizzards and all the ravages of time and tempest. The passing seasons and pressure of environmental forces so move upon the tree that often it barely survives the stresses and strains of its formidable setting.

Such solitary trees, wind-twisted and storm-tossed, are not always the perfectly shaped specimens of their kind.

To the onlooker they may appear contorted, mis-shapen, yes, sometimes even broken and blasted by ice and hail and winter gales. Yet they own a special glory born of adversity. They reflect a unique strength that has stood the stress of a thousand mountain storms. They possess a beauty that can emerge only out of great agony and solitary suffering.

God's people, who suffer adversity, are like that. *Lord, may I emerge from my "crucible" as beautiful in character as they!*

20 —— The Purpose of Pain

And after you have suffered a little while, the God of all grace, who has called you to his eternal glory in Christ, will himself restore, establish, and strengthen you.

1 Peter 5:10 RSV

At times the very life of the Living Christ which comes to us may appear clouded, maybe even murky. We cannot fully comprehend why the stream of daily events flowing over our little lives resembles the cold, chill glacial streams that bear their burden of "glacial flour." Yet this is the polishing compound that puts the fine polish and smooth satin patina over every stone it touches.

It is the minute pangs of human misunderstandings, the crude, persistent rub of rudeness from others, the little lapses of ingratitude that press in upon us, the subconscious grief of insensitivity that move over us. These are all our Father's "glacial flour" for polishing people in their pangs of pain.

Out of all this there has come to me an acute awareness that nothing is permitted to touch my life except in the gracious good will of my Father for me. In His infinite concern He is shaping a character that not only in time here, but in eternity to come, will reflect something of the wondrous work He did in me.

Out of my stony spirit He has brought something of beauty and worth. It has taken sorrow and suffering. But anything of great value costs a great deal to create and shape.

21 —— Learning to Love Him

Whoever claims to live in him must walk as Jesus did.

1 John 2:6 NIV; *read 1 John 2:3–6*

Our Lord invited men and women from every walk of life to come and join Him. There was something to learn. He said emphatically that if anyone became His child, His follower, His disciple, His companion, His student, he would daily discover that he was learning to have His outlook, His attitudes, His approach to life.

Walking with Christ implies, therefore, that as I come to learn what His character really is I shall comply with His wishes and carry out His commands.

Do you know Him this well? Are you this familiar with His will? Have you learned that to love Him is to obey Him? (WG)

22 —— The Wonder of It All!

This is the promise that he hath promised us, even eternal life. . . .
And this is the record, that God hath given to us eternal life,
and this life is in his Son.

1 John 2:25; 5:11 KJV; *read 1 John 2:18–29*

Some days the shore, glistening like polished gold, has draped along its edge a delicate lacework of silver filigree. A thousand tiny wavelets moving on and across the sand like a master weaver's loom, fashion a blue-and-white embroidery on the beach. Its fabric flashes with the brilliant sequins of ten million bubbles that reflect the light as they burst into splinters in the surf.

The pattern of the spume that spreads itself upon the sand is of infinite, interacting fragments of white foam. It lasts but a few moments, caught briefly in intense beauty upon the eye of the onlooker. Then it is swept clean, carried away into the next incoming wave, to be replaced by another, equally arresting.

December

Everywhere there is action, motion, life and design. Picture upon picture is created in rapid succession on the shore. No two are identical, no two even appear similar. Each is a unique creation formed by the ebb and flow of the sea upon the sand. The shore is the Master Artist's canvas, the wavelets His sure, swift, brush strokes.

In a similar way, our Father impacts our little lives. No two of us are exactly alike. Each of us is a unique creation. And yet He thought enough of us, His creation, to send His only Son to die for us, to open the way to eternity with Him. If I had been the only one who needed Him, still He would have died for me. O the wonder of it all!

23 —— A Way to Rest

> *He who says he abides in him ought to walk*
> *in the same way in which he walked.*
>
> 1 John 2:6 RSV

It is not always easy simply to step aside into solitude and rest and quietness. But unless I learn how, my entire growth in God will be endangered.

As a simple preliminary step in this direction may I suggest the reader take twenty minutes each day to go out and walk alone—a brisk walk—only smiling to strangers—deliberately looking for the beauty and handiwork of God in the natural world about him, and inwardly adoring the Lord for who He is. Leave the worries and work at home or in the office. It will prove to be a tonic, a rest that results in growth in God. (ATG)

24 —— From Glory to Glory

> *Beloved, now are we the children of God; and it has not yet been*
> *revealed what we shall be, but we know that when He is revealed*
> *we shall be like Him, for we shall see Him as He is.*
>
> 1 John 3:2 NKJV; read 1 John 3:1–3

In his constant exposure to a human parent, the young person actually takes on the traits and characteristics of the parent. We become like those we live with.

It is precisely the same in our life with Christ! We actually *become like Him*. We take on His very character. We are matured by exposure to

His company. We are conformed and perfected in His companionship. It is all a part of the perfect union of His life and love. What a wonder!

"('The Lord' means the Spirit, and wherever the Spirit of the Lord is, there is open freedom.) But we all mirror the glory of the Lord with face unveiled, and so we are being transformed into the same likeness as himself, passing from one glory to another—for this comes of the Lord the Spirit" (2 Corinthians 3:17–18, Moffatt).   (LOVE)

25 —— Humble Hearts

Hereby perceive we the love of God, because he laid down his life for us: and we ought to lay down our lives for the brethren.

1 John 3:16 KJV; *read 1 John 3:11–18*

It is a straightforward case of cause and effect, not some complicated formula or technique. In fact, not until the impact of the laid-down life of the Babe of Bethlehem comes crashing through the crust around our hard, self-centered hearts will humility ever displace our despicable self-preoccupation. Then and only then will the expulsive power of humility's presence displace our selfishness, enabling us to go out into a broken, shattered, bleeding, wounded world as suffering servants.

The humility of Christ, the meekness of His gracious Spirit, the gentleness of our God can only be known, seen, felt, and experienced by a tough world in the lives of God's people. If the society of our twentieth century finds God at all they will have to find Him at work in the garden of His children's lives. It is there His fruits should flourish and abound. It is there they should be readily found.

26 —— Known by the Father

For if our heart condemns us, God is greater than our heart, and knows all things.

1 John 3:20 NKJV; *read 1 Corinthians 4:1–5*

Only God in Christ, by His Spirit, is fully aware of all the environmental influences which have been brought to bear upon my life since the day of conception.

No human being is, not even my own mother.

It is this infinite, incredible *knowing* that enables Christ to deal with me in dignity, forgiveness, and love. He knows all the strains, stresses, and pressures that shaped me.

He alone can properly appraise the impact made on me by my parents, my home, my siblings, my schools, my playmates, my teachers, my friends, and all other human associates. He knows the experiences, the griefs, the triumphs, the adventures, the work, the impact of books and films and thousand other influences that molded me as a man.

No one else does or can.

Not even I can fully know myself or understand my behavior. Is it any wonder, then, He cried from the cross, *"Father, forgive them; for they know not what they do"* (Luke 23:34 KJV)?

Only God in Christ can clearly comprehend all my thoughts, all my hopes, all my fears, all my imaginations, all my emotions, all my deliberate choices, all my subconscious impulses.

And because He does, He deals with me in mercy, kindness, patience, long-suffering, justice, and total integrity. O the grandeur and graciousness of such a Savior, such a Friend, such a *Father!*   (LOVE)

27 —— God Is Love

He who does not love does not know God; for God is love.

1 John 4:8 RSV; *read 1 John 4:7–21*

In looking back to my youth, I am reminded again and again of the tremendous impact made on my own life by watching the growth in my father's Christian character. As a small lad I knew him to be a hard-driving, hot-headed, impulsive, impatient man. But as I grew up and passed through my teens I watched, awestruck, at a steady transformation taking place in my father. It was obvious that the love of God was being shed abroad more and more in his life and in responding to that love, his character was changed. He became one of the most gentle, endearing, considerate, and warm-hearted people I ever knew.

In the Christian life, the counterpart of physical warmth is love or affection. It is the other side of the character of God Himself—"for God is love" (1 John 4:8).

Just as God is light, which reveals to us His character of holiness, purity, justice, and righteousness, so God is love, which discloses His character of compassion, mercy, tenderness, and kindness.

There are Christians who know all about God in a clinical way. They can dispute doctrines and discuss all the details related to the divine life. There is no end to the light they have, but it has never produced growth because it was not combined with a warm, personal love for Christ.   (ATG)

28 —— Overcoming Faith

> . . . *for everyone born of God overcomes the world. This is the*
> *victory that has overcome the world, even our faith.*
>
> 1 John 5:4 NIV; read 1 John 5:1–12

The storms of life come and go. The winter weather is but for a short season. The dark squalls and gusting winds are passing phenomena. When they are gone, the rainbow of God's blessing and reassurance reminds us of His presence. The unique peace which He alone can provide for His people pervades our spirits. And the rest he promises us endures as our legacy. All of us have winter weather. We face those formidable interludes in life when everything looks dark and depressing. We all have times when our days are strewn with the apparent wreckage of wrong choices and derelict decisions. The best of men and women know what it is to be stripped down to the bedrock of sheer survival.

Yet amid all such storms what a consolation to know our Father has His strong hand upon us for our own good. What an assurance to recognize that Christ can be counted on to control the final outcome of our apparent calamities. What a strength to see His gracious Spirit bring great glory and beauty out of what to us may have seemed only disastrous!

Tomorrow is always His. It belongs to Him.

He can make it mine as well!

29 —— Growing in Godliness

> . . . *this is the victory that overcomes the world, our faith.*
> *Who is it that overcomes the world but he who*
> *believes that Jesus is the Son of God?*
>
> 1 John 5:4 RSV

If I want my faith in God to grow, the way to stimulate it vigorously is to remind myself always of His absolute faithfulness and utter reliability to me, His child.

God cannot betray either Himself or His children.

As I act on this realization, He unfailingly imparts to me, by the Spirit, His own abounding resurrection life of growth in godliness that counteracts every peril and perplexity. I know of a surety that *He is alive* and because He is alive I, too, shall live. (ATG)

December

30 —— The Son and a Seed

> *He who has the Son has life;*
> *he who does not have the Son of God does not have life.*
>
> *1 John 5:12* NIV

"The spirit gives life; the flesh counts for nothing. The words I have spoken to you are spirit and they are life. Yet there are some of you who do not believe" (John 6:63–64 NIV).

This inheritance of eternal life is a mystery and marvel that even surpasses the hereditary process within the seed of a cedar. No more does the frail, minute, inert-looking seed lying on the ground resemble the magnificent tree towering above it than does a newborn Christian (believer in Christ) resemble the mighty God, the Heavenly Father, whose will it is that he, likewise, should develop into His likeness. It is not the outer appearance which matters. It is, rather, the imparting of God's own life to mortal man, enabling him to have correspondence with God, that counts.

The vital question is, Do I have this *life?*

The verse above this meditation puts it very plainly: "He who does not possess the Son of God does not have that life." (ATG)

31 —— Promises from the Lamb

> *To him who overcomes, I will give the right to sit with me*
> *on my throne, just as I overcame and sat down*
> *with my Father on his throne.*
>
> *Revelation 3:21* NIV; *read Revelation 3:19–22*

It is the *person* of the Lamb of God in heaven which guarantees that there shall never again be any night there. Gone forever are the sorrows which comprise so great a part of our earth days. He, the Man of Sorrows, has long since borne them all away. Instead He now wipes away every tear, dries every eye, gives to His own the oil of gladness in the place of mourning.

It is in the *presence* of the Lamb of God in glory that all separation ceases. Never again will we be torn by the painful tugs of parting or the deep wounds of distance that so often distress us here.

The *power* of the Lamb of God guarantees the total extinction of all evil in His domain. Never, ever again shall sin or selfishness or evil hold sway. He has conquered all of these. He has subdued them to His sovereign purposes. His followers are set free in a new dimension of divine delight.

The *purity* of the Lamb of God assures us for all time that there can be no curse there. Nothing that defiles, deceives or diverts us from Himself can enter there. Never again will His people have to contend with the wiles of the wicked one. The enemy of our souls will be banished forever, while the blood-bought children of the Lamb clap their hands with joy, giving glory, honor, and adoration to Him who lives forever and forever. (LAMB)

TITLE INDEX

Title Index

Title Index

Title Index

Title Index

SUBJECT INDEX

Readings arranged chronologically under each subject heading.

Subject Index

Subject Index

Subject Index

Subject Index

Subject Index

Subject Index

Subject Index